THE COMPLEAT ANGLER

Izaak Walton

Charles Cotton

THE COMPLEAT ANGLER

or
The Contemplative
Man's Recreation

---◆---

Izaak Walton
& Charles Cotton

with illustrations by
EDMUND H. NEW

WORDSWORTH CLASSICS

This edition published 1996 by
Wordsworth Editions Limited
Cumberland House, Crib Street
Ware, Hertfordshire SG12 9ET

ISBN 1 85326 180 7

Typeset by Antony Gray
Printed and bound in Great Britain by
Mackays of Chatham plc, Chatham, Kent

> Lord of the Madeley peace, the quiet grass,
> The lilied pond, and muffled sleepy mill;
> Lord of each legendary fish that swims
> Deep down and swift beneath that emerald glass;
> While, soft as shadows, round its grassy rims
> The patient anglers move from east to west,
> Patient at morn, at evening patient still –
> Peace, if not fish, was theirs, and peace is best:
> To you, John Offley's far-descended son,
> What to your grandsire – past computing 'great' –
> Our Walton gave is here re-dedicate;
> Heirloom of ancient friendship friendly still
> In this old book, though all the talk be done.

R. Le. G.

CONTENTS

THE COMPLEAT ANGLER

Part One

❦

Being a Discourse of Rivers, Fishponds,
Fish and Fishing

A Dedication to the
Right Worshipful John Offley

To the Reader of this Discourse, but especially
to the Honest Angler

To my dear Brother, Mr Isaac Walton, upon his
Compleat Angler

To the Reader of The Compleat Angler

To my dear friend, Mr Iz. Walton, in praise of
Angling, which we both love

To the Readers of my most ingenious Friend's book
The Compleat Angler

To my dear Brother, Mr Iz. Walton,
on his Compleat Angler

Clarissimo amicissimoque; Fratri, Domino Isaaco
Walton Artis Piscatoriae pertissimo

The Fourth Day

THE COMPLEAT ANGLER

Part Two

❦

Introduction

by
Richard Le Gallienne

Izaak Walton

PART ONE

Outlines of Walton's Life

In his address to the reader of the first collected edition of his lives, Walton says: 'And now I wish, that as that learned Jew, Josephus, and others, so these men had also writ their own lives; but since it is not the fashion of these times, I wish their relations or friends would do it for them, before delays make it too difficult.' It was but natural that so good a biographer should desire to establish biography as a family duty, or at all events as one of those duteous 'courtesies that are done to the dead', to borrow a phrase of the younger Donne's. Had Walton lived to our day, as there seemed some possibility of his doing, he would no doubt have been somewhat more than satisfied with the activity of biographers; and perhaps have noted for particular remark the biographic conscientiousness of the modern interviewer, eager to catch and record every minute of a great man's life as it flies. Perhaps it is a little strange that his friend Cotton, or his son the Canon, did not remember Walton's words, and note for us some of the ways and talk of a man who must have been as good a subject for, as he was an artist in, biography. No doubt, Cotton, who was to survive his master but four years, dying amid debts and difficulties, had more instant demands upon his faculties; but Canon Izaak Walton, in his long quiet life in Salisbury Close, might surely have written some notes of a father to whose biographical faculty, and consequent acceptability with bishops, he owed his canonry.

Later on Dr Johnson talked of writing Walton's life, but his well-known admiration for the *Lives* found no other expression than possibly a certain influence on the form of his own *Lives of the Poets*, and his suggestion to Moses Browne that he should reprint *The Compleat Angler*, then somewhat fallen into neglect. Browne published his edition in 1750, having weeded the text of what he was pleased to regard as certain 'redundancies', 'superfluities', and 'absurdities', an editorial proceeding to which we owe the first authoritative life of our author, as it prompted Sir John Hawkins to publish his edition (1760), in which the text was restored to its original integrity, and to which were for the first time prefixed 'The Lives of the Authors'. Browne had supplied what Westwood calls 'some loose biographical litter', but the honour of being Walton's first serious biographer belongs to Sir John Hawkins, on whose biography all subsequent biographies have been founded. According to Mr R. B. Marston, however, this is an honour which he should from the beginning have shared with the famous antiquary William Oldys, to whose collections he owed most of his Walton material, and by whom entirely was written the life of Cotton. Dr Thomas Zouch was Walton's next original biographer, his life being prefixed to his edition of the *Lives* in 1796; and then in 1836 came Sir Harris Nicolas, who, if Sir John Hawkins was the first, may almost be said to be the first and last of Walton's biographers. For the scientific thoroughness of his research has left hardly a single stone unturned for subsequent editors, and, compared with his elaborately minute narrative, every fact reinforced by a phalanx of notes Sir John Hawkins's work seems a mere outline, with the occasional vagueness of myth.

Thus, for later editors there is little left to be done anew with the life of Izaak Walton, either in the way of fact or reflection. Sir Harris Nicolas has recorded nearly all the facts, and Dr Zouch and Mr R. B. Marston have made all the appropriate reflections. In the following resetting of the old narrative, so far as our common nature permits, I shall limit myself to facts, or the conjectures of facts, remembering Walton's admonition that 'the mind of man is best satisfied by the knowledge of events'.

Izaak Walton was born at Stafford, in the parish of St Mary, on August 9, 1593. Till recently two houses competed for the honour of being his birthplace, one a noble old Elizabethan house in Greengate Street, and the other a humble little house in East Gate Street, pulled down within the last seven or eight years. Tradition and probability were most strongly in favour of the latter. Of his father, Jervis Walton, nothing is known beyond the fact that he died in February, 1596–7, of his mother nothing at all, not even her name, though Dr Zouch makes out that she was a daughter of Edmund Cranmer, Archdeacon of Canterbury, a statement which seems entirely without foundation, and which probably arose from some traditional confusion due to Walton's own marriage into the Cranmer family.

A conjectural pedigree of Walton's father is to be found in Sir Harris Nicolas's Life, by which it would appear that he was the son

Walton's birthplace

of George Walton, bailiff, of Yoxall, who may have been related to Richard Walton of Hanbury, whose will was dated October 31, 1557 – the earliest date in Waltonian genealogy.

From his baptism (which is thus recorded in the register of St Mary's: '1593 Septemb. Baptiz. fuit Isaac Filius Jervis Walton 21° die mensis et anni praedict.') till we find him a London apprentice probably at the age of sixteen, and for many years after that, and for occasional long periods all through his life, his history is mainly conjecture. That he was educated at the Grammar School of his native town seems likely. What that education amounted to we can only judge from his writings. Lowell has been somewhat scornful of his poor attainments. Walton 'could never have been taught even the rudiments of Latin,' he says, with startling erudition, 'for he spells the third person singular of the perfect tense of *obire*, *obiet*; *separate*, *seperate*; and *divided*, *devided*'!* Sir Harris Nicolas is more

* Lowell might have instanced a much better known example of strange Waltonian Latin in the 'piscatoribys' for 'piscatoribus' in the well-known inscription on the Dovedale fishing-house. But then that is probably stonemason Latin, unless Cotton, the author of the *Virgil Travestie*, was responsible for it.

hopeful of poor Walton's Latin. 'It is not probable,' he thinks, 'that he received a regular classical education; but although translations existed of nearly all the Latin works which he quotes, it is nevertheless certain that he had some knowledge of that language. His reading in English literature was various and extensive, particularly in divinity.' However, apart from the fact that the printer, of whom Walton had frequent occasion to complain, might easily account for that eccentric conjugation of *obire*, and the bad spelling, it is of small consequence how much or little Latin, or other technical learning, Walton possessed. It is only important to realise that he was sufficiently familiar with such models of good and beautiful style in literature, as to have written English with classic dignity and distinction (such as Lowell, in the rather common essay from which I quote is far from attaining), not to speak of an immortalising charm, which even a more correct conjugation of Latin verbs could hardly have increased.

That Walton was devoted to literature at quite an early age, and that among his youthful friends he was a marked man because of that devotion, are among the first facts that we become aware of after his baptism. In 1619 was published a short poem, entitled *The Loves of Amos and Laura*, by S.P. (conjectured to be Samuel Purchas, author of the famous *Pilgrimage*), and this was dedicated to Walton in the following poem:

To My Approved and Much Respected Friend, Iz. Wa.

To thee, thou more than thrice beloved friend,
    I too unworthy of so great a bliss;
These harsh-tun'd lines I here to thee commend,
    Thou being cause it is now as it is:
For hadst thou held thy tongue, by silence might
These have been buried in oblivious night.

If they were pleasing, I would call them thine,
    And disavow my title to the verse:
But being bad, I needs must call them mine.
    No ill thing can be clothed in thy verse.
Accept them then, and where I have offended,
Rase thou it out, and let it be amended,

                                                      S.P.

This dedication does not occur in the only known copy of the first edition (1613), which, however, is imperfect, and from which it may have been lost, but Sir Harris Nicolas points out that, as the

text is precisely the same in both editions, any obligations to Walton acknowledged by 'S.P.', in 1619, must have been equally due in 1613; from which he further deduces that, 'as Walton was only twenty years of age in 1613, the love of literature, which never deserted him, must have commenced at a very early period of his life'.

The date of Walton's first coming to London, and the business in which he became engaged, have been matters of much speculation and research. The usual statement has been that at about the age of twenty he was apprenticed to a kinsman of his, Henry Walton, a Whitechapel haberdasher. The only authority I can find for this statement is Sir Harris Nicolas's elaborate genealogical guess. There was a Henry Walton, haberdasher, in Whitechapel about this time, whom we come at through the will of a cousin Samuel Walton, of St Mary's Cray, in Kent, and whose connection with Staffordshire is further deduced from the same document. Henry Walton *may* have been a kinsman of Izaak Walton, and Izaak Walton *may* have been his apprentice, and there are other mays and mights still more conjectural. One fact against the haberdasher or 'sempster' theory is that the records of the Haberdashers' Company do not contain the names of Henry or Izaak Walton, between 1600 and 1630, whereas it has been discovered that the records of the *Ironmongers*' Company for 1618 do contain the name of Izaak.* Still more conclusive is the fact dwelt upon by Mr Marston, that in his marriage licence with Rachel Floud, dated December 27, 1626, he is described as of the 'Cittie of London, Ironmonger'. Why a man who was a haberdasher should describe himself as an ironmonger in his marriage licence is certainly difficult to determine – except on the unlikely theory that Rachel Floud had a partiality for ironmongers.

Sir John Hawkins had supposed that Walton first settled in London as a shopkeeper in the Royal Exchange, under the patronage of Sir Thomas Gresham, but this seems to be a fable. Haberdasher, sempster, 'wholesale linen draper, or Hamburg merchant', these have been the traditional descriptions of Walton's business; but I fear that these graceful and fanciful professions must cease to claim him, and that in future he must be written down an ironmonger. 'Let no one,' to quote the impassioned words of Dr Zouch, who, along with one or two other editors, seems to have been uncomfortable because Walton was a tradesman, 'however elevated in rank or station, however accomplished with learning, or exalted in genius, esteem him the less for that.'

Well, if Walton became 'apprentice of Thomas Grinsell' at the usual age, he would have commenced his life in London at the age of sixteen, in the year 1611. So conjectures Mr Marston, and so we can leave the matter.

Though Walton's manner of business be still uncertain, the place of it has long been known, and Walton's residence in Chancery Lane and Fleet Street a matter of familiar tradition. Sir John Hawkins states that in 1624, 'Walton dwelt on the north side of Fleet Street in a house two doors west of the end of Chancery Lane, and abutting on a messuage known by the sign of the *Harrow*, and that this house was then in the joint occupation of himself and a hosier called John Mason.' 'Half a shop was sufficient for the business of Walton,' comments one of his old editors. From 1628 to 1644 he seems to have lived in Chancery Lane itself, in 'about the seventh house on the left-hand side', but Sir Harris Nicolas points out that in the parish-books of Saint Dunstan's his house is not, like the others, described as a shop. From the same parish records it has been unearthed that during the years from 1632 to 1640, Walton fulfilled the ordinary civic duties of a householder, as scavenger,

---

* 1618. 12th November. Isaac Walton, late apprentice to Thomas Grinsell, was now 'admitted and sworn a free brother of this companie and paid for his admittance xiij^d, and for default of presentm^t and enrollment X$^{s'}$.

juryman, constable, grand juryman, overseer of the poor, sidesman and vestryman – facts of humble biographical importance.

But long before Walton filled any of these posts of public usefulness, his residence in the parish of St Dunstan's had brought him into acquaintance and lifelong friendship with its famous vicar, Dr John Donne, a friendship of the first importance in Walton's life, as to it he probably owed his introduction to that literary and ecclesiastical society, in which, haberdasher or ironmonger as he might be, he was so evidently *persona grata*. That this should be so has not unnaturally been a matter of surprise to his editors, and Dr Johnson remarked that 'it was wonderful that Walton, who was in a very low station in life, should have been familiarly received by so many great men, and that at a time when the ranks of society were kept more separate than they are now'. Johnson suggests as explanation that he was no longer a tradesman but had become a professional author, but actually his retirement from business did not take place till 1643. After all, the circumstance need not have so greatly surprised a man who similarly owed his position to his own personality and talents.

However it be, we find him, while still living in Fleet Street, on terms of intimacy and affection with such men as Sir Henry Wotton, Dr Henry King (son of the Bishop of London), John Hales of Eton, and certain eminent divines – for Walton, as Lowell has said, had 'a special genius for bishops'.

Was it this episcopal bias that led him on December 27, 1626, to take to wife Rachel Floud, of Canterbury, closely connected by descent with the Cranmers, including the famous Archbishop? Through his wife's family Walton probably still further widened his episcopal connection. With Rachel Walton he lived, apparently in an entirely happy union, for nearly fourteen years, during which, however, he suffered severe domestic affliction in the loss of no less than seven children. His wife's mother had also died during their residence in Chancery Lane, and on the July 10, 1640, his wife was to die too, having survived only six weeks the birth of another daughter. But death seems to have come merely as a solemn incident of life to Walton's serene, unimpassioned, and devoutly religious spirit. A literal, undoubting faith such as his, and a preoccupation in little hobbies, must afford a great shelter from the keenness of life's tragedy and pathos.

Six years after this Walton was to marry again, to be again bereaved in April 1662. His second wife, like his first, was found among the bishops, being Anne Ken, of the Kens of Somersetshire, and half-sister to that Bishop Ken whose name has become a synonym for piety. She bore him one daughter Ann, married to Dr Hawkins, of Winchester, and two sons, one of whom died in infancy, and one Isaac, the Canon, who survived him. She was buried in Worcester Cathedral, Walton himself writing for her the following epitaph.

Ex terris

✠

Here lyeth buryed soe much as
could dye of ANNE the wife of
IZAAK WALTON
who was
a woman of remarkable prudence,
and of the *Primitive Piety*; her great
and general knowledge being adorned
with such true humility, and blest
with soe much Christian *meeknesse*, as
made her worthy of a more memorable
Monument.

She dyed (*Alas that she is dead!*)
the 17th of Aprill 1662, aged 52.

Study *to be like her*.

In his life of Hooker, Walton speaks of 'a secret sacred wheel of Providence – most visible in marriages – guided by His hand that "allows not the race to the swift", nor "bread to the wise", *nor good wives to good men*', his view apparently being that bad wives are allotted to good men to exercise their virtues. It would seem, however, that the remark had no reference to his own matrimonial experience.

Walton had left Chancery Lane in August 1644, finding it 'dangerous for honest men to be there', and for some years his place of residence is doubtful. Some have surmised that he retired to Stafford, to pass long days by Shawford brook, but Sir Harris Nicolas is of opinion that, except for occasional visits to Stafford, he did not leave London till after the Restoration.

In 1650 he was probably living in Clerkenwell, and in 1651, soon after the battle of Worcester, his pacific contemplative life comes for a moment in contact with the danger and trouble of the time. The King's baggage had fallen into Cromwell's hands, but a certain Colonel Blague had managed to save one of Charles's rings, known as 'the lesser George'. Having taken shelter at Blore Pipe House, near Eccleshall, Blague had handed it to his host Mr George Barlow, who passed it on to one Robert Milward, who again gave it into the 'trusty hands' of Mr Izaak Walton. Blague was meanwhile a prisoner in the Tower, but, effecting his escape, he received the ring again from Walton, and succeeded in restoring it to the King over the water. This is Walton's first and only appearance as a man of action, so we must make the most of it.

In 1655 we catch a glimpse of him once again in the more congenial society of the clergy, that famous glimpse of him talking with Bishop Sanderson in Little Britain, a meeting which he has thus described with so much charm:

About the time of his printing this excellent preface, I met him accidentally in London, in sad-coloured clothes, and God knows, far from being costly. The place of our meeting was near to Little Britain, where he had been to buy a book which he then had in his hand. We had no inclination to part presently, and therefore turned to stand in a corner under a penthouse (for it began to rain), and immediately the wind rose, and the wind increased so much, that both became so inconvenient, as to force us into a cleanly house, where we had bread, cheese, ale, and a fire for our ready money. The rain and wind were so obliging to me, as to force our stay here for at least an hour, to my great content and advantage; for in that time he made to me many useful observations of the present times with much clearness and conscientious freedom.

Fuller's *Church History* was published in 1655, and it was soon after its publication that we get another similar glimpse of Walton in conversation with its author:

Walton being asked by Fuller, who was aware of his being intimate with several bishops and other eminent clergymen, what he thought of that work himself, and what opinions he had heard his friends express of it, Walton replied 'he thought it should be acceptable to all tempers, because there were shades in it for the warm, and sunshine for those of a cold constitution, that with youthful readers, the facetious parts would be profitable to make the serious more palatable; while some reverend old readers might fancy themselves in his History of the Church, as in a flower-garden or one full of evergreens.' 'And why not,' said Fuller, 'the *Church History* so decked as well as the Church itself at a most holy season, on the Tabernacle of old at the feast of boughs.' 'That was but for a season,' said Walton; 'in your feast of boughs they may conceive we are so overshowed throughout, that the parson is more seen than the congregation, and this, sometimes invisible to his own acquaintance, who may wander in the search, till they are lost in the labyrinth.' 'Oh,' said Fuller, 'the very children of our Israel may find their way out of this wilderness.' 'True,' replied Walton, 'as, indeed, they have here such a Moses to conduct them.'

In the December of 1662, the year in which his wife died, Walton obtained from Gilbert Sheldon, Bishop of London (still another episcopal friend), a forty years' lease of a new building, adjoining a house called the 'Cross Keys', in Paternoster Row. This building was burnt down in the Great Fire, and on July 1, 1670, Walton presented a petition to the Court of Judicature, asking for extension of lease on condition of his rebuilding it; which petition was granted. On this occasion Walton was described as 'Isaac Walton, gentleman'.

Of one of Walton's closest friends mention has yet to be made. This was Dr George Morley, whom Walton first knew as a canon of Christchurch, Oxford. He was, however, expelled from his canonry somewhere about 1648, for refusing to take the covenant. There was a story that he took shelter with Walton at his Staffordshire cottage from April 1648 to May 1649; but for this there is no authority. He was one of Ben Jonson's twelve adopted 'sons', and wrote some commendatory verses prefixed to *The Compleat Angler*. His friendship with Walton was destined to be lifelong. On the Restoration he was made Dean of Christchurch, and presently Bishop of Worcester, and it was during a visit to him at Worcester that Walton's second wife is supposed to have died. Very shortly after her death Morley was made Bishop of Winchester, and invited Walton to make his home with him. The invitation was accepted, and Walton continued to live with him at Winchester, with occasional visits to London and to Morley's episcopal residence of Farnham Castle, till the end of his life. That he spent the Christmas of 1678 at Farnham Castle seems likely from the following inscription in a copy of the fifth edition of *The Compleat Angler* given to his friend, Mrs Wallop:

FOR MRS WALLOP – I think I did some years past, send you a booke of Angling: This is printed since, and I think better; and, because nothing that I can pretend a tytell too, can be too good for you: pray accept of this also, from me that am really,

Madam, yo[r] most affectionate friend;

and most humble servant,

IZAAK WALTON
*Farnham Castell,
Decem[r] 19°, 1678*

It was under one of Bishop Morley's roofs, and at his suggestion, that he wrote the lives of Hooker, Herbert and Sanderson; and it is likely that the Hooker – and possibly the Herbert – were written at Morley's house at Chelsea.

On May 26, 1683, we find him again at Farnham Castle; but this seems to have been his last journey, for there is no record of his again leaving Winchester.

On August 9, in the same year, he was ninety years old, and on that day he commenced to make his will. It was finished on the 16th and executed on the 24th, and is written throughout in his own hand, with several erasures. Not the least characteristic of his writings, it ran as follows:

August the 9°, 1683

In the name of God, Amen. I, Izaak Walton, the elder, of Winchester, being this present day in the neintyeth yeare of my age, and in perfect memory, for wich praysed be God: but Considering how sodainly I may be deprived of boeth, doe therfore make this my last will and testament as followeth. And first, I doe [declare]* my beliefe to be, that their is only one God, who hath made the whole world, and me and all mankinde; to whome I shall give an acount of all my actions, which are not to be justified, but I hope pardoned, for the merits of my saviour Jesus. – And because [the profession of] Cristianity does, at this time, seime to be subdevided into papist and protestant, I take it to be at least convenient to declare my beleife to be, in all poynts of faith, as the Church of England now professeth. And this I doe the rather because of a very long and very trew friendship with some of the Roman Church.

And for my worldly estate (which I have nether got by falshood or flattery, or the extreme crewelty of the law of this nation), I doe hereby give and bequeth it as followeth: First, I give my son-in-law, Doc^r Hawkins, and to his Wife, to them I give all my tytell and right of or in a part of a howse and shop in Pater-noster-rowe, in London, which I hold by lease from the Lord Bishop of London for about 50 years to come. and I doe also give to them all my right and tytell of or to a howse in Chancery-lane, London, where in Mrs Greinwood now dwelleth, in which is now about 16 years to come. I give these two leases to them, they saving my executor from all damage concerning the same.

[And I doe also give to my saide dafter all my books this day at Winchester and Droxford: and what ever ells I can call mine their, except a trunk of linen wch I give my son Izaak Walton. but if he doe not marry, or use the saide linen himselfe, then I give the same to my grand-doughter Anne Hawkins.]

And I give to my son Izaak all my right and tytell to a lease of Norington farme, which I hold from the lord B^p of Winton: And I doe also give him all my right and tytell to a farme or land nere to Stafford, which I bought of Mr Walter Noell; I say, I give it to him and [his] heares for ever; but upon the condition following, namely: if my sone shall not marry before he shall be of the age of forty and one yeare, or, being marryed, shall dye before the saide age, and leve noe son to inherit the saide farme or land, or if his son [or sonns]

---

* The words and sentences in square brackets were interlineations, and a passage in double square brackets was erased because 'twice repeated'.

shall not live to ataine the age of twentie and one yeare, to dispose otherwayes of it, then I give the saide farme or land to the towne or corperation of Stafford, (in which I was borne), for the good and benifit of some of the saide towne, as I shall direct, and as followeth (but first note, that it is at this present time rented for 21 pound 10^s a yeare, and is like to hold the said rent, if care be taken to keipe the barne and howsing in repaire). And I wood have and doe give ten pownd of the saide rent to binde out yearely two boyes, the sons of honest and pore parents, to be apprentises to some tradesmen or handycraft-men, to the intent the saide boyes [may] the better afterward get their owne living. And I doe also give five pownd yearly out of the said rent, to be given to some meade-servant that hath attain'd the age of twenty and [one] yeare, (not les), and dwelt long in one servis, or to some honest pore man's daughter that hath attain'd to that age, to [be] paide her at or on the day of her marriage. And this being done, my will is, that what rent shall remaine of the saide farme or land, shall be disposed of as followeth:

First, I doe give twenty shillings yearely, to be spent by the maior of Stafford, and those that shall colect the said rent and dispose of it as I have and shall hereafter direct; and that what mony or rent shall remaine undisposed offe, shall be imployed to buie coles for some pore people, that shall most neide them, in the said towne; the said coles to be delivered the last weike in Janewary, or in every first weike in Febrewary; I say then, because I take that time to be the hardest and most pinching times with pore people; and God reward those that shall doe this without partialitie, and with honestie and a good contience.

And if the saide maior and others of the saide town of Stafford shall prove so necligent, or dishonest, as not to imply the rent by me given as intended and exprest in this my will, which God forbid, then I give the saide rents and profits of the saide farme or land to the towne and chief magestrats or governers of Ecles-hall, to be disposed by them in such manner as I have ordered the disposall of it by the towne of Stafford, the said Farme or land being nere the town of Ecles-hall.

And I give to my son-in-law, Doctor Hawkins, whome I love as my owne son; and to my dafter, his wife; and my son Izaak; to each of them a ring, with these words or moto: 'Love my memory. I. W., *obiet*'; to the Lord B^p of Winton a ring, with this motto: 'A mite for a million. I. W., *obiet*'; and to the friends hearafter named, I give to each of them a ring, with this motto: 'A friends farewell. I. W., *obiet*.' And my will is, the said rings be delivered within fortie days after my deth; and that the price or valew of all the saide rings shall be 13ˢ 4ᵈ a piece.

I give to Doctor Hawkins Doctoᵣ Donnus Sermons, which I have hear'd preach and read with much content. To my son Izaak I give Docᵣ Sibbs his 'Soules Conflict'; and to my doughter his 'Brewsed Reide;' desiring them to reade them so as to be well acquainted with them. And I also give to her all my bookes at Winchester and Droxford, and what ever in those two places are or I can call mine, except a trunk of linen, which I give to my son Izaak; but if he doe not live to [marry or] make use of it, then I give the same to my grand-dafter, Anne Hawkins. And I give my dafter Docᵣ Halls Works, which be now at Farnham.

To my son Izaak I give all my books, not yet given, at Farnham Castell; and a deske of prints and pickters; also a cabinet nere my beds head, in wᶜʰ are som littell things that he will valew, tho of noe greate worth.

And my will and desyre is, that he will be kinde to his Ante Beacham, and his ant Rose Ken, by alowing the first about fiftie shilling a yeare, in or for bacon and cheise, not more, and paying 4 a yeare toward the bordin of her son's dyut to Mr John Whitehead: for his Ante Ken, I desyre him to be kinde to her acording to her necessitie and his owne abillitie; and I comend one of her children, to breide up as I have saide I intend to doe, if he shall be able to doe it, as I know he will; for they be good folke.

I give to Mr John Darbishire the Sermons of Mr Antony Faringdon or of doᵣ Sanderson, which my executor thinks fit. To my servant, Thomas Edghill, I give five pownd in mony, and all my clothes, linen and wollen – except one sute of clothes, which I give to Mr Holinshed and forty shiling – if the saide Thomas be my servant at my deth; if not, my cloths only.

And I give my old friend, Mr Richard Marriot, ten pownd in mony, to be paid him within 3 months after my deth; and I desyre my son to shew kindenes to him if he shall neide, and my son can spare it.

And I doe hereby will and declare my son Izaak to be my sole executoᵣ of this my last will and testament; and Doᵣ Hawkins to see that he performs it, which I doubt not but he will.

I desyre my buriall may be nere the place of my deth, and free from any ostentation or charg, but privately. This I make to be my last will (to which I shall only add the codicell for rings), this 16. day of August, 1683.

IZAAK WALTON

Izaac Walton's House
on the N: side of Fleet St·

The rings I give are as on the other side.

To my brother Jon Ken
to my sister his wife
to my brother Doc^r Ken
to my sister Pye
to Mr Francis Morley
to Sr George Vernon
to his wife
to his 3 dafters
to Mrs Nelson
to Mr Rich Walton
to Mr Palmer
to Mr Taylor
to Mr Tho. Garrard
to the Lord B^p of Sarum
to my brother Beacham
to my sister his wife
to the lady Anne How
to Mrs King Do^r Philips wife
to Mr Valantine Harecourt
to Mrs Elyza Johnson

to Mrs Mary Rogers
to Mrs Elyza Milward
to Mrs Doro. Wallop
to Mr Will. Milward, of
    Christchurch, Oxford
to Mr John Darbeshire
to Mrs Vuedvill
to Mrs Rock
to Mr Rede his servant
to my Coz. Dorothy Kenrick
to my Coz. Lewin
to Mr Walter Higgs
to Mr Cha. Cotton
to Mr Rich. Marryot
to Mr Peter White
to Mr John Lloyde
to my cozen Greinsells widow

Mrs Dalbin must not be forgotten.

Note that severall lines are blotted out of this will for they were twice repeted: And, that this will is now signed and sealed, this twenty and fourth day of October 1683 in the presence of us:

Witnes: Abra. Markland   Jos. Taylor   Thomas Crawley

Probatum apud London, &c. Coram venli et egregio viro d'no Thoma Exton Milite Legum D'core surro &c., quarto die mensis, Februarii Anno D'ni (stylo Angliae) 1683 juramento Isaaci Walton jun^{ris} filii d'ci def'ti et Extoris &c., cui &c., de bene &c. Jurat.

His will was thus endorsed by himself:

Izaak Walton's last will, octo_r, 1683.

Izaak Walton's Burialplace.

On December 15th Walton was dead. His death seems to have taken place at the house of his son-in-law, Dr Hawkins, a prebendary of Winchester.

He was buried in Winchester Cathedral, in a chapel in the south transept, called Prior Silkstead's Chapel. A large black marble slab bears the following inscription:

HERE RESTETH THE BODY OF
MR ISAAC WALTON
WHO DYED THE 15TH OF DECEMBER
1683

Alas he's gone before.
Gone to returne no more!
Our panting Breasts aspire
After their aged Sire,
Whose well spent life did last,
Full ninety yeares and past,
But now he hath begun
That which will ne're be done
Crown'd with eternall blisse:
We wish our Souls with his.

VOTIS MODESTIS SIC FLERUNT LIBERI

And now we may pass on to the record of his literary life, and to a fuller account of his relations with those friends whom so far we have but mentioned.

PART TWO

Walton's Literary Life and Friendships

If Walton had a 'special genius for bishops', he had an even rarer genius for friendship. His literary life may be said to have been begotten of two particularly interesting friendships, for his first appearance in print was in the form of an elegy upon Donne,* prefixed to the 1633 edition of Donne's poems, of which it is probable he was the editor; and when later, in 1640, he prefixed his life of Donne to a volume of Donne's sermons, it was because Sir Henry Wotton had died in 1639, without fulfilling his intention of himself writing the life of the great dean. Walton had been busy, at Wotton's request, collecting materials for that life, and had on one occasion jogged his memory about the matter. Wotton's reply, preserved in the *Reliquiae Wottonianae*, can hardly be spared here, for the illustration it affords of the familiar intercourse between the two men:

[Date, probably early part of 1639]

MY WORTHY FRIEND – I am not able to yield any reason; no, not so much as may satisfy myself, why a most ingenious letter of yours hath lain so long by me (as it were in lavender) without an answer, save this only, the pleasure I have taken in your style and conceptions, together with a meditation of the subject you propound, may seem to have cast me into a gentle slumber. But being now awaked, I do herein return you most hearty thanks for the kind prosecution of your first motion, touching a just office due to the memory of our ever memorable friend, to whose good fame, though it be needless to add anything (and my age considered, almost hopeless from my pen;) yet I will endeavour to perform my promise, if it were but even for this cause, that in saying somewhat of the life of so deserving a man, I may perchance over-live mine own. That which you add of Dr King (now made Dean of Rochester, and by that translated into my native soil) is a great spur unto me: with whom I hope shortly to confer about it in my passage towards Boughton Malherb, which was my genial air, and invite him to a friendship with that family where his predecessor was familiarly acquainted. I shall write to you at large by the next messenger (being at present a little in business), and then I shall set down certain general heads, wherein I desire information by your loving diligence; hoping shortly to enjoy your own ever welcome company in this approaching time of the *Fly* and the *Cork*. And so I rest,

Your very hearty poor friend to serve you,

H. WOTTON

In addition to the Elegy, Walton had meanwhile written some lines for the portrait of Donne in the second edition of Donne's poems (1635), and had also contributed complimentary verses to *The Merchant's Map of Commerce*, 1638; but it is with his life of Donne that his literary work really commences. It appears to have won immediate and unanimous praise. Charles I spoke of it with approbation; John Hales told Dr King that 'he had not seen a life written with more advantage to the subject, or more reputation to the writer than that of Dr Donne'. A letter from Donne's son, expressing his gratitude, is to be found in Nicholas's 'Life', and, long after, Dr Johnson gave it as his opinion that Walton was 'a great panegyrist', and that Donne's was the best life he had written. Of the closeness of Walton's friendship with Donne, the fact that

Walton was among the three or four friends gathered round his deathbed is evidence, and also that Donne left him the quaint memorial seal which he ever afterwards used, and which will be found engraved at the foot of his will.

For the next ten years, Walton's literary work is confined to stray verses and prefaces. In 1642 he is supposed to have published a letter by George Cranmer to Hooker, concerning 'the new Church discipline'; in 1643 he wrote some lines on the death of his friend, the poet William Cartwright, first published in the 1651 edition of Cartwright's poems; in 1646 there is little doubt that he contributed the charming address 'To the Reader' (so much in his own pretty style) in Francis Quarles's *Shepherd's Eclogues*, its signature, 'John Marriott', being probably an innocent literary deception; for the year 1650 his literary output was a couplet found written in his copy of Dr Richard Sibbes's *The Returning Backslider*, preserved at Salisbury. But in 1651 he published another of his incomparable biographies, the charming life of Sir Henry Wotton prefixed to the *Reliquiae Wottonianae*, of which also he was the editor.

Sir Henry Wotton is one of the most fascinating figures of the seventeenth century, and his *Reliquiae* are curiously illustrative of his wandering life and his sensitive many-sided character; for never was such a quaint jumble of materials – notes on Italian architecture, 'characters' of contemporary statesmen, reminiscences of diplomatic missions to Venice, 'meditations' upon Christmas day, and the twenty-second chapter of Genesis, delightful gay letters to familiar friends, grave letters of business to 'my Lord Zouch', and in the midst, like a little bunch of myrrh, a handful of lyrics of a rare meditative sweetness. In one of these, prettily entitled 'On a Bank as I sat a-Fishing', he very likely refers to Walton, for he is doubtless the 'friend' of these lines:

> The jealous Trout, that low did lie,
> Rose at a well dissembled fly:
> There stood my friend, with patient skill
> Attending of his trembling quill.

Probably a reminiscence of one of the many fishing excursions Walton and his friend used to make together along the Thames near Eton, where Wotton had a fishing-house. The *Reliquiae* contain two letters to 'Iz. Wa'. One has already been quoted. The other ran as follows:

MY WORTHY FRIEND – Since I last saw you I have been confined to my chamber by a quotidian fever, I thank God, of more contumacy than malignity. It had once left me, as I thought, but it was only to fetch more company, returning with a surcrew of those splenetic vapours, that are called hypochondriacal; of which most say the cure is good company; and I desire no better physician than yourself. I have in one of those fits endeavoured to make it more easy by composing a short Hymn; and since I have apparelled my best thoughts so lightly as in verse, I hope I shall be pardoned a second vanity, if I communicate it with such a friend as yourself; to whom I wish a cheerful spirit, and a thankful heart to value it, as one of the greatest blessings of our good God, in whose dear love I leave you, remaining,

Your poor friend to serve you,

H. WOTTON

Oh thou great Power! in whom I move,
For whom I live, to whom I die,
Behold me through thy beams of love,
Whilst on this couch of tears I lie;
    And cleanse my sordid soul within,
    By thy Christ's blood, the bath of sin.

No hallowed oils, no grains I need,
No rags of saints, no purging fire,
Our rosy drop from David's seed,
Was world's of seas to quench thine ire.
    Oh! precious Ransom! which once paid
    That Consummatum est was said.

And said by him, that said no more,
But seal'd it with his sacred breath;
Thou then that has despung'd my score,
And dying wast the death of death,
    Be to me now, on thee I call,
    My life, my strength, my joy, my all.

H. WOTTON

In 1652 Walton seems to have contributed an Address to the Reader to 'The Heroe of Lorenzo, or The way to Eminencie and Perfection. A piece of serious Spanish wit Originally in that language

At Stafford

written, and in English. By Sir John Skeffington, Kt. and Barronet;'
and in the same year he contributed some commendatory verses to
the 'Scintillula Altaris' of his 'worthy friend' Edward Sparke.

With the year 1653 came the charming classic, which in the
present volume is published for the hundred and twenty-first time.
It was a troublous year in which this 'contemplative man's recreation' was born. For us, looking back, it seems hard to realise that
quiet men might go a-angling by tranquil rivers, and that there
should be a sale, and a ready one, for so peaceful a book; but one
remembers Sir Thomas Browne meditating in alike quietude at
Norwich; one thinks, too, to take an example from a later time, of
Théophile Gautier bringing out a new edition of his poems during
the siege of Paris, and it is healing to reflect that even in such
troublous times there is always peace somewhere in the world for
peaceable men.

I shall deal more particularly with *The Compleat Angler* later on.

Meanwhile let us proceed with Walton's quiet history.

In 1654 appeared an enlarged a second edition of the *Reliquiae Wottonianae*, in 1655 an enlarged second edition of *The Compleat Angler*, and in 1658 a second edition of The *Life of Donne*, also revised and enlarged. In 1660 Walton's satisfaction at the Restoration was expressed in a 'humble eclogue', addressed to 'my ingenious friend, Mr Brome, on his various and excellent poems', 'written the 29 of May 1660', and first published in the first edition of Alexander Brome's *Songs and Other Poems*, 1661. In 1661 came a third edition of *The Compleat Angler*, and in that year Walton also contributed some verses to the fourth edition of a religious poem, entitled *The Synagogue*, by the Revd Christopher Harvie, who had paid Walton a similar compliment in the second edition of *The Compleat Angler*. In 1665 appeared *The Life of Mr Richard Hooker*, which Walton had written during the first two years of his residence with Bishop Morley at Winchester. To the Life was prefixed that delightful letter from Dr King, Bishop of Chichester, from which one of Walton's many soubriquets of affection is borrowed. 'Honest Izaak,' it began:

> Though a familiarity of more than forty years continuance, and the constant experience of your love, even in the worst of the late sad times, be sufficient to endear our friendship, yet, I must confess my affection much improved, not only by evidences of private respect to many that know and love you, but by your new demonstration of a public spirit, testified in a diligent, true and useful collection of so many material passages as you have now afforded me in the life of venerable Mr Hooker, of which, since desired by such a friend as yourself, I shall not deny to give the testimony of what I know concerning him and his learned books; but shall first here take a fair occasion to tell you, that you have been happy in choosing to write the lives of three such persons as posterity hath just cause to honour; which they will do the more for the true relation of them by your happy pen; of all which I shall give you my unfeigned censure.

Walton's preface is particularly interesting from the allusion he makes to some other friendships. The friend who had persuaded him to the task, 'a friend whom I reverence, and ought to obey', was, of course, Bishop Morley. He goes on to speak of his long 'happy affinity with William Cranmer – now with God – a grand-nephew unto the great Archbishop of that name', and 'I had also,' he continues, 'a friendship with the Reverend Dr Usher, the late learned

Archbishop of Armagh; and with Dr Morton, the late learned and charitable Bishop of Durham; as also the learned John Hales, of Eton College; and with them also – who loved the very name of Mr Hooker – I have had many discourses concerning him . . . '

The year 1668 is marked by a fourth edition of *The Compleat Angler*, and in 1670 appeared *The Life of Mr George Herbert*. This year also appeared the first collected edition of the *Lives*, dedicated to Bishop Morley. In 1673 appeared a third edition of the *Reliquiae*

Wottonianae, and from a letter to his publisher, Marriott, it appears that Walton was then collecting materials for a life of John Hales.

In 1674 appeared an edition of Herbert's *Temple*, with Walton's Life prefixed, and in 1675 appeared the second collected edition of the *Lives*, on which occasion Cotton addressed a long and affectionate poem to Walton, which he had written apparently on January 17, 1672–3.

In 1676 appeared the fifth and finally revised edition of *The Compleat Angler*, to which further reference will be made.

In 1678 Walton published his *Life of Robert Sanderson, Bishop of Lincoln*, being then in his eighty-fifth year, but as vigorous mentally as ever. This Life is of particular interest for the personal glimpses which it gives us of Walton, and his attitude to the movements of his own day. I have already quoted the charming picture of Walton and Sanderson meeting in Little Britain in 'that dangerous year, 1655', but this charming valedictory reference to his own length of years, as he finishes telling of Sanderson's dying, should not be omitted: 'Thus this pattern of meekness and primitive innocence changed this for a better life. 'Tis now too late to wish that my life may be like his; for I am in the eighty-fifth year of my age; but I humbly beseech Almighty God that my death may; and do as earnestly beg of every reader to say Amen. "Blessed is the man in whose spirit there is no guile." Psalms XXXII. 2.'

In 1680 was published a pamphlet entitled 'Love and Truth: in two modest and peacable Letters, concerning the distempers of the Present Times: written from a quiet and conformable Citizen of London to Two Busie and Factious Shopkeepers in Coventry.' These letters have been attributed to Walton (confidently by Zouch) and there has been much controversy on the matter. Their style certainly recalls Walton, and Sir Harris Nicolas hesitates to decide. William Pickering, in an interesting MS note to his copy now in the British Museum, decides unhesitatingly against Walton's authorship, and the balance of opinion seems to be that way. Space forbids our discussing the pros and cons here, the more so as the matter is of no great importance, for even if the letters were proved to be Walton's, the fact could hardly persuade one that they are exciting to read.

In 1680, however, it is certain that Walton did no great service to the memory of Ben Jonson by sending the following data, or rather gossip, to his friend Aubrey, the antiquary, who, it would appear, had applied to him for the information.

Temple Bar before the fire

FFOR Y^R FFRIENDS Q^UE THIS

I only knew Ben Jonson: But my Lord of Winton knew him very well; and says, he was in the 6°, that is, the uppermost fforme in Westminster scole, at which time his father dyed, and his mother married a bricklayer, who made him (much against his will) help him in his trade; but in a short time, his scolemaister, Mr Camden, got him a better imployment, which was to attend or accompany a son of Sir Walter Rauley's on his travills. Within a short time after their return, they parted (I think not in cole bloud) and with a love sutable to what they had in their travilles (not to be commended). And then Ben began to set up for himself in the trade by which he got his subsistance and fame, of which I need not give any account. He got in time to have a 100£ a yeare from the King, also a pension from the cittie, and the like from many of the nobilitie and some of the gentry, wch was well pay'd, for love or fere of his railing in verse, or prose, or boeth. My lord told me, he told him he was (in his long retyrement and sickness, when he saw him, which was often) much afflickted, that he had profaned the Scripture in his playes, and lamented it with horror:

yet that, at that time of his long retyrement, his pension (so much
as came in) was giuen to a woman that gouern'd him (with
whome he liv'd and dyed near the Abie in Westminster); and that
nether he nor she tooke too much care for next weike: and wood
be sure not to want wine, of wch he usually tooke too much before
he went to bed, if not oftener and soner. My Lord tells me, he
knowes not, but thinks he was born in Westminster. The question may be put to Mr Wood very easily upon what grounds he is
positive as to his being born their; he is a friendly man, and will
resolve it. So much for braue Ben. You will not think the rest so
tedyous as I doe this.

I. W.
Nou^r. 22, 80

Gifford's criticism upon this is justifiably severe. 'Izaak Walton,'
he writes, 'cannot be mentioned without respect; but his letter was
written nearly half a century after Jonson's death, and when the
writer was in his eighty-seventh year. It is made up of the common
stories of the time, and a few anecdotes procured, while he was
writing, from the Bishop of Winchester, who must himself, at the
date of Izaak's letter, have been verging on ninety. It is not easy to
discover what was the Bishop's and what was Walton's, but on these
Wood constructed his Life of Jonson. He brings little of his own
but a few dates.'

In 1683 Walton had reached the advanced age of ninety, and if
the theory which makes himself the real author of '*Thealma and
Clearchus*, a Pastoral History, in smooth and easie verse', which he
published this year, be true, it may well be an example of that
second childhood's tenderness towards their early verses which is
often observed to overcome the aging prose-writer. However,
Walton declared the poem to have been 'written long since, by John
Chalkhill Esqre; an Acquaint and Friend of Edmund Spencer', and
as there were more than one John Chalkhill among his second
wife's connections, and as even so innocent a dissimulation would
probably have been repugnant to Walton, there seems no good
ground for doubting his statement. Sir Harris Nicolas will not hear
of Walton being the author, but Lowell, on the other hand, is of
opinion that Walton very much tinkered his friend's poem and that
it is 'mainly Walton's as it now stands'.

The publication of *Thealma and Clearchus* brings Walton's literary
life to an end, and here I may take the opportunity of remarking
that Walton's poetry, which the reader may study for himself, has

perhaps been a little unduly depreciated. It is often no doubt little
more than versified prose, but 'poetry' of this order shares the
advantage of the necessity imposed upon prose of having something, however prosaic, to say. Moreover, the same downright
sincerity of feeling, which so often makes poetry of his prose, comes
to the rescue of his verse also, verse which seldom lacks the prose
excellence of apt and pithy phrase. On the other hand, in Lowell's
opinion, Walton's prose, like that of many another prose-writer,
owes no little to the secret practice of verse. 'I think,' he says, 'that
Walton's prose owes much of its charm to the poetic sentiment in
him which was denied a refuge in verse, and that his practice in
metres may have given to his happier periods a measure and a music
they would otherwise have wanted.'

Lowell's own success and failure were so parallel to this that his
judgement is the more authoritative. His remarks on Walton's
Elegy upon Donne are equally worth noting. 'The versification of

At Shallowford

this,' he says, 'if sometimes rather stiff, is for the most part firm and not inharmonious. It is easier in its gait than that of Donne in his *Satires*, and shows the manly influence of Jonson. Walton, at any rate, in course of time, attained, at least in prose, to something which, if it may not be called style, was a very charming way of writing, all the more so that he has an innocent air of not knowing how it is done. Natural endowment and predisposition may count for nine in ten of the chances of success in this competition; but no man ever achieved, as Walton sometimes did, a simplicity which leaves criticism helpless, by the even light of nature alone.'

To the number of Walton's friends before mentioned must be added the poet Drayton, of whom he twice speaks with affection in *The Compleat Angler*, once as his 'honest old friend', and again as 'his old deceased friend'; also Walter, Lord Aston, to whom he presented a copy of his collected *Lives*, still preserved, with this note beneath Walton's inscription:

> Izake Walton gift to me,
> June y^e 14, 1670,
> wch I most thankfully for
> his memmory off mee acknowledge
> a greate kindnesse.
> WALTER ASTON

Walton's cottage
Shallowford

PART THREE

The Compleat Angler

The history of *The Compleat Angler* is a romance in itself, and it has been written once and for all by Thomas Westwood, in his *Chronicle of the Compleat Angler*, a model of what one might call devotional bibliography. That so restful a pastoral should have been published in so turbulent a time has already been commented upon. Some have suggested that that very paradox may have accounted for its immediate success, so welcome was such a note of peace. Certainly its quietist message was one pertinent to the moment, and it had the rare fortune to be heard. The sale of the first edition seems to have been immediate, and the second speedily called for. This second is really the first of the book as we know it today, and that perhaps accounts for its greater rarity, for Walton had increased its length by at least a third, and made many changes and additions. In the first edition the interlocutors had been but two, 'Piscator' and 'Viator', and in the second they are three, as we know them, 'Venator' taking the place of 'Viator', whom, however, Cotton resuscitates in his second part. In some respects Walton would have done well to allow his book to remain in the form it had now attained, for I must agree with Sir Harris Nicolas that the changes and additions made in the fifth edition (the third and fourth having practically been reprints of the second) were somewhat short of improvements. 'The garrulity and sentiments,' says Nicolas, 'of an octogenarian are very apparent in some of the alterations; and the subdued colouring of religious feeling which prevails throughout the former editions, and forms one of the charms of the piece, is, in this impression, so much heightened as to become almost obtrusive;' and he gives as an example the homiletical passage in the last chapter, immediately after Venator's recipe for colouring rods, which, he says truly, is in fact a religious essay. In this fifth edition also he made the artistic mistake of inviting Cotton to write an unnecessary second part, but it was so he decreed that his book should take its final shape, and it is on this fifth edition that all subsequent editions have been based. To some copies of this edition still a third part was added, namely *The Experienc'd Angler, or Angling Improved*, by Colonel Richard Venables. When including this third part, the book is entitled *The Universal Angler*, but Venables's portion was not retained in later editions. Of these the most important have been those of Moses Browne, Sir John Hawkins, John Major, Sir Harris Nicolas, Dr Bethune and Mr R. B. Marston. Sir Harris Nicolas's is the most complete, and will probably remain the authoritative edition, John Major's is the daintiest (but greatly marred by its shopkeeper's preface) and Dr Bethune's is the most learned.

Perhaps no English book except *The Pilgrim's Progress* and *Robinson Crusoe* has been so beloved. Generation after generation has brought to it its young affections, and there seems every reason to suppose that the average of something like a new edition for every two and a half years, which so far *The Compleat Angler* has maintained, will even be surpassed in the future.

This veneration for Walton is one of the curious phenomena of literature. Perhaps Dr Johnson set the fashion by saying that he considered 'the preservation and elucidation of Walton' 'a pious work'. He himself has become the god of a similar idolatry, and Lamb perhaps is the only other writer who has inspired quite the same kind of devotion. For it is not mere hero-worship, it is an actually religious sentiment on the part of the Waltonian. In his loving imagination Saint Izaak is as truly a saint as any in the Calendar. We can observe the same process of canonisation going on in the case of Lamb.

Lamb's question to Coleridge, 'Among all your quaint readings,

Bishop Morley's Palace, Winchester

did you ever light upon Walton's *Complete Angler*? . . . it breathes the very spirit of innocence, purity, and simplicity of heart; there are many choice old verses interspersed in it; it would sweeten a man's temper at any time to read it; it would Christianise every discordant angry passion: pray make yourself acquainted with it' – and his many references to Walton in his essays have no doubt swelled his fame even more than the pontifical praise of Johnson. Then he has had Scott for his panegyrist and Wordsworth for his sonneteer. Nor should we forget the poet Bowles.

All his admirers have not written so wisely or so well as these. Like Burns, Walton has suffered from maudlin devotees, he has been slapped on the back by the robustious, cooed to in the voice of the sucking dove by the sentimental, some have written in the 'man and a brother', grand lodge 'masonic' vein, others as though he were a sort of aged pet lamb; but that was inevitable – fame is no fame without the plebs, and the paths of glory must often pass beneath triumphal arches not always in the best taste. Besides, however absurd the form it may take, this devotion to the memory of a lovely soul is surely far from absurd. For, after all, Walton is a sentiment, at least as an angler; for I understand that the ordinary Philistine angler, to whom all that pretty warbling talk of birds and honeysuckle hedges has no appeal in comparison with a creel full of speckled trout, thinks but small beer of poor Izaak's antiquated angling methods. It is probably among those who have never cast a line (like the present editor), or, like Washington Irving, have but fished 'to satisfy the sentiment', that the majority of Waltonians are to be found.

As a practical guide to angling, *The Compleat Angler* was exploded even in its own day. Robert Franck belonged to the order of Philistine, as distinct from that of contemplative, anglers, and naturally he had little patience with Walton's unpractical digressions. He vents his spleen in a curious book, entitled *Northern Memoirs*, written in dialogue between Theophilus and Arnoldus, published in 1694, and re-edited by Sir Walter Scott, in 1821. Arnoldus complains that Walton 'stuffs his book with morals from Dubravius and others, not giving us one precedent of his own practical experiments'. Theophilus loftily rejoins: 'I remember the book, but you inculcate his errata; however, it may pass muster among common muddlers.' But Arnoldus thinks not, 'For,' he continues, 'I remember in Stafford, I urged his own argument upon him, that pickerel weed of itself breeds pickerel. Which question was no sooner stated, but he transmits himself to his authority, viz., Gesner, Dubravius and Aldrovandus, which I readily opposed, and offered my reasons to prove the contrary.' Arnoldus finally relates how the Compleat Angler, getting the worst of the argument, dropped it, 'and leaves Gesner to defend it', and 'so huffed away'.

Of course, from his point of view Franck was perfectly justified. For one might as well consult a fifteenth-century pharmacopoeia on Russian influenza as consult 'Honest Izaak' on any of the higher branches of his art. But who minds that? Angling was simply an excuse for Walton's artless garrulity, a peg on which to hang his ever-fragrant discourse of stream and meadow. He followed angling, as indeed any such sport is most intelligently followed, as a pretext for a day or two in the fields, not so much to fill his basket as to refresh his spirit, and store his memory with the sweetness of country sights and sounds. The angler who merely angles for the sake of what he can catch is not so much an angler as a fishmonger. The truer angler is more often like Scott and Mr Lang, 'no fisher, but a well-wisher to the game', such a one as Mr Bridges describes in one of his prettiest verses –

Farnham Castle

> Sometimes an angler comes, and drops his hook
>   Within its hidden depths, and 'gainst a tree
> Leaning his rod, reads in some pleasant book,
>   Forgetting soon his pride of fishery;
>   And dreams, or falls asleep,
>   While curious fishes peep
> About his nibbled bait, or scornfully
>   Dart off and rise and leap.

How much better to be this angler who only dreams, to have one's creel empty indeed, but one's head sweetly giddy with the shining 'ghosts of fish' – the angler who fishes for the sake of doing something else, to 'some incognisable end', which certainly is not trout.

It is curious to note that that fantastic natural history, which was the scorn of the fierce scientific Franck, is one of the features of *The Compleat Angler* which most attracts us today. Aldrovandus, Aelianus, Dubravius, Rondeletius – what names had the scientists of those days! Names monstrous to the eye as the monsters they celebrate. It is hard sometimes to make up one's mind whether Walton's solemn deference to these extinct naturalists of the extinct is not a form of humour with him, as indeed one sometimes wonders too of his no less fantastic piety. Take, for instance, his familiar argument in favour of anglers that four of Christ's disciples were fishermen, and 'first, that He never reproved these for their employment or calling, as He did scribes and the money-changers. And secondly, He found that the hearts of such men by nature were fitted for contemplation and quietness; men of mild, and sweet and peaceable spirits, as indeed most anglers are . . . And it is observable, that it was our Saviour's will, that these our four Fishermen should have a priority of nomination in the catalogue of His Twelve Apostles, Matt. x. 2-4, Acts i. 13, as namely, first St Peter, St Andrew, St James, and St John, and then the rest in their order.'

It is difficult for us to realise that Walton probably meant all this quite seriously, so hard is it by any stretch of imagination to transport oneself into that atmosphere of primitive innocence in which the childlike soul of Walton breathed. But to doubt Walton's absolute seriousness in such a passage is to miss one of the essential conditions of his temperament, its complete, unquestioning reliance upon authority. He was entirely the product of the old order. We see in him an exquisite example of that perfection of character which that old order not infrequently developed. He is perhaps more the ideal Churchman than the ideal Christian, a respecter of castes and an unquestioning supporter of the powers that be. He is the type of man who grows obediently as he is trained, and gives God the glory. It is inevitable that such a type has its limitations. It is apt to be hard on merely human feelings, and one encounters Walton's limitations when he comes to deal with such a matter as Donne's beautiful passionate love-story. Donne's wife married him against the open hostility of her family, and their life together to the very end (even when she had become the mother of twelve children) was an idyll of devoted love – yet Walton declares their marriage to have been 'the remarkable error' of Donne's life, and even goes so far as to say, 'a marriage, too, without the allowance of those friends, whose approbation always was, and ever will be, necessary, to make even a virtuous love become lawful'! One would have expected the gentle fisherman to have treated so charming a love-story more tenderly, but I am afraid 'Honest Izaak's' view of woman was much like that of Mr Coventry Patmore, and his respect for social usage and dividing-lines as inexorable.

But a saint is, of necessity, somewhat inhuman, and Izaak, being a true saint, he was not, doubtless, without saintly drawbacks – though they are hard to discover. To adapt Wordsworth's sonnet, he was a saint who wrote with a quill 'dropt from an angel's wing'.

Walton's Cottage

One can hardly think of one so innocent-minded writing so well. There always seems a spice of the devil in any form of skill, and we don't readily think of the good man being clever as well. It seems a sort of wickedness in him, somehow. But perhaps Walton was not quite so artless in this matter as he seemed. No artist can be really artless. Take, for instance, that apparently simple sentence in the life of Herbert, where, speaking of certain of Donne's hymns, he says, 'These hymns are now lost to us; but doubtless they were such as they two now Sing in heaven.' How touchingly quaint, we say, how primitive in its old-world innocency! And yet Lowell has pointed out, that on the inside of his Eusebius, preserved at Salisbury, Walton has written three attempts at this sentence, each of them very far from the concise beauty to which he at last constrained himself. In his prayer-book are to be found his studies for his wife's epitaph, and his account of the death of Hooker and the *Lives* generally received considerable retouching. We have seen him working at *The Compleat Angler* till the last; and if it was artlessness that planned his pastoral, managed his dialogues, and introduced his variations from his chosen theme, it was that artlessness which is one with art. So much nature was never got into a book without a corresponding outlay of art – and has anyone else brought the singing of birds, the fragrance of meadows, the meditative peace of the riverside, into a book, with so undying a freshness as he? And how well he knew daintily to set a sprig of 'old-fashioned poetry, but choicely good', here and there among his pages, poetry thus immortalised by the association – for no other writer so hallows his quotations.

But it is in vain we strive by critical reagents to analyse the unfading charm of this old book; is it not simply that the soul of a good man still breathes through its pages like lavender?

Bentley Hall

PART FOUR

Charles Cotton

I have elsewhere ventured to express the opinion that Cotton's so-called 'second part' of *The Compleat Angler*, whatever the literary skill with which the style of Walton is imitated, not to say parodied, whatever its illustrative and associative value, or its importance as a contribution to the art and science of fly-fishing, is nevertheless – printed as an integral part of that charming classic – an impertinence. Its proper place is an appendix, whither I should have relegated it in this edition, had not tradition been too strong to be gainsaid. Whom fame has joined together let no man put asunder.

Yet, as I have said, I cannot be 'the only reader of the book for whom it ends with that gentle benediction: "And upon all that are lovers of virtue, and dare trust in his providence, and be quiet, and go a Angling"; and that sweet exhortation from 1 Thess. iv. 11, "Study to be quiet."

'After the exquisite quietism of this farewell, it is distracting to come precipitately upon the fine gentleman with the great wig and the Frenchified airs.'

But I resent the arbitrary wedlock for Cotton, too. It has caused him to be preached at for years by sententiously pious editors, who, it is plain, feel him no fit company for Walton, and only tolerate him at all because Walton's affection 'pleads against oblivion for his name'.

Dr Bethune's sanctimonious horror on the matter is so delicious that I cannot forbear quoting him:

> The friendship which our venerated Walton had for Cotton, besides his being the author of the following amusing and excellent treatise, will naturally lead the reader to desire a better knowledge of him; but, it must be confessed, that the duty thus laid upon the editor is by no means so pleasant as he could wish. The character of the adopted son differs so widely from that of his pure-minded father, as to make it a mystery how even a common taste for angling could have made the friend of Wotton bear with the habits of the younger man. Perhaps the friendship Walton had for Cotton's father was affectionately entailed upon the offspring; perhaps similarity of political opinions may have biased even the very sober judgement; perhaps a charitable hope to do the reckless wit good by a close association made the merciful heart more tolerant; no doubt the venerable presence restrained the tongue from the licence of the pen which the burlesque poet made a second nature; but however it came about, an affectionate intercourse was maintained between them, as the reader already knows, and will soon know further. Let us hope that Walton's serious occupations and intercourse with pious men of learning kept him happily away from companions where loose writings would be named; and that, ignorant of Cotton's vicious folly, he judged him rather by the truly beautiful sentiments breathed through the 'Stanzes Irreguliers'.

One would like to hear 'hearty, cheerful Mr Cotton's' laughter – and remarks – on this passage.

The incongruity of the friendship is obvious, and we may be sure, with Lowell, that 'there must have been delicately understood and mutually respectful conventions of silence in an intimacy between the placidly believing author of the *Lives* and the translator of him who created the essay'.

But saint and sinner have been friends before and after Walton and Cotton, and the likeableness of a friend is more important to a friendship than his opinions, or even his morals. Besides, if Walton was a saint, he had plainly not forgotten the good gospel advice given to unpractical children of light, and Lowell no doubt indicates one bond between him and Cotton, when he says that, 'Walton loved a gentleman of the blood as honestly as Johnson did, and was, I am sure, as sturdily independent withal . . . himself of obscurest lineage, there was nothing he relished more keenly than the long pedigrees of other people.' When that gentleman of the blood was an angler, with one of the best trout streams in England rippling through his lands, a man of taste, a staunch cavalier, a loyal Churchman, and a kind, hearty, good-natured young man, reverent to age and respectful towards sanctities, if perhaps a thought too gay and giddy in his life and poems, as young men will be – well, why shouldn't even the Bishop of Chichester's 'Honest Izaak' take him for his friend?

For Cotton Walton probably had that charm of antithesis which is so attractive to men of the world, who by a sort of intellectual urbanity often understand and interpret goodness and purity better than the good and pure themselves. Probably he had the man of the world's delight in character for its own sake, independent of the particular type's likeness or unlikeness to himself. There must have been times when, mentally, Walton made him yawn tremendously; times when he would smother his smiles at the old man's prudishness; times even when he may have been tempted to 'damn' his sententiousness. The same happens with Walton's readers to this day, but they go on loving him all the same; and so it was, no doubt, with Cotton.

Besides, it must not be forgotten that Walton had been a friend of the father before the son,* a father so closely repeated in the son, that the same description will almost literally serve for both – though, of the two, the father seems to have been the more brilliant man. That description, stately yet almost tender, is supplied by Lord Clarendon in the following passage, quoted from his autobiography:

Charles Cotton was a gentleman born to a competent fortune, and so qualified in his person and education, that for many years

* In Cotton's poem to Walton, he says, *à propos* of the lives of Donne and Wotton:

> How happy was my father, then, to see
> Those men he lov'd, by him he lov'd, to be
> Rescued from frailties and mortality.

he continued the greatest ornament of the town, in the esteem of those who had been best bred. His natural parts were very great, his wit flowing in all the parts of conversation; the superstructure of learning not raised to a considerable height: but having passed some years in Cambridge, and then in France, and conversing always with learned men, his expressions were ever proper and significant, and gave great lustre to his discourse upon any argument; so that he was thought by those who were not intimate with him, to have been much better acquainted with books than he was. He had all those qualities which in youth raise men to the reputation of being fine gentlemen; such a pleasantness and gaiety of humour, such a sweetness and gentleness of nature, and such a civility and delightfulness in conversation, that no man, in court or out of it, appeared a more accomplished person: all these extraordinary qualifications being supported by as extraordinary a clearness of courage and fearlessness of spirit, of which he gave too often manifestation. Some unhappy suits in law, and waste of his fortune in those suits, made some impression on his mind which, being impaired by domestic afflictions, and those indulgences to himself which naturally attend those afflictions, rendered his age less reverenced than his youth had been, and gave his best friends cause to have wished that he had not lived so long.

The fortunate son of this delightful father, and by him and his mother, Olive Stanhope, sprung from some of the noblest Derbyshire and Staffordshire families, Charles Cotton was born at Beresford, April 28, 1630. Particulars of his youth are almost as vague as particulars of the youth of Walton; but in his case, on account of his birth, they are more safely conjecturable. That he was sent to Cambridge is likely, though not definitely known; it being surmised, however, from his affection for his tutor, Ralph Rawson, as expressed in a dedication to a translation of an ode by Joannes Secundus, included in his *Poems on Several Occasions* (1689). It seems certain, however, that he took no degree; but, like many who have done the same, his acquaintance with and love for literature at an early age seems to have been none the less. His classical attainments and his knowledge of French and Italian, combined with the usual polite accomplishments of his time, appear to have been considerable; and he seems to have written poetry from his youth, though little of it was published till after the Restoration. He boasted two poets among his family connections – Colonel Richard Lovelace, a

The Fishing House

E·H·N·

friend of his father's, and Sir Aston Cockayne, a cousin of his mother's. Lovelace, who had written an elegy on his aunt Cassandra Cotton, and had likewise addressed an ode on 'The Grasshopper' to his father, later on inscribed 'The Triumphs of Philamore and Amoret, to the noblest of our youth and best of friends, Charles Cotton, Esquire, being at Beresford, at his house in Staffordshire, from London'. Cotton is supposed to have befriended him in his poverty, and he wrote an elegy to his memory, which was printed at the end of *Lucasta and Posthume Poems* in 1659.

   Sir Aston Cockayne, if but a very minor poet, had a pretty gift for flattering his friends. He seems from the first to have taken the praise of Cotton for his mission in life, and his poem, 'To my most honoured cousin, Mr Charles Cotton the Younger, upon his excellent Poems', is a by no means despicable piece of hyperbole. I quote the greater part of it for its references to Cotton's beauty and accomplishments, but also for its own intrinsic curiosity:

   To my Most Honoured Cousin, Mr Charles Cotton, the Younger,
   upon his Excellent Poems.

       Bear back, you crowd of wits, that have so long
       Been the prime glory of the English tongue,
       And room for our arch-poet make, and follow
       His steps, as you would do your great Apollo.
       Nor is he his inferior, for see
       His picture, and you'll say that this is he;
       So young and handsome both, so tress'd alike,
       That curious Lilly, or most skill'd Vandyke,
       Would prefer neither, only here's the odds,
       This gives us better verse, than that the Gods.
       Beware, you poets, that (at distance) you
       The reverence afford him that is due
       Unto his mighty merit, and not dare
       Your puny threads with his lines to compare . . .
       The Greek and Latin language he commands,
       So all that then was writ in both these lands;
       The French and the Italian he hath gain'd
       And all the wit that in them is contain'd.
       So, if he pleases to translate a piece
       From France or Italy, old Rome or Greece,
       The understanding reader soon will find,
       It is the best of any of that kind;
       But when he lets his own rare fancy loose,
       There is no flight so noble as his muse.
       Treats he of war? Bellona doth advance,
       And leads his march with her refulgent lance.
       Sings he of love? Cupid about him lurks,
       And Venus in her chariot draws his works.

Whate'er his subject be, he'll make it fit
To live hereafter emperor of wit.
He is the Muses' darling, all the nine
Phoebus disclaim, and term him more divine.
The wondrous Tasso, that so long hath borne
The sacred laurel, shall remain forlorn.
Alonso de Ercilla, that in strong
And mighty lines hath Araucana sung,
And Sallust, that the ancient Hebrew story
Hath poetis'd, submit unto your glory.
So the chief swans of Tagus, Arne, and Seine,
Must yield to Thames, and veil unto your strain.
Hail, generous magazine of wit, you bright
Planet of learning, dissipate the night
Of dullness, wherein us this age involves,
And (from our ignorance) redeem our souls.
A word at parting, Sir, I could not choose
Thus to congratulate your happy muse;
And (though I vilify your worth) my zeal
(And so in mercy think) intended well.
The world will find your lines are great and strong,
The nihil ultra of the English tongue.

Cotton's young manhood seems to have been spent like the manhood of other young men of his class and time: college, foreign travel and the town, with a touch of such graver interests as angling, gardening and planting. (He wrote an admirable *Planters' Manual* in 1675.)

In 1656 he married his cousin Isabella, daughter of Sir Thomas Hutchinson, and in 1658 his father died.

On the Restoration he began his public career as author by a prose panegyric of the king, and in 1664 he published his *Scarronides, or the First Book of Virgil Travestie*, a burlesque, neither brighter nor duller than the average wit of his day, but which, however, enjoyed great popularity (going through no less than fourteen editions), possibly on account of its indecencies. In these, however, it cannot be said to have been singular in that liberal age.

From this time onwards, Cotton became a fairly busy literary man. He seems to have been driven to translating as a means of enlivening the 'vacancy of a country life', of which he frequently complains, rather than from any profit it brought him. A list of his writings will be found at the end of this note.

In 1670 his wife died, leaving him with three sons and five daughters, and in 1675 we find him married again, his second wife being Mary, daughter of Sir William Russell, and widow of the Earl of Ardglass. Like his father before him, his life seems to have been much harassed by the narrowness of his means. On two occasions he found it necessary to petition Parliament to sanction the sale of portions of his estate, and there is a cave near where Beresford Hall stood, in which, according to local tradition, he used to hide from his creditors; a story generally discredited by his biographers, but somewhat borne out by this passage from a poem addressed to Alexander Brome, complaining of his country exile, with no company –

> But such, as I still pray, I may not see,
> Such craggy rough-hewn rogues, as do not fit,
> Sharpen and set, but blunt the edge of wit;
> Any of which (and fear has a quick eye)
> If through a perspective I chance to spy,
> Though a mile off, I take the alarm and run
> As if I saw the devil, or a dun;
> And in the neighbouring rocks take sanctuary,
> Praying the hills to fall and cover me;
> So that my solace lies amongst my grounds,
> And my best company's my horse and hounds.

Another story represents him scribbling the following not very brilliant quatrain on the walls of a debtor's prison in London:

> A prison is a place of cure
>   Wherein no one can thrive;
> A touchstone sure to try a friend,
>   A grave for men alive.

Cotton's friendship with Walton, as we have seen, probably dated from his boyhood, and had found poetical expression before, preparing a fifth edition of his pastoral, Walton had invited him to contribute those 'Instructions how to angle for a trout or grayling in a clear stream', which Cotton, he himself tells us, wrote in about ten days, and sent back to his friend. In the same year in which the joint *Compleat Angler* appeared, Cotton had finished building the little fishing-house which still stands among its trees, in a bend of the Dove, sacred to anglers and ancient friendship. Mr New's illustrations make unnecessary any more modern description than Cotton's own (Part Two, Chap. III), and indeed the place is to this

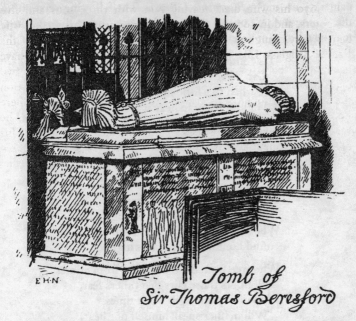

Tomb of Sir Thomas Beresford

day so pleasant that one may still say of it in Walton's words that 'the pleasantness of the river, mountains and meadows about it, cannot be described; unless Sir Philip Sidney or Mr Cotton's father were alive again to do it'.

Cotton survived his old friend but four years, dying of a fever on some date uncertain during 1687, but said to be February 13.

He is entirely remembered today by his association with Walton, and his translation of Montaigne, which have carried down to us the tradition of his handsome person and courtly manners, but which have hardly won due recognition for his poetry. Without declaring it, with Sir Aston Cockayne, 'the *nihil ultra* of the English tongue', we may still feel that it has charms and excellencies, real if modest, which make forgetfulness of it unjust, and which justify Cotton's long-neglected claim to a recognised place among English poets, a claim which a new edition of his poems might establish; though it is to be feared, that he would shine best in a judicious selection. His bane was fluency, and not seldom we have to plod through deserts of mediocre verse before we reach any poetry worth while. But the poetry is there, and when with Cotton the moment of literary projection did come, the product had a charming inevitability, and is marked by a rare excellence of simplicity, to which Coleridge has

paid a tribute in the *Biographia Literaria*. The following verses from
the 'Contentation', one of the several poems 'directed' to Walton,
may be taken as an example:

> 'Tis contentation that alone
>   Can make us happy here below,
> And when this little life is gone,
>   Will lift us up to heav'n too.
>
> A very little satisfies
>   An honest and a grateful heart;
> And who would more than will suffice,
>   Does covet more than is his part.
>
> That man is happy in his share,
>   Who is warm clad, and cleanly fed;
> Whose necessaries bound his care,
>   And honest labour makes his bed.
>
> Who free from debt, and clear from crimes,
>   Honours those laws that others fear;
> Who ill of princes, in worst times,
>   Will neither speak himself nor hear.
>
> Who from the busy world retires
>   To be more useful to it still,
> And to no greater good aspires,
>   But only the eschewing ill.
>
> Who with his angle and his books
>   Can think the longest day well spent,
> And praises God when back he looks,
>   And finds that all was innocent.
>
> This man is happier far than he,
>   Whom public business oft betrays,
> Through labyrinths of policy
>   To crooked and forbidden ways.
>
> The world is full of beaten roads,
>   But yet so slippery withall,
> That where one walks secure, 'tis odds
>   A hundred and a hundred fall.
>
> Untrodden paths are then the best,
>   Where the frequented are unsure,

And he comes soonest to rest,
  Whose journey has been most secure.

It is content alone that makes
  Our pilgrimage a pleasure here,
And who buys sorrow cheapest, takes
  An ill commodity too dear.

Nor was Cotton's muse always so mild, as this manly rebuke of Waller, censure so well-deserved, will show:

To Poet E. W., occasioned for his writing
a Panegyric on Oliver Cromwell.

From whence, vile Poet, didst thou glean the wit,
And words for such a vitious poem fit?
Where couldst thou paper find was not too white,
Or ink that could be black enough to write?
What servile devil tempted thee to be
A flatterer of thine own slavery?
To kiss thy bondage and extol the deed,
At once that made thy prince and country bleed?
I wonder much thy false heart did not dread,
And shame to write what all men blush to read;
Thus with a base ingratitude to rear
Trophies unto thy master's murtherer?
Who called thee coward – much mistook
The characters of thy pedantic look;
Thou hast at once abused thyself and us,
He's stout that dares to flatter a tyranne thus.
  Put up thy pen and ink, muzzle thy muse,
Adulterate hag fit for the common stews,
No good man's library; writ thou hast,
Treason in rhyme, has all thy works defaced;
Such is thy fault, that when I think to find
A punishment of the severest kind
For thy offence, my malice cannot name
A greater, than once to commit the same.
  Where was thy reason then, when thou began
To write against the sense of God and man?
Within thy guilty breast despair took place,
Thou wouldst despairing die despite of grace,

At once thou'rt judge and malefactor shown,
Each sentence in thy poem is thine own.
Then what thou hast pronounced go execute,
Hang up thyself, and say I bid thee do it,
Fear not thy memory, that cannot die,
This panegyric is thy elegy,
Which shall be when or wheresoever read,
A living poem to upbraid the dead.

Cotton's Literary Works

[This list is reprinted from Mr R. B. Marston's 'Lea and Dove' edition]

1649   An *Elegy* upon the Death of Henry, Lord Hastings.

1651   Verses prefixed to Edmund Prestwich's translation to the *Hippolitus* of Seneca.

1651   Verses on the Execution of James, Earl of Derby.

1654   Verses in which he castigates Waller for writing a panegyric on the Protector.

1664   *Scarronides*, or *Virgil Travestie*, being the first book of Virgil's *Aeneid*, in English burlesque. 8vo.

1667   A translation of *The Moral Philosophy of the Stoics*, from the French of Du Vaix.
        Some verses on the *Poems* of his friend, Alexander Brome.

1670   *Scarronides*, second edition.
        Translation of Gerard's *History of the Life of the Duke of Espernon*, dedicated to Dr Gilbert Sheldon, Archbishop of Canterbury.

1671   A translation of Corneille's tragedy, *Les Horaces*.
        Voyage to Ireland, in burlesque.

1670–4 Translation of the Commentaries of Blaise de Montluc, Marshal of France.
        The Compleat Gamester (attributed to him).
        The Fair One of Tunis, a novel, translated from the French.

1675   *Burlesque upon Burlesque; or the Scoffer Scoff'd.*
        The Planter's Manual, being instructions for cultivating all sorts of fruit trees. 8vo.

1676   The Second Part of *The Compleat Angler; Being Instructions how to Angle for a Trout or Grayling in a clear Stream.*

1681   *The Wonders of the Peak*. A description in verse of the natural wonders of the Peak District in Derbyshire.

1685   Translation of the *Essays* of Montaigne.

1687   Was engaged in translating the *Memoirs* of the Sieur de Pontis at the time of his death, in February 1687. This work was published in 1694, by his son, Beresford Cotton. In 1689 *Poems on Several Occasions*, a collection of some of his poems, was published.

Cotton's Cave

THE COMPLEAT ANGLER

Part One

Being a Discourse of Rivers,
Fishponds, Fish and Fishing

IZAAK
WALTON

TO THE RIGHT WORSHIPFUL
JOHN OFFLEY
OF MADELEY MANOR,
IN THE COUNTY OF STAFFORD, ESQ.
MY MOST HONOURED FRIEND

Sir – I have made so ill use of your former favours, as by them to be encouraged to entreat, that they may be enlarged to the *patronage* and *protection* of this book: and I have put on a modest confidence, that I shall not be denied, because it is a discourse of *fish* and *fishing*, which you know so well, and both love and practise so much.

You are assured (though there be ignorant men of another belief) that *angling* is an *art*: and you know that art better than others; and that this truth is demonstrated by the fruits of that pleasant labour which you enjoy, when you purpose to give rest to your mind, and divest yourself of your more serious business, and (which is often) dedicate a day or two to this *recreation*.

At which time, if *common Anglers* should attend you, and be eye-witnesses of the success, not of your *fortune* but your *skill*, it would doubtless beget in them an emulation to be like you, and that emulation might beget an industrious diligence to be so; but I know it is not attainable by common capacities. And there be now many men of great *wisdom*, *learning*, and *experience*, which love and practise this art, that know I speak the truth.

Sir, this pleasant curiosity of fish and fishing (of which you are so great a master) has been thought worthy the *pens* and *practices* of divers in other nations, that have been reputed men of great *learning* and *wisdom*: and amongst those of this nation, I remember Sir Henry Wotton (a dear lover of this art) has told me, that his intentions were to write a discourse of the art, and in praise of *angling*; and doubtless he had done so, if death had not prevented him; the remembrance of which hath often made me sorry; for if he had lived to do it, then the unlearned *angler* had seen some better treatise of this art, a treatise that might have proved worthy his perusal, which (though some have undertaken) I could never yet see in English.

But mine may be thought as *weak*, and as *unworthy* of common view; and I do here freely confess, that I should rather excuse myself, than censure others, my own discourse being liable to so many exceptions; against which you, sir, might make this one, *that it can contribute nothing to your knowledge.* And lest a longer epistle may diminish your pleasure, I shall make this no longer than to add this following truth, *that I am really,*

Sir,
Your most affectionate friend,
And most humble servant,

Iz. Wa.

Ruins of Madeley Manor

To the Reader of this Discourse,
but especially
to the Honest Angler

I think fit to tell thee these following truths, that I did neither *undertake*, nor *write*, nor *publish*, and much less own, this Discourse to please myself; and, having been too easily drawn to do all to please others, as I proposed not the gaining of credit by this undertaking, so I would not willingly lose any part of that to which I had a just title before I began it, and do therefore desire and hope, if I deserve not commendations, yet I may obtain pardon.

And though this Discourse may be liable to some exceptions, yet I cannot doubt but that most readers may receive so much *pleasure* or *profit* by it, as may make it worthy the time of their perusal, if they be not too grave or too busy men. And this is all the confidence that I can put on, concerning the merit of what is here offered to their consideration and censure; and if the last prove too severe, as I have a liberty, so I am resolved to use it, and neglect all sour censures.

And I wish the reader also to take notice, that in writing of it I have made myself a *recreation* of a *recreation*; and that it might prove so to him, and not dull and tediously, I have in several places mixed, not any scurrility, but some innocent, harmless mirth, of which, if thou be a severe, sour-complexioned man, then I here disallow thee to be a competent judge; for divines say, *there are offences given, and offences not given but taken.*

And I am the willinger to justify the pleasant part of it, because, though it is known, I can be serious at seasonable times, yet the whole Discourse is, or rather was, a picture of my own disposition, especially in such days and times as I have laid aside business, and gone a-fishing with honest *Nat.* and *R. Roe*; but they are gone, and with them most of my pleasant hours, even as a shadow that passeth away and returns not.

And next, let me add this, that he that likes not the book, should like the excellent picture of the trout, and some of the other fish; which I may take a liberty to commend, because they concern not myself.

Next, let me tell the reader, that in that which is the more useful part of this *Discourse*, that is to say, the observations of the nature, and breeding, and seasons, and catching of fish, I am not so simple as not to know that a captious reader may find exceptions against something said of some of these; and therefore, I must entreat him to consider that experience teaches us to know that several countries alter the time, and I think almost the manner of fishes' breeding, but doubtless of their being in season; as may appear by three rivers in *Monmouthshire*, namely, *Severn*, *Wye*, and *Usk*, where *Camden* (*British Fishes*, 633) observes, that in the river Wye, salmon are in season from *September* to *April*; and we are certain that in *Thames* and *Trent*, and in most other rivers, they be in season the six hotter months.

Now for the art of catching fish, that is to say, how to make a man – that was none – to be an angler by a book; he that undertakes it shall undertake a harder task than *Mr Hales* (a most valiant and excellent fencer) who, in a printed book called *A Private School of Defence*, undertook to teach that art or science, and was laughed at for his labour. Not but that many useful things might be learnt by that book, but he was laughed at because that art was not to be taught by words, but practice; and so must angling. And note also, that in this Discourse, I do not undertake to say all that is known, or may be said of it, but I undertake to acquaint the reader with many things that are not usually known to every angler; and I shall leave gleanings and observations enough to be made out of the experience of all that love and practise this recreation, to which I shall encourage them. For *angling* may be said to be so like the *mathematics*, that it can never be fully learnt; at least not so fully, but that there will still be more new experiments left for the trial of other men that succeed us.

But I think all that love this game may here learn something that may be worth their money, if they be not poor and needy men; and in case they be, I then wish them to forbear to buy it, for I write, not to get money, but for pleasure, and this Discourse boasts of no more; for I hate to promise much and deceive the reader.

And however it proves to him, yet I am sure I have found a high content in the search and conference of what is here offered to the reader's view and censure; I wish him as much in the perusal of it, and so I might here take my leave; but will stay a little and tell him, that whereas it is said by many that in fly-fishing for a trout the angler must observe his twelve several flies for the twelve months of the year: I say, he that follows that rule shall be as sure to catch fish, and be as wise, as he that makes hay by the fair days in an almanac, and no surer; for those very flies that used to appear about and on the water in one month of the year, may the following year come almost a month sooner or later, as the same year proves colder or hotter; and yet, in the following Discourse, I have set down the twelve flies that are in reputation with many anglers, and they may serve to give him some

Madeley church

observations concerning them. And he may note, that there are in *Wales* and other countries, peculiar flies, proper to the particular place or country; and doubtless unless a man makes a fly to counterfeit that very fly in that place, he is like to lose his labour, or much of it; but for the generality, three or four flies, neat and rightly made, and not too big, serve for a trout in most rivers all the summer. And for winter fly-fishing – it is as useful as an almanac out of date! And of these (because as no man is born an artist, so no man is born an angler) I thought fit to give thee this notice.

When I have told the reader that in this fifth impression there are many enlargements, gathered both by my own observation and the communication with friends, I shall stay him no longer than to wish him *a rainy evening to read this following Discourse*; and that (if he be an honest angler) *the east wind may never blow when he goes a-fishing*.

I. W.

To my dear Brother
Mr Isaac Walton
upon his Compleat Angler

Erasmus in his learned Colloquies,
Has mixt some toys, that by varieties
He might entice all readers: for in him
Each child may wade, or tallest giant swim.
And such is this discourse: there's none so low
Or highly learn'd, to whom hence may not flow
Pleasure and information: both which are
Taught us with so much art, that I might swear
Safely, the choicest critic cannot tell,
Whether your matchless judgement most excel
In angling or its praise: where commendation
First charms, then makes an art a recreation.

'Twas so to me: who saw the cheerful Spring
Pictur'd in every meadow, heard birds sing
Sonnets in every grove, saw fishes play
In cool crystal streams, like lambs in May:
And they may play, till anglers read this book;
But after, 'tis a wise fish 'scapes a hook.

                              Io. Floud, Master of Arts

To the Reader of The Compleat Angler

First mark the title well; my friend that gave it
Has made it good; this book deserves to have it.
For he that views it with judicious looks,
Shall find it full of art, baits, lines, and hooks.

The world the river is; both you and I,
And all mankind, are either fish or fry:
If we pretend to reason, first or last
His baits will tempt us, and his hooks hold fast.
Pleasure or profit, either prose or rhyme,
If not at first, will doubtless take in time.

He sits in secret blest theology,
Waited upon by grave philosophy,
Both natural and moral; history,
Deck'd and adorn'd with flowers of poetry;
The matter and expression striving which
Shall most excel in worth, yet not seem rich.
There is no danger in his baits; that hook
Will prove the safest that is surest took.

Nor are we caught alone, (which is best)
We shall wholesome, and be toothsome, drest:
Drest to be fed, not be fed upon;
And danger of a surfeit here is none.
The solid food of serious contemplation
Is sauc'd, here, with such harmless recreation,
That an ingenuous and religious mind
Cannot enquire for more than it may find
Ready at once prepared either t' excite
Or satisfy a curious appetite.

More praise is due; for 'tis both positive
And truth, which once was interrogative,
And utter'd by the poet then in jest,
ET PISCATOREM PISCIS AMARE POTEST.

Ch. Harvie, Master of Arts

To my dear friend,
Mr Iz. Walton, in praise of Angling,
which we both love

Down by this smooth stream's wand'ring side,
Adorn'd and perfum'd with the pride
Of Flora's wardrobe, where the shrill
Aërial choir express their skill,
First in alternate melody,
And then in chorus all agree.
Whilst the charm'd fish, as extasy'd
With sounds, to his own throat deny'd,
Scorns his dull element, and springs
I' th' air, as if his fins were wings.

'Tis here that the pleasures sweet and high
Prostrate to our embraces lie.
Such as a body, soul, or frame
Create no sickness, sin, or shame.
Roses not fenc'd with pricks grow here,
No sting to th' honey-bag is near.
But (what's perhaps their prejudice)
The difficulty, want and price.

An obvious rod, a twist of hair
With hook hid in an insect, are
Engines of sport, would fit the wish
O' th' epicure, and fill his dish.

In this clear stream let fall a grub;
And straight take up a dace or chub.
I' th' mud your worm provokes a snig,
Which being fast, if it prove big
The Gotham folly will be found
Discreet, ere ta'en she must be drown'd
The tench (physician of the brook)
In yon dead hole expects your hook,
Which having first your pastime been,
Serves then for meat or medicine.
Ambush'd behind that root doth stay
A pike, to catch and be a prey.

The treacherous quill in this slow stream
Betrays the hunger of a bream.
And at that nimbler ford (no doubt)
Your false fly cheats a speckled trout.
When you these creatures wisely choose
To practise on, which to your use
Owe their creation, and when
Fish from your arts do rescue men;
To plot, delude, and circumvent,
Ensnare and spoil, is innocent.
Here by these crystal streams you may
Preserve a conscience clear as they;
And when by sullen thoughts you find
Your harassed, not busied, mind
In sable melancholy clad,
Distemper'd, serious, turning sad;
Hence fetch your cure, cast in your bait,
All anxious thoughts and cares shall straight
Fly with such speed they'll seem to be
Possest with the hydrophobie.
The water's calmness in your breast,
And smoothness on your brow shall rest.

Away with sports of charge and noise,
And give me cheap and silent joys;
Such as Actaeon's game pursue
Their fate oft make the tale seem true.
The sick or sullen hawk, today
Flies not; tomorrow, quite away.
Patience and purse to cards and dice
Too oft are made a sacrifice:
The daughter's dower, th' inheritance
O' th' son, depend on one mad chance.
The harms and mischiefs which the abuse
Of wine doth every day produce,
Make good the doctrine of the Turks,
That in each grape a devil lurks.
And by yon fading, sapless tree,
'Bout which the ivy twin'd you see,
His fate's foretold, who fondly places
His bliss in woman's soft embraces.
All pleasures, but the angler's, bring,

I' th' tail, repentance like a sting.

Then on these banks let me sit down,
Free from the toilsome sword and gown,
And pity those that do affect
To conquer nations and protect.
My reed affords such true content,
Delights so sweet and innocent,
As seldom fall into the lot
Of sceptres, though they're justly got.

Tho. Weaver, Master of Arts

Colts-foot.

To the Readers of my most ingenious Friend's book The Compleat Angler

He that both knew and writ the lives of men,
Such as were once, but must not be again:
Witness is matchless Donne and Wotton, by
Whose aid he could their speculations try:
He that conversed with angels, such as were
Ouldsworth and Featley, each a shining star
Showing the way to Bethlem; east a saint;
(Compar'd to whom our zealots, now, but paint).
He that our pious and learn'd Morley knew,
And from him suck'd wit and devotion too:
He that from these such excellencies fetch'd,
That he could tell how high and far they reach'd;
What learning this, what graces th' other had;
And in what several dress each soul was clad.

Reader, this HE, this fisherman comes forth,
And in these fisher's weeds would shroud his worth.
Now his mute harp is on a willow hung,
With which when finely touch'd, and fitly strung,
He could friends' passions for these times allay;
Or chain his fellow-anglers from their prey.
But now the music of his pen is still,
And he sits by a brook watching a quill:
Where with a fixt eye, and a ready hand,
He studies first to hook, and then to land
Some trout, or perch, or pike; and having done,
Sits on a bank, and tells how this was won,
And that escap'd his hook, which with a wile
Did eat the bait, and fishermen beguile.
Thus whilst some vex they from their lands are thrown,
He joys to think the waters are his own,
And like the Dutch, he gladly can agree
To live at peace now, and have fishing free,

April 3, 1650
Edw. Powel, Master of Arts

To my dear Brother,
Mr Iz. Walton, on his Compleat Angler

This book is so like you, and you like it,
For harmless mirth, expression, art, and wit,
That I protest ingeniously 'tis true,
I love this mirth, art, wit, the book and you.

Rob. Floud, C.

Madeley Church

E·H·N·

Clarissimo amicissimoque;
Fratri, Domino Isaaco Walton
Artis Piscatoriae pertissimo

Unicus est medicus reliquorum piscis, et istis
Fas quibis est medicum tangere, certa salus
Hic typus est salvatoris mirandus Jesu,
Litera mysterium quaelibet hujus habet.

Hunc cupio, hunc cupias (bone frater arundis) ιχφὺν;
Solverit hic pro me debita, teque Deo.
Piscis is est, et piscator (mihi credito) qualena
Vel piscatorem piscis amare velit.

Henry Bayley, *Artium Magister*

Ad Virum optimum,
et Piscatorem peritissimum
Isaacum Waltonum

Magister artis docte piscatoriae,
Waltone salve, magne arundis,
Seu tu reductâ valle solus ambulas,
Praeterfluentes interim observans aquas,
Seu fortè puri stans in amnis margine,
Sive in tenaci gramine et ripâ sedens,
Fallis peritâ squameum pecus manu;
O te beautum! qui procul negotiis,
Forique et urbis pulvere et strepitu carens,
Extraque turbam, ad lenè manantes aquas
Vagos honestâ fraude pisces discipis.
Dum caetera ergo paenè gens mortalium
Aut retia invicem sibi et technas struunt,
Donis, ut hamo, aut divites captant senes,
Gregi natantûm tu interim nectis dolos,
Voracem inescas advenam hamo lucium,
Avidamvè percam parvulo alberno capis,
Aut verme ruffo, muscula aut truttam levi,
Cautumvè cyprinum, et ferè indocilem capi
Calamoque linoque (ars at hunc superat tua)
Medicamvè tincam, gobium aut esca trahis,
Gratum palato gobium, parvum licet,
Praedamvè, non acque salubrem barbulum,
Etsi ampliorem, et mystace insignem gravi.
Hae sunt tibi artes, dum annus et tempus sinunt,
Et nulla transit absque linea dies.
Nec sola praxis, sed theoria et tibi
Nota artis hujus; unde tu simul bonus
Piscator, idem et scriptor; et calami potens
Utriusque necdum et ictus, et tamen sapis,
Ut hamiotam nempe tironem instruas!
Stylo eleganti scribus en Halientica
Oppianus alter, artis et methodum tuae, et
Praecepta promis rite piscatoria,
Varias et escas piscium, indolem, et genus.

Nec tradere artem sat putas piscariam,
(Virtutis est haec et tamen quaedam docet),
Documenta quin majora das, et regulas
Sublimioris artis, et perennia
Monimenta morem, vitae et exempla optima;
Dum tu profundum scribis Hookerum, et pium
Domum ac disertum, sanctum et Herbertum, sacrum
Vatem; hos videmus nam penicillo tuo
Graphicè, et perità, Isaace, depictos manu.
Post fata factos hosce per te Virbios.
O quae voluptas est legere in scriptis tuis!
Sic tu libris nos, lineis pisces capis,
Musisque litterisque dum incumbis, licet
Intentus hamo, interque piscandum studes.

Alliud ad Isaacum Waltonum, Virum et Piscatorem Optimum.

Isaace, macte hac arte piscatoriâ;
Hac arte Petrus principi censum dedit;
Hac arte princeps nec Petro multo prior,
Tranquillus ille, teste Tranquillo, pater
Patriae, solebat recreare se lubens
Augustus, hamo instructus ac arundine.
Tu nunc, amice, proximum clari est decus
Post Caesarem hami, gentis ac Halienticae:
Euge O professor artis haud ingloriae,
Doctor cathedrae, perlegens piscariam!
Nae tu magister, et ego disciplus tuus,
Nam candidatum et me ferunt arundinis,
Socium hâc in arte nobilem nacti sumus,
Quid amplius, Waltone, nam dici potest?
Ipsi hamiota Dominus en orbis fuit!

                                        Iaco: Dup. D. D.

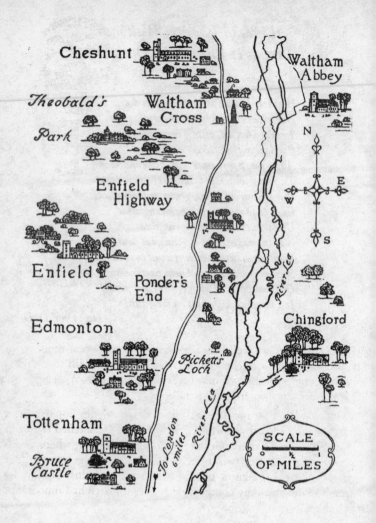

CHAPTER I

Conference betwixt an Angler, a Hunter, and a Falconer; each commending his Recreation.

PISCATOR, VENATOR, AUCEPS

PISCATOR. You are well overtaken, gentlemen; a good-morning to you both; I have stretched my legs up Tottenham Hill to overtake you, hoping your business may occasion you towards Ware, whither I am going this fine, fresh May morning

VENATOR. Sir, I for my part shall almost answer your hopes; for my purpose is to drink my morning's draught at the Thatched House in Hoddesden, and I think not to rest till I come thither, where I have appointed a friend or two to meet me: but for this gentleman that you see with me, I know not how far he intends his journey; he came so lately into my company, that I have scarce had time to ask him the question.

AUCEPS. Sir, I shall, by your favour, bear you company as far as Theobald's, and there leave you; for then I turn up to a friend's house who mews a hawk for me, which I now long to see.

VEN. Sir, we are all so happy as to have a fine, fresh, cool morning; and I hope we shall each be the happier in the other's company. And, gentlemen, that I may not lose yours, I shall either abate or amend my pace to enjoy it; knowing that (as the Italians say) 'Good company in a journey makes the way to seem the shorter.'

Auc. It may do so, sir, with the help of good discourse, which methinks we may promise from you that both look and speak so cheerfully; and for my part I promise you, as an invitation to it, that I will be as free and open-hearted as discretion will allow me to be with strangers.

Ven. And, sir, I promise the like.

Pisc. I am right glad to hear your answers, and in confidence you speak the truth, I shall put on a boldness to ask you, sir, whether business or pleasure caused you to be so early up, and walk so fast; for this other gentleman hath declared that he is going to see a hawk that a friend mews for him.

Ven. Sir, mine is a mixture of both, a little business and more pleasure; for I intend this day to do all my business and then bestow another day or two in hunting the Otter which a friend, that I go to meet, tells me is much pleasanter than any other chase whatsoever: howsoever, I mean to try it; for tomorrow morning we shall meet a pack of Otter-dogs of noble Mr Sadler's, upon Amwell Hill, who will be there so early that they intend to prevent the sun rising.

Pisc. Sir, my fortune has answered my desires, and my purpose is to bestow a day or two in helping to destroy some of those villainous vermin; for I hate them perfectly, because they love fish so well, or rather, because they destroy so much; indeed so much that, in my judgement, all men that keep Otter-dogs ought to have pensions from the king, to encourage them to destroy the very breed of those base Otters, they do so much mischief.

Ven. But what say you to the Foxes of the Nation, would not you as willingly have them destroyed? for doubtless they do as much mischief as Otters do.

Pisc. Oh sir, if they do, it is not so much to me and my fraternity, as those base vermin the Otters do.

Auc. Why, sir, I pray, of what fraternity are you, that you are so angry with the poor Otters?

Pisc. I am, sir, a brother of the Angle, and therefore an enemy to the Otter: for you are to note that we Anglers all love one another, and therefore do I hate the Otter, both for my own and for their sakes who are of my brotherhood.

Ven. And I am a lover of Hounds; I have followed many a pack of dogs many a mile, and heard many merry huntsmen make sport and scoff at Anglers.

Tottenham High Cross

E·H·N·

Auc. And I profess myself a Falconer, and have heard many grave serious men pity them, 'tis such a heavy, contemptible, dull, recreation.

Pisc. You know, gentlemen, 'tis an easy thing to scoff at any art or recreation; a little wit, mixed with ill-nature, confidence, and malice, will do it; but though they often venture boldly, yet they are often caught, even in their own trap, according to that of Lucian, the father of the family of scoffers.

> Lucian, well skill'd in scoffing, this hath writ,
> Friend, that's your folly, which you think your wit;
> This, you vent oft, void both of wit and fear,
> Meaning another, when yourself you jeer.

If to this you add what Solomon says of scoffers, that 'they are an abomination to mankind', let them that think fit scoff on, and be a scoffer still; but I account them enemies to me and to all that love virtue and angling.

And for you, that have heard many grave, serious men, pity Anglers; let me tell you, sir, there be many men that are by others taken to be serious and grave men, which we contemn and pity. Men that are taken to be grave, because nature hath made them of a sour complexion; money-getting men, men that spend all their time, first in getting, and next in anxious care to keep it; men that are condemned to be rich, and then always busy or discontented; for these poor rich men, we Anglers pity them perfectly, and stand in no need to borrow their thought to think ourselves so happy. No, no, sir, we enjoy a contentedness above the reach of such dispositions, and as the learned and ingenuous Montaigne says – like himself, freely, 'When my cat and I entertain each other with mutual apish tricks, as playing with a garter, who knows but that I make my cat more sport than she makes me? Shall I conclude her to be simple, that has her time to begin or refuse to play as freely as I myself have? Nay, who knows but that it is a defect of my not understanding her language (for doubtless cats talk and reason with one another), that we agree no better? And who knows but that she pities me for being no wiser than to play with her, and laughs and censures my folly for making sport for her, when we two play together?'

Thus freely speaks Montaigne concerning cats; and I hope I may take as great a liberty to blame any man, and laugh at him too, let him be never so grave, that hath not heard what Anglers can say in the justification of their art and recreation; which I may again tell

Sbandon the seat of Sir Ralf Sadler

E·H·N·

you is so full of pleasure, that we need not borrow their thoughts to make ourselves happy.

Ven. Sir, you have almost amazed me: for though I am no scoffer, yet I have (I pray let me speak it without offence) always looked upon Anglers as more patient and more simple men, than I fear I shall find you to be.

Pisc. Sir, I hope you will not judge my earnestness to be impatience: and for my simplicity, if by that you mean a harmlessness, or that simplicity which was usually found in the primitive Christians, who were, as most Anglers are, quiet men, and followers of peace; men that were so simply wise, as not to sell their consciences to buy riches, and with them vexation and a fear to die; if you mean such simple men as lived in those times when there were fewer lawyers, when men might have had a lordship safely conveyed to them in a piece of parchment no bigger than your hand, though several sheets will not do it safely in this wiser age: I say, sir, if you take us Anglers to be such simple men as I have spoken of, then myself and those of my profession will be glad to be so understood: but if by simplicity you meant to express a general defect in those that profess and practise the excellent art of angling, I hope in time to disabuse you, and make the contrary appear so evidently, that, if you will but have patience to hear me, I shall remove all the anticipations that discourse, or time, or prejudice, have possessed you with against that laudable and ancient art; for I know it worthy the knowledge and practice of a wise man.

But, gentlemen, though I be able to do this, I am not so

unmannerly as to engross all the discourse to myself; and, therefore, you two having declared yourselves, the one to be a lover of hawks, the other of hounds, I shall be most glad to hear what you can say in the commendation of that recreation which each of you love and practise; and having heard what you can say, I shall be glad to exercise your attention with what I can say concerning my own recreation and art of angling, and by this means we shall make the way to seem the shorter; and if you like my motion, I would have Mr Falconer to begin.

Auc. Your motion is consented to with all my heart; and to testify it, I will begin as you have desired me.

And first, for the element that I use to trade in, which is the air, an element of more worth than weight, an element that doubtless exceeds both the earth and water; for though I sometimes deal in both, yet the air is most properly mine, I and my hawks use that most, and it yields us most recreation: it stops not the high soaring of my noble, generous falcon; in it she ascends to such a height as the dull eyes of beasts and fish are not able to reach to; their bodies are too gross for such high elevations: in the air my troops of hawks soar up on high, and when they are lost in the sight of men, then they attend upon and converse with the gods; therefore I think my eagle is so justly styled 'Jove's servant in ordinary;' and that very falcon that I am now going to see, deserves no meaner title, for she usually in her flight endangers herself, like the son of Daedalus, to have her wings scorched by the sun's heat, she flies so near it; but her mettle makes her careless of danger; for then she heeds nothing, but makes her nimble pinions cut the fluid air, and so makes her highway over the steepest mountains and deepest rivers, and in her glorious career looks with contempt upon those high steeples and magnificent palaces which we adore and wonder at; from which height I can make her to descend by a word from my mouth (which she both knows and obeys), to accept of meat from my hand, to own me for her master, to go home with me, and be willing the next day to afford me the like recreation.

And more: this element of air which I profess to trade in, the worth of it is such, and it is of such necessity, that no creature whatsoever, not only those numerous creatures that feed on the face of the earth, but those various creatures that have their dwelling within the waters, every creature that hath life in its nostrils, stands in need of my element. The waters cannot preserve the fish without air, witness the not breaking of ice in an extreme frost: the reason is,

Tottenham High Cross

for that if the inspiring and expiring organ of an animal be stopped, it suddenly yields to nature, and dies. Thus necessary is air to the existence both of fish and beasts, nay, even to man himself; the air or breath of life with which God at first inspired mankind, he, if he wants it, dies presently, becomes a sad object to all that loved and beheld him, and in an instant turns to putrefaction.

Nay more, the very birds of the air (those that be not hawks) are both so many and so useful and pleasant to mankind, that I must not let them pass without some observations. They both feed and refresh him – feed him with their choice bodies, and refresh him with their heavenly voices. I will not undertake to mention the several kinds of fowl by which this is done; and his curious palate pleased by day, and which with their very excrements afford him a soft lodging at night. These I will pass by; but not those little nimble musicians of the air, that warble forth their curious ditties, with which nature hath furnished them to the shame of art.

As, first, the lark, when she means to rejoice, to cheer herself and those that hear her; she then quits the earth, and sings as she ascends higher into the air, and having ended her heavenly employment, grows then mute and sad, to think she must descend to the dull earth, which she would not touch, but for necessity.

How do the blackbird and thrassel, with their melodious voices, bid welcome to the cheerful spring, and in their fixed months warble forth such ditties as no art or instrument can reach to?

Nay, the smaller birds also do the like in their particular seasons, as, namely, the leverock, the titlark, the little linnet, and the honest robin, that loves mankind both alive and dead.

But the nightingale (another of my airy creatures) breathes such sweet loud music out of her little instrumental throat, that it might make mankind to think miracles are not ceased. He that at midnight, when the very labourer sleeps securely, should hear, as I have very often, the clear airs, the sweet descants, the natural rising and falling, the doubling and redoubling of her voice, might well be lifted above earth, and say, 'Lord, what music hast Thou provided for the saints in heaven, when Thou affordest bad men such music on earth?'

And this makes me the less to wonder at the many aviaries in Italy, or at the great charge of Varro his aviary, the ruins of which are yet to be seen in Rome, and is still so famous there, that it is reckoned for one of those notables which men of foreign nations either record, or lay up in their memories, when they return from travel.

Tottenham Hill

This for the birds of pleasure, of which very much more might be said. My next shall be of birds of political use. I think 'tis not to be doubted that swallows have been taught to carry letters betwixt two armies. But 'tis certain, that when the Turks besieged Malta or Rhodes (I now remember not which 'twas), pigeons are then related to carry and recarry letters. And Mr G. Sandys, in his *Travels* (fol. 269) relates it to be done betwixt Aleppo and Babylon. But if that be disbelieved, 'tis not to be doubted that the dove was sent out of the ark by Noah, to give him notice of land, when to him all appeared to be sea; and the dove proved a faithful and comfortable messenger. And for the sacrifices of the law, a pair of turtle-doves or young pigeons were as well accepted as costly bulls and rams. And when God would feed the prophet Elijah (1 Kings, XVII) after a kind of miraculous manner, he did it by ravens, who brought him meat morning and evening. Lastly, the Holy Ghost, when He descended visibly upon our Saviour, did it by assuming the shape of a dove. And to conclude this part of my discourse, pray remember these wonders were done by the birds of the air, the element in which they and I take so much pleasure.

There is also a little contemptible winged creature (an inhabitant of my aërial element), namely, the laborious bee, of whose prudence, policy, and regular government of their own commonwealth I might say much, as also of their several kinds, and how useful their honey and wax are both for meat and medicines to mankind; but I will leave them to their sweet labour, without the least disturbance, believing them to be all very busy at this very time amongst the herbs and flowers that we see nature puts forth this May morning.

And now to return to my hawks, from whom I have made too long a digression; you are to note, that they are usually distinguished into two kinds; namely, the long-winged and the short-winged hawk: of the first kind, there be chiefly in use amongst us in this nation,

> The Gerfalcon and Jerkin,
> The Falcon and Tassel-gentel,
> The Laner and Lanaret,
> The Bockerel and Bockeret,
> The Saker and Sacaret,
> The Merlin and Jack Merlin,
> The Hobby and Jack:
> There is the Stelletto of Spain,
> The Blood-red Rook from Turkey,
> The Waskite from Virginia:
> And there is of short-winged hawks,
> The Eagle and Iron,
> The Goshawk and Tarcel,
> The Sparhawk and Musket,
> *The French Pye, of two sorts.*

These are reckoned hawks of note and worth; but we have also hawks of an inferior rank,

> The Stanyel, the Ringtail,
> The Raven, the Buzzard,
> The Forked Kite, the Bald Buzzard,
> The Hen-driver, and others that I forbear to name.

Gentlemen, if I should enlarge my discourse to the observation of the eiries, the brancher, the ramish hawk, the haggard, and the two sorts of lentners, and then treat of their several ayries, their mewings, rare order of casting, and the renovation of their feathers: their reclaiming, dieting, and then come to their rare stories of practice; I say, if I should enter into these, and many other observations that I could make, it would be much, very much pleasure to me: but lest I should break the rules of civility to you, by taking up more than the proportion of time allotted to me, I will

BruceCastle Tottenham

here break off, and entreat you, Mr Venator, to say what you are able in the commendation of hunting, to which you are so much affected; and, if time will serve, I will beg your favour for a further enlargement of some of those several heads of which I have spoken. But no more at present.

VEN. Well, sir, and I will now take my turn, and will first begin with a commendation of the Earth, as you have done most excellently of the Air: the earth being that element upon which I drive my pleasant, wholesome, hungry trade. The earth is a solid, settled element: an element most universally beneficial both to man and beast: to men who have their several recreations upon it, as horse-races, hunting, sweet smells, pleasant walks: the earth feeds man, and all those several beasts that both feed him and afford him recreation. What pleasure doth man take in hunting the stately stag, the generous buck, the wild boar, the cunning otter, the crafty fox, and the fearful hare? And if I may descend to a lower game, what pleasure is it sometimes with gins to betray the very vermin of the earth? as, namely, the fitchet, the fulimart, the ferret, the pole-cat, the mould-warp, and the like creatures that live upon the face and within the bowels of the earth. How doth the earth bring forth herbs, flowers, and fruits, both for physic and the pleasure of mankind! and above all, to me at least, the fruitful vine, of which, when I drink moderately, it clears my brain, cheers my heart, and sharpens my wit. How could Cleopatra have feasted Mark Antony, with eight wild boars roasted whole at one supper, and other meat suitable, if the earth had not been a bountiful mother? But to pass by the mighty elephant, which the earth breeds and nourisheth, and descend to the least of creatures, how doth the earth afford us a doctrinal example in the little pismire, who in the summer provides and lays up her winter provision, and teaches man to do the like! The earth feeds and carries those horses that carry us. If I would be prodigal of my time and your patience, what might not I say in commendations of the earth? that puts limits to the proud and raging sea, and by that means preserves both man and beast, that it destroys them not, as we see it daily doth those that venture upon the sea, and are there shipwrecked, drowned, and left to feed haddocks; when we that are so wise as to keep ourselves on the earth, walk, and talk, and live, and eat, and drink, and go a-hunting: of which recreation I will say a little, and then leave Mr Piscator to the commendation of angling.

Hunting is a game for princes and noble persons; it hath been highly prized in all ages; it was one of the qualifications that Xenophon bestowed on his Cyrus, that he was a hunter of wild beasts. Hunting trains up the younger nobility to the use of manly exercises in their riper age. What more manly exercise than hunting the wild boar, the stag, the buck, the fox, or the hare? How doth it preserve health, and increase strength and activity!

And for the dogs that we use, who can commend their excellency to that height which they deserve? How perfect is the hound at smelling, who never leaves or forsakes his first scent, but follows it through so many changes and varieties of other scents, even over and in the water, and into the earth! What music doth a pack of dogs then make to any man, whose heart and ears are so happy as to be set to the tune of such instruments! How will a right greyhound fix his eye on the best buck in a herd, single him out, and follow him, and him only, through a whole herd of rascal game, and still know and then kill him! For my hounds, I know the language of them, and they know the language and meaning of one another as perfectly as we know the voices of those with whom we discourse daily.

I might enlarge myself in the commendation of hunting, and of the noble hound especially, as also of the docibleness of dogs in

Tottenham Church

general; and I might make many observations of land creatures, that for composition, order, figure, and constitution, approach nearest to the completeness and understanding of man; especially of those creatures which Moses in the law permitted to the Jews, which have cloven hoofs, and chew the cud; which I shall forbear to name, because I will not be so uncivil to Mr Piscator, as not to allow him a time for the commendation of angling, which he calls an art; but doubtless 'tis an easy one; and, Mr Auceps, I doubt we shall hear a watery discourse of it, but I hope it will not be a long one.

AUC. And I hope so too, though I fear it will.

PISC. Gentlemen, let not prejudice prepossess you. I confess my discourse is like to prove suitable to my recreation, calm and quiet; we seldom take the name of God into our mouths but it is either to praise Him or pray to Him; if others use it vainly in the midst of their recreations, so vainly as if they meant to conjure, I must tell you it is neither our fault nor our custom; we protest against it. But pray remember I accuse nobody; for as I would not make a 'watery discourse', so I would not put too much vinegar into it, nor would I raise the reputation of my own art by the diminution or ruin of another's. And so much for the prologue to what I mean to say.

And now for the water, the element that I trade in. The water is the eldest daughter of the creation, the element upon which the

Spirit of God did first move, the element which God commanded to bring forth living creatures abundantly; and without which, those that inhabit the land, even all creatures that have breath in their nostrils, must suddenly return to putrefaction. Moses, the great lawgiver, and chief philosopher, skilled in all the learning of the Egyptians, who was called the friend of God, and knew the mind of the Almighty, names this element the first in the creation: this is the element upon which the Spirit of God did first move, and is the chief ingredient in the creation: many philosophers have made it to comprehend all the other elements, and most allow it the chiefest in the mixtion of all living creatures.

There be that profess to believe that all bodies are made of water, and may be reduced back again to water only: they endeavour to demonstrate it thus:

Take a willow (or any like speedy growing plant) newly rooted in a box or barrel full of earth, weigh them all together exactly when the tree begins to grow, and then weigh all together after the tree is increased from its first rooting, to weigh a hundred pound weight more than when it was first rooted and weighed; and you shall find this augment of the tree to be without the diminution of one drachm weight of the earth. Hence they infer this increase of wood to be from water of rain, or from dew, and not to be from any other element. And they affirm they can reduce this wood back again to water; and they affirm also the same may be done in any animal or vegetable. And this I take to be a fair testimony of the excellency of my element of water.

The water is more productive than the earth. Nay, the earth hath no fruitfulness without showers or dews; for all the herbs and flowers and fruit are produced, and thrive by the water; and the very minerals are fed by streams that run under ground, whose natural course carries them to the tops of many high mountains, as we see by several springs breaking forth on the tops of the highest hills; and this is also witnessed by the daily trial and testimony of several miners.

Nay, the increase of those creatures that are bred and fed in the water is not only more and more miraculous, but more advantageous to man, not only for the lengthening of his life, but for preventing of sickness, for it is observed by the most learned physicians, that the casting off of Lent and other fish days (which hath not only given the lie to so many learned, pious, wise founders of colleges, for which we should be ashamed) hath doubtless been the chief cause of those many putrid, shaking, intermitting agues, unto which this nation of ours is now more subject than those wiser countries that feed on herbs, salads, and plenty of fish; of which it is observed in story, that the greatest part of the world now do. And it may be fit to remember that Moses (Lev. XI: 9, Deut. XIV: 9) appointed fish to be the chief diet for the best commonwealth that ever yet was.

And it is observable, not only that there are fish, as, namely, the whale, three times as big as the mighty elephant, that is so fierce in battle, but that the mightiest feasts have been of fish. The Romans in the height of their glory have made fish the mistress of all their entertainments; they have had music to usher in their sturgeons, lampreys, and mullets, which they would purchase at rates rather to be wondered at than believed. He that shall view the writings of Macrobius or Varro may be confirmed and informed of this, and of the incredible value of their fish and fishponds.

But, gentlemen, I have almost lost myself, which I confess I may easily do in this philosophical discourse; I met with most of it very lately (and I hope happily) in a conference with a most learned physician, Dr Wharton, a dear friend, that loves both me and my art of angling. But, however, I will wade no deeper in these

mysterious arguments, but pass to such observations as I can manage with more pleasure, and less fear of running into error. But I must not yet forsake the waters, by whose help we have so many known advantages.

And first, to pass by the miraculous cures of our known baths, how advantageous is the sea for our daily traffic, without which we could not now subsist! How does it not only furnish us with food and physic for the bodies, but with such observations for the mind as ingenious persons would not want!

How ignorant had we been of the beauty of Florence, of the monuments, urns, and rarities that yet remain in and near unto old and new Rome (so many as it is said will take up a year's time to view, and afford to each of them but a convenient consideration); and therefore it is not to be wondered at that so learned and devout a father as St Jerome, after his wish to have seen Christ in the flesh, and to have heard St Paul preach, makes his third wish, to have seen Rome in her glory; and that glory is not yet all lost, for what pleasure is it to see the monuments of Livy, the choicest of the historians; of Tully, the best of orators; and to see the bay trees that now grow out of the very tomb of Virgil! These, to any that love learning, must be pleasing. But what pleasure is it to a devout Christian to see there the humble house in which St Paul was content to dwell, and to view the many rich statues that are made in honour of his memory! nay, to see the very place in which St Peter and he lie buried together! These are in and near to Rome. And how much more doth it please the pious curiosity of a Christian to see that place on which the blessed Saviour of the world was pleased to humble himself, and to take our nature upon him, and to converse with men: to see Mount Zion, Jerusalem, and the very sepulchre of our Lord Jesus? How may it beget and heighten the zeal of a Christian to see the devotions that are daily paid to him at that place! Gentlemen, lest I forget myself I will stop here and remember you, that but for my element of water, the inhabitants of this poor island must remain ignorant that such things ever were, or that any of them have yet a being.

Gentlemen, I might both enlarge and lose myself in suchlike arguments; I might tell you that Almighty God is said to have spoken to a fish but never to a beast; that he hath made a whale a ship to carry, and set his prophet Jonah safe on the appointed shore. Of these I might speak, but I must in manners break off, for I see Theobald's house. I cry your mercy for being so long, and thank you for your patience.

Almshouses Edmonton Church Yard

AUC. Sir, my pardon is easily granted you: I except against nothing that you have said; nevertheless I must part with you at this park wall, for which I am very sorry; but I assure you, Mr Piscator, I now part with you full of good thoughts, not only of yourself, but your recreation. And so, gentlemen, God keep you both.

PISC. Well now, Mr Venator, you shall neither want time nor my attention to hear you enlarge your discourse concerning hunting.

VEN. Not I, sir: I remember you said that angling itself was of great antiquity and a perfect art, and an art not easily attained to; and you have so won upon me in your former discourse, that I am very desirous to hear what you can say farther concerning those particulars.

PISC. Sir, I did say so: and I doubt not but if you and I did converse together but a few hours, to leave you possessed with the same high and happy thoughts that now possess me of it; not only of the antiquity of angling, but that it deserves commendations; and that it is an art, and an art worthy the knowledge and practice of a wise man.

VEN. Pray, sir, speak of them what you think fit, for we have yet five miles to the Thatched House; during which walk I dare promise you my patience and diligent attention shall not be wanting. And if you shall make that to appear which you have undertaken – first that it is an art, and an art worth the learning, I shall beg that I may attend you a day or two a-fishing, and that I may become your scholar and be instructed in the art itself which you so much magnify.

PISC. O sir, doubt not that angling is an art. Is it not an art to deceive a trout with an artificial fly? a trout! that is more sharp-sighted than any hawk you have named, and more watchful and timorous than your high-mettled merlin is bold; and yet I doubt not to catch a brace or two tomorrow for a friend's breakfast: doubt not, therefore, sir, but that angling is an art, and an art worth your learning. The question is rather, whether you be capable of learning it? for angling is somewhat like poetry, men are to be born so: I mean, with inclinations to it, though both may be heightened by discourse and practice: but he that hopes to be a good angler, must not only bring an enquiring, searching, observing wit, but he must bring a large measure of hope and patience, and a love and propensity to the art itself; but having once got and practised it, then doubt not but angling will prove to be so pleasant, that it will prove to be like virtue, a reward to itself.

VEN. Sir, I am now become so full of expectation, that I long much to have you proceed; and in the order you propose.

PISC. Then first, for the antiquity of angling, of which I shall not say much, but only this: some say it is as ancient as Deucalion's flood; others, that Belus, who was the first inventor of godly and virtuous recreations, was the first inventor of angling; and some others say (for former times have had their disquisitions about the antiquity of it) that Seth, one of the sons of Adam, taught it to his sons, and that by them it was derived to posterity: others say, that he left it engraven on those pillars which he erected, and trusted to preserve the knowledge of the mathematics, music, and the rest of that precious knowledge and those useful arts which by God's appointment or allowance and his noble industry, were thereby preserved from perishing in Noah's flood.

These, sir, have been the opinions of several men that have possibly endeavoured to make angling more ancient than is needful, or may well be warranted; but for my part, I shall content myself in telling you, that angling is much more ancient than the Incarnation of our Saviour; for in the prophet Amos mention is made of fish-hooks; and in the book of Job (which was long before the days of Amos, for that book is said to be writ by Moses) mention is made also of fish-hooks, which must imply anglers in those times.

But, my worthy friend, as I would rather prove myself a gentle-man, by being learned and humble, valiant and inoffensive, virtuous and communicable, than by any fond ostentation of riches; or, wanting those virtues myself, boast that these were in my ancestors (and yet I grant that where a noble and ancient descent, and such merit meet in any man, it is a double dignification of that person); so if this antiquity of angling (which for my part I have not forced) shall, like an ancient family, be either an honour or an ornament to this virtuous art which I profess to love and practise, I shall be the gladder that I made an accidental mention of the antiquity of it, of which I shall say no more, but proceed to that just commendation which I think it deserves.

And for that, I shall tell you, that in ancient times a debate hath arisen, and it remains yet unresolved: whether the happiness of man in this world doth consist more in contemplation or action?

Concerning which some have endeavoured to maintain their opinion of the first; by saying, that the nearer we mortals come to God by way of imitation, the more happy we are. And they say that God enjoys himself only, by a contemplation of his own infiniteness, eternity, power, and goodness, and the like. And upon this ground, many

JOHN TRADESCANT

cloisteral men of great learning and devotion, prefer contemplation before action. And many of the fathers seem to approve this opinion, as may appear in their commentaries upon the words of our Saviour to Martha (Luke 10: 41-2).

And on the contrary, there want not men of equal authority and credit, that prefer action to be the more excellent; as namely, experiments in physic, and the application of it, both for the ease and prolongation of man's life; by which each man is enabled to act and do good to others, either to serve his country or do good to particular persons: and they say also that action is doctrinal, and teaches both art and virtue, and is a maintainer of human society; and for these, and other like reasons, to be preferred before contemplation.

Concerning which two opinions, I shall forbear to add a third, by declaring my own: and rest myself contented in telling you, my very worthy friend, that both these meet together, and do most properly belong to the most honest, ingenious, quiet, and harmless art of angling.

And first, I shall tell you what some have observed (and I have found it to be a real truth) that the very sitting by the river's side is not only the quietest and fittest place for contemplation, but will invite an angler to it: and this seems to be maintained by the learned Pet. Du Moulin, who (in his discourse of the fulfilling of prophecies) observes, that when God intended to reveal any future events or high notions to his prophets, he then carried them either to the deserts or the sea-shore, that having so separated them from amidst the press of people and business, and the cares of the world, he might settle their minds in a quiet repose, and there make them fit for revelation.

And this seems also to be intimated by the Children of Israel (Psal. 137), who, having in a sad condition banished all mirth and music from their pensive hearts, and having hung up their then mute harps upon the willow trees growing by the rivers of Babylon, sat down upon these banks bemoaning the ruins of Sion, and contemplating their own sad condition.

And an ingenious Spaniard says, that 'rivers and the inhabitants of the watery element were made for wise men to contemplate and fools to pass by without consideration.' And though I will not rank myself in the number of the first, yet give me leave to free myself from the last, by offering to you a short contemplation, first of rivers and then of fish; concerning which I doubt not but to give you many observations that will appear very considerable: I am sure they have appeared so to me, and made many an hour to pass away more pleasantly, as I have sat quietly on a flowery bank by a calm river, and contemplated what I shall now relate to you.

And first, concerning rivers: there be so many wonders reported and written of them, and of the several creatures that be bred and live in them; and those by authors of so good credit, that we need not to deny them an historical faith.

As namely of a river in Epirus, that puts out any lighted torch, and kindles any torch that was not lighted. Some waters being drank cause madness, some drunkenness, and some laughter to death. The

river Selarus in a few hours turns a rod or wand to stone; and our Camden mentions the like in England, and the like in Lochmere in Ireland. There is also a river in Arabia, of which all the sheep that drink thereof have their wool turned into a vermilion colour. And one of no less credit than Aristotle tells us of a merry river (the river Elusina) that dances at the noise of music, for with music it bubbles, dances, and grows sandy, and so continues till the music ceases, but then it presently returns to its wonted calmness and clearness. And Camden tells us of a well near to Kirby in Westmoreland, that ebbs and flows several times every day: and he tells us of a river in Surrey (it is called Mole), that after it has run several miles, being opposed by hills, finds or makes itself a way under ground, and breaks out again so far off, that the inhabitants thereabout boast (as the Spaniards do of their river Anus) that they feed divers flocks of sheep upon a bridge. And lastly, for I would not tire your patience, one of no less authority than Josephus, that learned Jew, tells us of a river in Judea that runs swiftly all the six days of the week, and stands still and rests all their sabbath.

But I will lay aside my discourse of rivers, and tell you some things of the monsters, or fish, call them what you will, that they breed and feed in them. Pliny, the philosopher, says (in the third chapter of his ninth book) that in the Indian Sea, the fish called the *balaena* or whirlpool, is so long and broad as to take up more in length and breadth than two acres of ground; and of other fish of two hundred cubits long; and that, in the river Ganges, there be eels of thirty feet long. He says there, that these monsters appear in the sea only when tempestuous winds oppose the torrents of water falling from the rocks into it, and so turning what lay at the bottom to be seen on the water's top. And he says that the people of Cadara (an island near this place) make the timber for their houses of those fishbones. He there tells us that there are sometimes a thousand of these great eels found wrapt or interwoven together. He tells us there that it appears that dolphins love music, and will come when called for, by some men or boys that know, and use to feed them; and that they can swim as swift as an arrow can be shot out of a bow; and much of this is spoken concerning the dolphin, and other fish, as may be found also in the learned Dr Casaubon's *Discourse of Credulity and Incredulity*, printed by him about the year 1670.

I know we islanders are averse to the belief of these wonders; but there be so many strange creatures to be now seen (many collected by John Tradescant, and others added by my friend Elias Ashmole, Esq., who now keeps them carefully and methodically at his house near to Lambeth near London) as may get some belief of some of the other wonders I mentioned. I will tell you some of the wonders that you may now see, and not till then believe, unless you think fit.

You may see the hog-fish, the dog-fish, the dolphin, the coney-fish, the parrot fish, the shark, the poison-fish, sword-fish, and not only other incredible fish, but you may there see the salamander, several sorts of barnacles, and Solan geese, the bird of Paradise, such sorts of snakes, and such birds'-nests, and of so various forms, and so wonderfully made, as may beget wonder and amusement in any beholder: and so many hundred of other rarities in that collection, as will make the other wonders I spake of the less incredible; for you may note that the waters are nature's store-house, in which she locks up her wonders.

But, sir, lest this discourse may seem tedious, I shall give it a sweet conclusion out of that holy poet Mr George Herbert his divine *Contemplation on God's Providence*.

> Lord, who hath praise enough; nay, who hath any?
> None can express thy works but he that knows them;
> And none can know thy works, they are so many,
> And so complete, but only he that owes them.
>
> We all acknowledge both thy power and love
> To be exact, transcendent and divine;

Ashmole's house in Ship yard.

Who dost so strangely and so sweetly move,
 Whilst all things have their end, yet none but thine.

Wherefore, most sacred Spirit, I here present,
 For me, and all my fellow, praise to thee;
And just it is that I should pay the rent,
 Because the benefit accrues to me.

And as concerning fish, in that psalm (Psalm 104) wherein, for height of poetry and wonders, the prophet David seems even to exceed himself; how doth he there express himself in choice metaphors, even to the amazement of a contemplative reader, concerning the sea, the rivers, and the fish therein contained! And the great naturalist, Pliny, says, 'that nature's great and wonderful power is more demonstrated in the sea than on the land.' And this may appear by the numerous and various creatures inhabiting both in and about that element; as to the readers of Gesner, Rondeletius, Pliny, Ausonius, Aristotle, and others, may be demonstrated. But I will sweeten this discourse also out of a contemplation in divine Du Bartas (in the fifth day), who says –

> God quicken'd in the sea, and in the rivers,
> So many fishes of so many features,
> That in the waters we may see all creatures,
> Even all that on earth are to be found,
> As if the world were in deep waters drown'd.
> For seas (as well as skies) have sun, moon, stars:
> (As well as air) swallows, rooks and stares:
> (As well as earth) vines, roses, nettles, melons,
> Mushrooms, pinks, gilliflowers, and many millions
> Of other plants, more rare, more strange than these,
> As very fishes, living in the seas;
> As also rams, calves, horses, hares, and hogs,
> Wolves, urchins, lions, elephants, and dogs;
> Yea, men and maids; and, which I most admire,
> The mitred bishop and the cowled friar;
> Of which, examples, but a few years since,
> Were shown the Norway and Polonian Prince.

These seem to be wonders, but have had so many confirmations from men of learning and credit, that you need not doubt them; nor are the number, nor the various shapes of fishes, more strange or more fit for contemplation than their different natures, inclinations, and actions; concerning which I shall beg your patient ear a little longer.

The cuttle-fish will cast a long gut out of her throat, which (like as an angler doth his line) she sendeth forth and pulleth in again at her pleasure, according as she sees some little fish come near her; and the cuttle-fish (being then hid in the gravel) lets the smaller fish nibble and bite the end of it, at which time she by little and little draws the smaller fish so near to her that she may leap upon her, and then catches and devours her: and for this reason some have called this fish the sea-angler.

And there is a fish called a hermit, that at a certain age gets into a dead fish's shell, and like a hermit dwells there alone, studying the wind and weather, and so turns her shell, that she makes it defend her from the injuries that they would bring upon her.

ELIAS ASHMOLE

There is also a fish called, by Aelian (in his ninth book of *Living Creatures*, chap. 16), the Adonis, or darling of the sea; so called because it is a loving and innocent fish, a fish that hurts nothing that hath life, and is at peace with all the numerous inhabitants of that vast watery element: and truly I think most anglers are so disposed to most of mankind.

And there are also lustful and chaste fishes, of which I shall give you examples.

And first Du Bartas says of a fish called the sargus; which (because none can express it better than he does) I shall give you in his own words; supposing it shall not have the less credit for being in verse; for he hath gathered this and other observations out of authors that have been great and industrious searchers into the secrets of nature.

> The adulterous sargus doth not only change
> Wives every day, in the deep streams, but, strange,
> As if the honey of sea-love delight
> Could not suffice his raging appetite,
> Goes courting she-goats on the grassy shore,
> Horning their husbands that had horns before.

And the same author writes concerning the cantharus that which you shall also hear in his own words:

> But, contrary, the constant cantharus
> Is ever constant to his faithful spouse;
> In nuptial duties spending his chaste life;
> Never loves any but his own dear wife.

Sir, but a little, and I have done.

VEN. Sir, take what liberty you think fit, for your discourse seems to be music, and charms me to an attention.

PISC. Why then, sir, I will take a liberty to tell, or rather to remember you what is said of turtle-doves: first, that they silently plight their troth, and marry; and that then the survivor scorns (as the Thracian women are said to do) to outlive his or her mate, and this is taken for a truth; and if the survivor shall ever couple with another, then not only the living but the dead (be it either the he or the she) is denied the name and honour of a true turtle-dove.

And to parallel this land-rarity, and teach mankind moral faithfulness, and to condemn those that talk of religion, and yet come short of the moral faith of fish and fowl; men that violate the law affirmed by St Paul (Rom 2: 14–15), to be writ in their hearts, and which he says shall at the last day condemn and leave them without excuse; I pray hearken to what Du Bartas sings (for the hearing of such conjugal faithfulness will be music to all chaste ears), and therefore I pray hearken to what Du Bartas sings of the mullet.

> But for chaste love the Mullet hath no peer;
> For if the fisher hath surprised her pheer,
> As mad with woe to shore she followeth,
> Prest to consort him both in life and death.

On the contrary, what shall I say of the house-cock, which treads any hen, and then (contrary to the swan, the partridge, and pigeon) takes no care to hatch, to feed or to cherish his own brood, but is senseless, though they perish.

And 'tis considerable that the hen, which, because she also takes any cock, expects it not, who is sure the chickens be her own, hath by a moral impression her care and affection to her own brood more than doubled, even to such a height that our Saviour, in expressing his love to Jerusalem (Matt. 23: 37), quotes her for an example of tender affection; as his Father had done Job for a pattern of patience.

And to parallel this cock, there be divers fishes that cast their spawn on flags or stones, and then leave it uncovered and exposed to become a prey and be devoured by vermin, or other fishes; but other fishes (as namely the barbel) take such care for the preservation of their seed, that unlike to the cock or the cuckoo, they mutually labour, both the spawner and the melter, to cover the spawn with sand, or watch it, or hide it in some secret place, unfrequented by vermin or any fish but themselves.

Sir, these examples may to you and others seem strange, but they are testified, some by Aristotle, some by Pliny, some by Gesner, and by many others of credit; and are believed and known by divers both of wisdom and experience, to be a truth; and indeed are (as I said at the beginning) fit for the contemplation of a most serious and a most pious man. And doubtless this made the prophet David say, 'They that occupy themselves in deep waters see the wonderful works of God:' indeed such wonders and pleasures too, as the land affords not.

And that they be fit for the contemplation of the most prudent and pious and peaceable men, seems to be testified by the practice of so many devout and contemplative men, as the patriarchs and prophets of old; and of the apostles of our Saviour in our latter times, of which twelve, we are sure he chose four that were simple fishermen, whom he inspired and sent to publish his blessed will to the Gentiles; and inspired them also with a power to speak all languages, and by their powerful eloquence to beget faith in the unbelieving Jews; and themselves to suffer for that Saviour whom their forefathers and they had crucified; and, in their sufferings, to preach freedom from the encumbrances of the law, and a new way to everlasting life: this was the employment of these happy fishermen. Concerning which choice some have made these observations.

First, That he never reproved these for their employment or calling, as he did scribes and the money-changers. And secondly, he found that the hearts of such men by nature were fitted for contemplation and quietness; men of mild, and sweet, and peaceable spirits, as indeed most anglers are: these men our blessed Saviour (who is observed to love to plant grace in good natures), though indeed nothing be too hard for him; yet these men he chose to call from their irreprovable employment of fishing, and gave them grace to be his disciples, and to follow him and do wonders. I say four of twelve.

And it is observable, that it was our Saviour's will that these our four fishermen should have a priority of nomination in the catalogue of his twelve apostles (Matt: 10); as namely, first, St Peter, St Andrew, St James, and St John, and then the rest in their order.

And it is yet more observable, that when our blessed Saviour went up into the mount, when he left the rest of his disciples and chose only three to bear him company at his transfiguration, that those three were all fishermen. And it is to be believed, that all the other apostles, after they betook themselves to follow Christ, betook themselves to be fishermen too; for it is certain that the greater number of them were found together fishing by Jesus after his Resurrection, as it is recorded in the 21st chapter of St John's Gospel.

And since I have your promise to hear me with patience, I will take the liberty to look back upon an observation that hath been made by an ingenious and learned man, who observes that God hath been pleased to allow those whom he himself hath appointed to write his holy will in holy writ, yet to express his will in such metaphors as their former affections or practice had inclined them to; and he brings Solomon for an example, who before his conversion was remarkably carnally amorous; and after, by God's appointment, wrote that spiritual dialogue, or holy amorous love-song, the Canticles, betwixt God and his church; in which he says, his beloved had eyes like the fish-pools of Heshbon.

And if this hold in reason (as I see none to the contrary) then it may be probably concluded that Moses, who I told you before writ the book of Job, and the prophet Amos, who was a shepherd, were both anglers; for you shall, in all the Old Testament find fish-hooks,

I think, but twice mentioned: namely, by meek Moses, the friend of God, and by the humble prophet Amos.

Concerning which last, namely, the prophet Amos, I shall make but this observation; that he that shall read the humble, lowly, plain style of that prophet, and compare it with the high, glorious, eloquent style of the prophet Isaiah (though they both be equally true), may easily believe Amos to be, not only a shepherd, but a good-natured, plain fisherman.

Which I do the rather believe, by comparing the affectionate, loving, lowly, humble epistles of St Peter, St James, and St John, whom we know were all fishers, with the glorious language and high metaphors of St Paul, whom we may believe was not.

And for the lawfulness of fishing: it may very well be maintained by our Saviour's bidding St Peter cast his hook into the water and catch a fish, for money to pay tribute to Caesar. And let me tell you that angling is of high esteem and of much use in other nations. He that reads the voyages of Ferdinand Mendez Pinto, shall find, that there he declares to have found a king and several priests a-fishing.

And he that reads Plutarch shall find that angling was not contemptible in the days of Mark Anthony and Cleopatra, and that they, in the midst of their wonderful glory, used angling as a principal recreation. And let me tell you, that in the Scripture, angling is always taken in the best sense, and that though hunting may be sometimes so taken, yet it is but seldom to be so understood. And let me add this more, he that views the ancient ecclesiastical canons, shall find hunting to be forbidden to churchmen, as being a turbulent, toilsome, perplexing recreation; and shall find angling allowed to clergymen, as being a harmless recreation, a recreation that invites them to contemplation and quietness.

I might here enlarge myself by telling you what commendations our learned Perkins bestows on angling: and how dear a lover, and great a practiser of it our learned Doctor Whittaker was, as indeed many others of great learning have been. But I will content myself with two memorable men, that lived near to our own time, whom I also take to have been ornaments to the art of angling.

The first is Doctor Nowel, some time Dean of the Cathedral Church of St Paul's in London, where his monument stands yet undefaced: a man that in the reformation of Queen Elizabeth (not that of Henry VIII) was so noted for his meek spirit, deep learning, prudence, and piety, that the then Parliament and Convocation both, chose, enjoined, and trusted him to be the man to make a catechism for public use, such a one as should stand as a rule for faith and manners to their posterity. And the good old man (though he was very learned, yet knowing that God leads us not to Heaven by many nor by hard questions), like an honest angler, made that good, plain, unperplexed catechism, which is printed with our good old service-book. I say, this good old man was a dear lover and constant practiser of angling, as any age can produce: and his custom was to spend, besides his fixed hours of prayer (those hours which, by command of the church, were enjoined the clergy, and

voluntarily dedicated to devotion by many primitive Christians); I say, beside those hours, this good man was observed to spend a tenth part of his time in angling; and also (for I have conversed with those which have conversed with him) to bestow a tenth part of his revenue, and usually all his fish, amongst the poor that inhabited near to those rivers in which it was caught; saying often, 'that charity gave life to religion:' and, at his return to his house, would praise God he had spent that day free from worldly trouble; both harmlessly, and in recreation that became a churchman. And this good man was well content, if not desirous, that posterity should know he was an angler; as may appear by his picture, now to be seen, and carefully kept, in Brazennose College (to which he was a liberal benefactor). In which picture he was drawn, leaning on a desk, with his Bible before him, and on one hand of him his lines, hooks, and other tackling lying in a round; and on his other hand are his angle-rods of several sorts: and by them this is written, 'That he died Feb. 13, 1601, being aged 95 years, 44 of which he had been Dean of St Paul's Church; and that his age had neither impaired his hearing, nor dimmed his eyes, nor weakened his memory, nor made any of the faculties of his mind weak or useless.' 'Tis said that angling and temperance were great causes of these blessings, and I wish the like to all that imitate him, and love the memory of so good a man.

My next and last example shall be that under-valuer of money, the late provost of Eton College, Sir Henry Wotton (a man with whom I have often fished and conversed), a man whose foreign employments in the service of this nation, and whose experience, learning, wit, and cheerfulness, made his company to be esteemed one of the delights of mankind: this man, whose very approbation of angling were sufficient to convince any modest censurer of it, this man was also a most dear lover, and a frequent practiser of the art of angling; of which he would say, ' 'Twas an employment for his idle time, which was then not idly spent: for angling was, after tedious study, a rest to his mind, a cheerer of his spirits, a diverter of sadness, a calmer of unquiet thoughts, a moderator of passions, a procurer of contentedness: and that it begat habits of peace and patience in those that professed and practised it.' Indeed, my friend, you will find angling to be like the virtue of humility, which has a calmness of spirit, and a world of other blessings attending upon it.

Sir, this was the saying of that learned man, and I do easily believe, that peace and patience, and a calm content, did cohabit in the cheerful heart of Sir Henry Wotton; because I know that when he was beyond seventy years of age, he made this description of a part of the present pleasure that possessed him, as he sat quietly in a summer's evening, on a bank a-fishing. It is a description of the spring; which because it glided as soft and sweetly from his pen, as that river does at this time, by which it was then made, I shall repeat it unto you –

> This day dame Nature seem'd in love;
> The lusty sap began to move;
> Fresh juice did stir th' embracing vines;
> And birds had drawn their valentines.
> The jealous trout, that low did lie,
> Rose at a well-dissembled fly;
> There stood my friend with patient skill,
> Attending of his trembling quill;
> Already were the eaves possess'd
> With the swift pilgrim's daubèd nest;
> The groves already did rejoice
> In Philomel's triumphing voice,
> The showers were short, the weather mild,
> The morning fresh, the evening smiled.
> Joan takes her neat-rubbed pail, and now
> She trips to milk the sand-red cow;
> Where, for some sturdy football swain,
> Joan strokes a syllabub or twain.
> The fields and gardens were beset
> With tulip, crocus, violet;

And now, though late, the modest rose
Did more than half a blush disclose.
  Thus all looks gay and full of cheer,
To welcome the new-liveried year.

These were the thoughts that then possessed the undisturbed mind of Sir Henry Wotton. Will you hear the wish of another angler, and the commendation of his happy life, which he also sings in verse? – viz. Jo. Davors, Esq. –

> Let me live harmlessly; and near the brink
>   Of Trent or Avon have a dwelling place,
> Where I may see my quill or cork down sink
>   With eager bite of perch, or bleak, or dace;
> And on the world and my Creator think:
>   Whilst some men strive ill-gotten goods t' embrace,
> And others spend their time in base excess
> Of wine, or worse, in war and wantonness.
>
> Let them that list, these pastimes still pursue,
>   And on such pleasing fancies feed their fill;
> So I the fields and meadows green may view,
>   And daily by fresh rivers walk at will,
> Among the daisies and the violets blue,
>   Red hyacinth and yellow daffodil,
> Purple narcissus like the morning rays,
> Pale gander-grass, and azure culverkeys.

Chingford Church

I count it higher pleasure to behold
   The stately compass of the lofty sky;
And in the midst thereof (like burning gold)
   The flaming chariot of the world's great eye;
The watery clouds that, in the air up-roll'd,
   With sundry kinds of painted colours fly;
And fair Aurora, lifting up her head,
Still blushing, rise from old Tithonus' bed.

The hills and mountains raised from the plains,
   The plains extended level with the ground;
The grounds divided into sundry veins,
   The veins enclos'd with rivers running round;
These rivers making way through nature's chains
   With headlong course into the sea profound;
The raging sea, beneath the valleys low,
Where lakes and rills and rivulets do flow.

The lofty woods, the forests wide and long,
   Adorn'd with leaves and branches fresh and green,
In whose cool bowers the birds, with many a song,
   Do welcome with their choir the summer's queen;
The meadows fair, where Flora's gifts among
   Are intermixed, with verdant grass between;
The silver-scal'd fish that softly swim
Within the sweet brook's crystal watery stream.

At Waltham Cross

E·H·N·

All these, and many more of His creation
    That made the heavens, the angler oft doth see:
Taking therein no little delectation,
    To think how strange, how wonderful they be!
Framing thereof an inward contemplation
    To set his heart from other fancies free;
And whilst he looks on these with joyful eye,
His mind is wrapt above the starry sky.

Sir, I am glad my memory has not lost these last verses, because they are somewhat more pleasant and more suitable to May-day than my harsh discourse. And I am glad your patience hath held out so long, as to hear them and me; for both together have brought us within the sight of the Thatched House: and I must be your debtor (if you think it worth your attention) for the rest of my promised discourse, till some other opportunity, and a like time of leisure.

VEN. Sir, you have angled me on with much pleasure to the Thatched House; and I now find your words true, 'that good company makes the way seem short'; for trust me, sir, I thought we had wanted three miles of this house, till you showed it to me. But now we are at it, we'll turn into it, and refresh ourselves with a cup of drink, and a little rest.

PISC. Most gladly, sir, and we'll drink a civil cup to all the otter-hunters that are to meet you tomorrow.

VEN. That we will, sir, and to all the lovers of angling, of which number I am now willing to be one myself: for, by the help of your good discourse and company, I have put on new thoughts both of the art of angling, and of all that profess it; and if you will but meet me tomorrow, at the time and place appointed, and bestow one day with me and my friends in hunting the otter, I will dedicate the next two days to wait upon you, and we two will for that time do nothing but angle, and talk of fish and fishing.

PISC. 'Tis a match, sir; I'll not fail you, God willing, to be at Amwell Hill tomorrow morning before sunrising.

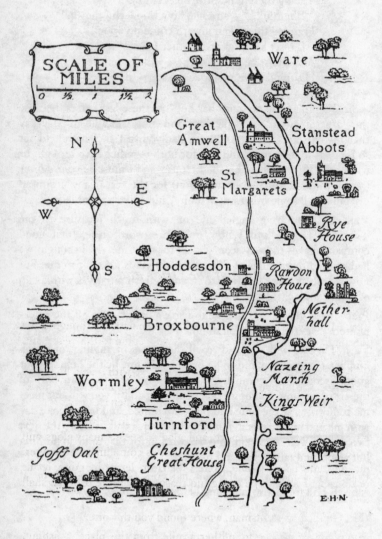

CHAPTER II

Observations of the Otter and Chub

VEN. My friend Piscator, you have kept time with my thoughts, for the sun is just rising, and I myself just now come to this place, and the dogs have just now put down an otter. Look down at the bottom of the hill there in that meadow, chequered with water-lilies and lady-smocks: there you may see what work they make: look! look! you may see all busy, men and dogs, dogs and men all busy.

PISC. Sir, I am right glad to meet you, and glad to have so fair an entrance into this day's sport, and glad to see so many dogs and more men all in pursuit of the otter. Let us compliment no longer, but join unto them. Come, honest Venator, let us be gone, let us make haste; I long to be doing; no reasonable hedge or ditch shall hold me.

VEN. Gentleman-huntsman, where found you this otter?

HUNT. Marry, sir, we found her a mile from this place, a-fishing. She has this morning eaten the greatest part of this trout; she has only left this much of it as you see, and was fishing for more; when we came we found her just at it; but we were here very early, we were here an hour before sunrise, and have given her no rest since we came; sure, she will hardly escape all these dogs and men. I am to have the skin if we kill her.

VEN. Why, sir, what is the skin worth?

HUNT. 'Tis worth ten shillings to make gloves; the gloves of an otter are the best fortification for your hands that can be thought on against wet weather.

PISC. I pray, honest huntsman, let me ask you a pleasant question: do you hunt a beast or a fish?

HUNT. Sir, it is not in my power to resolve you; I leave it to be resolved by the college of Carthusians, who have made their vows never to eat flesh. But I have heard the question hath been debated among many great clerks, and they seem to differ about it; yet most agree that her tail is fish; and if her body be fish too, then I may say that a fish will walk upon land; for an otter does so, sometimes, five or six or ten miles in a night, to catch for her young ones, or to glut herself with fish. And I can tell you that pigeons will fly forty miles for a breakfast; but, sir, I am sure the otter devours much fish, and kills and spoils much more than he eats. And I can tell you that this dog-fisher (for so the Latins call him) can smell a fish in the water a hundred yards from him: Gesner says much farther; and that his stones are good against the falling sickness; and that there is an herb, benione, which being hung in a linen cloth, near a fish pond, or any haunt that he uses, makes him to avoid the place; which proves he smells both by water and land; and I can tell you there is brave hunting this water-dog in Cornwall, where there have been so many, that our learned Camden says there is a river called Ottersey, which was so named by reason of the abundance of otters that bred and fed in it.

And thus much for my knowledge of the otter, which you may now see above water at vent, and the dogs close with him; I now see he will not last long, follow therefore my masters, follow, for Sweetlips was like to have him at this last vent.

VEN. Oh me! all the horse are got over the river, what shall we do now? Shall we follow them over the water?

HUNT. No, sir, no, be not so eager; stay a little and follow me, for both they and the dogs will be suddenly on this side again I warrant you; and the otter too, it may be: now have at him with Kilbuck, for he vents again.

VEN. Marry so he does, for look he vents in that corner. Now, poor

Ringwood has him: now he's gone again, and has bit the poor dog. Now Sweetlips has her; hold her, Sweetlips! now all the dogs have her, some above and some under water; but now, now she's tired, and past losing: come bring her to me, Sweetlips. Look, 'tis a bitch otter, and she has lately whelped, let's go to the place where she was put down, and not far from it you will find all her young ones, I dare warrant you, and kill them all too.

HUNT. Come, gentlemen, come all, let's go to the place where we put down the otter. Look you, hereabout it was that she kennelled; look you, here it was indeed, for here's her young ones, no less than five; come, let's kill them all.

PISC. No, I pray, sir, save me one, and I'll try if I can make her tame, as I know an ingenious gentleman in Leicestershire (Mr Nicholas Seagrave) has done; who hath not only made her tame, but to catch fish, and do many other things of much pleasure.

HUNT. Take one with all my heart, but let us kill the rest. And now let's go to an honest ale-house, where we may have a cup of good barley-wine, and sing Old Rose, and all of us rejoice together.

VEN. Come, my friend Piscator, let me invite you along with us; I'll bear your charges this night, and you shall bear mine tomorrow; for my intention is to accompany you a day or two in fishing.

PISC. Sir, your request is granted, and I shall be right glad both to exchange such a courtesy, and also to enjoy your company.

Marsh Marigolds

THIRD DAY

Ven. Well, now let's go to your sport of angling.

Pisc. Let's be going with all my heart. God keep you all, gentlemen, and send you meet this day with another bitch-otter, and kill her merrily, and all her young ones too.

Ven. Now, Piscator, where will you begin to fish?

Pisc. We are not yet come to a likely place, I must walk a mile further yet before I begin.

Ven. Well then, I pray, as we walk tell me freely, how do you like your lodging, and mine host, and the company? Is not mine host a witty man?

Pisc. Sir, I will tell you presently what I think of your host; but first, I will tell you, I am glad these otters were killed; but I am sorry there are no more otter-killers; for I know that the want of otter-killers, and the not keeping the fence-months for the preservation of fish, will, in time, prove the destruction of all rivers. And those very few that are left, that make conscience of the laws of the nation, and of keeping days of abstinence, will be forced to eat flesh, or suffer more inconveniences than are yet foreseen.

Ven. Why, sir, what be those that you call the fencemonths?

Pisc. Sir, they be principally three, namely, March, April, and May; for these be the usual months that salmon come out of the sea to spawn in most fresh rivers: and their fry would, about a certain time, return back to the salt water, if they were not hindered by weirs and unlawful gins, which the greedy fishermen set, and so destroy them by thousands; as they would (being so taught by nature) change the fresh for salt water. He that shall view the wise statutes, made in the 13th of Edward I, and the like in Richard III, may see several provisions made against the destruction of fish; and though I profess no knowledge of the law, yet I am sure the regulation of these defects might be easily mended. But I remember that a wise friend of mine did usually say, 'that which is everybody's business is nobody's business'. If it were otherwise, there could not be so many nets and fish, that are under the statute size, sold daily amongst us, and of which the conservators of the waters should be ashamed.

But, above all, the taking fish in spawning-time may be said to be against nature; it is like the taking the dam on the nest when she hatches her young: a sin so against nature that Almighty God hath in the Levitical law made a law against it.

But the poor fish have enemies enough besides such unnatural fishermen, as namely, the otters that I spake of, the cormorant, the bittern, the osprey, the seagull, the heron, the kingfisher, the gorara, the puet, the swan, goose, ducks, and the craber, which some call the water-rat: against all which any honest man might make a just quarrel, but I will not, I will leave them to be quarrelled with, and killed by others; for I am not of a cruel nature, I love to kill nothing but fish.

And now to your question concerning your host; to speak truly, he is not to me a good companion; for most of his conceits were either Scripture-jests, or lascivious jests, for which I count no man witty, for the devil will help a man that way inclined, to the first; and his own corrupt nature (which he always carries with him) to the latter. But a companion that feasts the company with wit and mirth, and leaves out the sin (which is usually mixed with them) he is the man; and indeed such a man should have his charges borne, and to such company I hope to bring you this night; for at Trout Hall, not far from this place, where I purpose to lodge tonight, there is usually an angler that proves good company: and let me tell you, good company and good discourse are the very sinews of virtue: but for such discourse as we heard last night, it infects others; the very boys will learn to talk and swear, as they heard mine host, and another of the company that shall be nameless; I am sorry the other is a gentleman; for less religion will not save their souls than a beggar's: I think more will be required at the last great day. Well! you know what example is able to do; and I know what the poet says in the like case, which is worthy to be noted by all parents and people of civility:

> . . . many a one
> Owes to his county his religion;
> And in another would as strongly grow,
> Had but his nurse or mother taught him so.

This is reason put into verse, and worthy the consideration of a wise man. But of this no more; for though I love civility, yet I hate severe censures. I'll to my own art; and I doubt not but at yonder tree I shall catch a chub: and then we'll turn to an honest cleanly hostess that I know right well; rest ourselves there; and dress it for our dinner.

VEN. Oh, sir! a chub is the worst fish that swims; I hoped for a trout for my dinner.

PISC. Trust me, sir, there is not a likely place for a trout hereabout: and we stayed so long to take leave of your huntsmen this morning, that the sun is got so high, and shines so clear, that I will not undertake the catching of a trout till evening; and though a chub be, by you and many others, reckoned the worst of fish; yet you shall see I'll make it a good fish by dressing it.

VEN. Why, how will you dress him?

PISC. I'll tell you by and by, when I have caught him. Look you here, sir, do you see? (but you must stand very close), there lie upon the top of the water, in this very hole, twenty chubs. I'll catch only one, and that shall be the biggest of them all; and that I will do so, I'll hold you twenty to one, and you shall see it done.

VEN. Ay, marry, sir, now you talk like an artist, and I'll say you are one, when I shall see you perform what you say you can do; but I yet doubt it.

PISC. You shall not doubt it long, for you shall see me do it presently: look, the biggest of these chubs has had some bruise upon his tail by a pike, or some other accident, and that looks like a white spot; that very chub I mean to put into your hands presently; sit you but down in the shade, and stay but a little while, and I'll warrant you I'll bring him to you.

VEN. I'll sit down, and hope well, because you seem to be so confident.

PISC. Look you, sir, there is a trial of my skill, there he is, that very chub that I showed you with the white spot on his tail: and I'll be as certain to make him a good dish of meat as I was to catch him. I'll now lead you to an honest ale-house where we shall find a cleanly room, lavender in the windows, and twenty ballads stuck about the wall; there my hostess (which, I may tell you, is both cleanly and handsome, and civil) hath dressed many a one for me, and shall now dress it after my fashion, and I warrant it good meat.

VEN. Come, sir, with all my heart, for I begin to be hungry, and long to be at it, and indeed to rest myself too; for though I have walked but four miles this morning, yet I begin to be weary; yesterday's hunting hangs still upon me.

PISC. Well, sir, you shall quickly be at rest, for yonder is the house I mean to bring you to.

Come, Hostess, how do you do? Will you first give us a cup of your best drink, and then dress this chub as you dressed my last, when I and my friend were here about eight or ten days ago? But you must do me one courtesy, it must be done instantly.

HOSTESS. I will do it, Mr Piscator, and with all the speed I can.

PISC. Now, sir, has not my hostess made haste? and does not the fish look lovely?

VEN. Both, upon my word, sir, and therefore let's say grace, and fall to eating of it.

PISC. Well, sir, how do you like it?

VEN. Trust me, 'tis as good meat as I ever tasted: now let me thank you for it, drink to you, and beg a courtesy of you; but it must not be denied me.

PISC. What is it, I pray, sir? You are so modest, that methinks I may promise to grant it before it is asked.

VEN. Why, sir, it is, that from henceforth you would allow me to call you Master, and that really I may be your scholar; for you are such a companion, and have so quickly caught, and so excellently cooked this fish, as makes me ambitious to be your scholar.

PISC. Give me your hand; from this time forward I will be your master, and teach you as much of this art as I am able; and will, as you desire me, tell you somewhat of the nature of most of the fish that we are to angle for; and I am sure I both can and will tell you more than any common Angler yet knows.

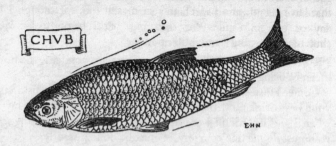

CHAPTER III

How to Fish for, and to Dress, the Chavender, or Chub

Pisc. The Chub, though he eat well thus dressed, yet as he is usually dressed he does not. He is objected against, not only for being full of small forked bones, dispersed through all his body, but that he eats waterish, and that the flesh of him is not firm, but short and tasteless. The French esteem him so mean as to call him *un vilain*; nevertheless, he may be so dressed as to make him very good meat; as, namely, if he be a large chub, then dress him thus:

First, scale him, and then wash him clean, and then take out his guts; and to that end make the hole as little and near to his gills as you may conveniently, and especially make clean his throat from the grass and weeds that are usually in it (for if that be not very clean, it will make him to taste very sour). Having so done, put some sweet herbs into his belly; and then tie him with two or three splinters to a spit, and roast him, basted often with vinegar, or rather verjuice and butter, with good store of salt mixed with it.

Being thus dressed, you will find him a much better dish of meat than you, or most folk, even than anglers themselves, do imagine: for this dries up the fluid watery humour with which all chubs do abound.

But take this rule with you, that a chub newly taken and newly dressed, is so much better than a chub of a day's keeping after he is dead, that I can compare him to nothing so fitly as to cherries newly gathered from a tree, and others that have been bruised and lain a day or two in water. But the chub being thus used, and dressed presently, and not washed after he is gutted (for note, that lying long in water, and washing the blood out of any fish after they be gutted, abates much of their sweetness), you will find the chub being dressed in the blood, and quickly, to be such meat as will recompense your labour, and disabuse your opinion.

Or you may dress the chavender or chub thus: When you have scaled him, and cut off his tail and fins, and washed him very clean, then chine or slit him through the middle, as a salt fish is usually cut; then give him three or four cuts or scotches on the back with your knife, and broil him on charcoal, or wood-coal that is free from smoke, and all the time he is a-broiling baste him with the best sweet butter, and good store of salt mixed with it; and to this add a little thyme cut exceeding small, or bruised into the butter. The cheven thus dressed hath the watery taste taken away, for which so many except against him. Thus was the cheven dressed that you now liked

so well, and commended so much. But note again, that if this chub that you ate of had been kept till tomorrow, he had not been worth a rush. And remember that his throat be washed very clean, I say very clean, and his body not washed after he is gutted, as indeed no fish should be.

Well, scholar, you see what pains I have taken to recover the lost credit of the poor despised chub. And now I will give you some rules how to catch him; and I am glad to enter you into the art of fishing by catching a chub, for there is no fish better to enter a young angler, he is so easily caught, but then it must be this particular way.

Go to the same hole in which I caught my chub, where in most hot days you will find a dozen or twenty chevens floating near the top of the water; get two or three grasshoppers as you go over the meadow, and get secretly behind the tree, and stand as free from motion as is possible; then put a grasshopper on your hook, and let your hook hang a quarter of a yard short of the water, to which end you must rest your rod on some bough of the tree. But it is likely the chubs will sink down towards the bottom of the water at the first shadow of your rod (for a chub is the fearfulest of fishes), and will do so if a bird flies over him and makes the least shadow on the water; but they will presently rise up to the top again, and there lie soaring till some shadow affrights them again. I say, when they lie upon the top of the water, look out the best chub (which you, setting yourself in a fit place, may very easily see), and move your rod as softly as a snail moves, to that chub you intend to catch; let your bait fall gently upon the water three or four inches before him, and he will infallibly take the bait, and you will be as sure to catch him; for he is one of the leather-mouthed fishes, of which a hook does scarce ever lose its hold; and therefore give him play enough before you offer to take him out of the water. Go your way presently; take my rod and do as I bid you; and I will sit down and mend my tackling till you return back.

VEN. Truly, my loving master, you have offered me as fair as I could wish. I'll go, and observe your directions.

Look you, master, what I have done, that which joys my heart, caught just such another chub as yours was.

PISC. Marry, and I am glad of it: I am like to have a towardly scholar of you. I now see that with advice and practice, you will make an angler in a short time. Have but a love to it; and I'll warrant you.

VEN. But, master, what if I could not have found a grasshopper?

PISC. Then I may tell you that a black snail, with his belly slit to show his white, or a piece of soft cheese, will usually do as well: nay, sometimes a worm, or any kind of fly, as the ant-fly, the flesh-fly, or wall-fly, or the dor or beetle (which you may find under cow-turd), or a bob, which you will find in the same place, and in time will be a beetle; it is a short white worm, like to and bigger than a gentle, or a

Harold's
Bridge
Waltham

cod-worm, or a case-worm, any of these will do very well to fish in such a manner. And after this manner you may catch a trout in a hot evening: when as you walk by a brook, and shall see or hear him leap at flies, then if you get a grasshopper, put it on your hook, with your line about two yards long, standing behind a bush or tree where his hole is, and make your bait stir up and down on the top of the water, you may, if you stand close, be sure of a bite, but not sure to catch him, for he is not a leather-mouthed fish: and after this manner you may fish for him with almost any kind of live fly, but especially with a grasshopper.

VEN. But before you go further, I pray, good master, what mean you by a leather-mouthed fish?

PISC. By a leather-mouthed fish I mean such as have their teeth in their throat, as the chub or cheven, and so the barbel, the gudgeon, and carp, and divers others have; and the hook being stuck into the leather or skin of the mouth of such fish, does very seldom or never lose its hold: but, on the contrary, a pike, a perch, or trout, and so some other fish, which have not their teeth in their throats, but in their mouths, which you shall observe to be very full of bones, and the skin very thin, and little of it; I say, of these fish the hook never takes so sure hold, but you often lose your fish, unless he have gorged it.

VEN. I thank you, good master, for this observation; but now, what shall be done with my chub or cheven that I have caught?

Pisc. Marry, sir, it shall be given away to some poor body, for I'll warrant you I'll give you a trout for your supper: and it is a good beginning of your art to offer your first-fruits to the poor, who will both thank God and you for it, which I see by your silence you seem to consent to. And for your willingness to part with it so charitably, I will also teach more concerning chub-fishing: you are to note that in March and April he is usually taken with worms; in May, June, and July, he will bite at any fly, or at cherries, or at beetles with their legs and wings cut off, or at any kind of snail, or at the black bee that breeds in clay walls; and he never refuses a grasshopper, on the top of a swift stream, nor, at the bottom, the young humble bee that breeds in long grass, and is ordinarily found by the mower of it. In August, and in the cooler months, a yellow paste made of the strongest cheese, and pounded in a mortar, with a little butter and saffron, so much of it, as being beaten small, will turn it to a lemon colour. And some make a paste, for the winter months, at which time the chub is accounted best (for then it is observed that the forked bones are lost, or turned into a kind of gristle, especially if he be baked), of cheese and turpentine. He will bite also at a minnow, or penk, as a trout will: of which I shall tell you more hereafter, and of divers other baits. But take this for a rule, that, in hot weather, he is to be fished for towards the mid-water, or near the top; and in colder weather nearer the bottom. And if you fish for him on the top, with a beetle or any fly, then be sure to let your line be very long, and keep out of sight. And having told you that his spawn is excellent meat, and that the head of a large cheven, the throat being well washed, is the best part of him, I will say no more of this fish at the present, but wish you may catch the next you fish for.

But, lest you may judge me too nice in urging to have the chub dressed so presently after he is taken, I will commend to your consideration how curious former times have been in the like kind.

You shall read in Seneca, his *Natural Questions* (Lib. 3, Cap. 17), that the ancients were so curious in the newness of their fish, that that seemed not new enough that was not put alive into the guest's hand; and he says that to that end they did usually keep them living in glass bottles in their dining-rooms: and they did glory much in their entertaining of friends, to have that fish taken from under their table alive that was instantly to be fed upon. And he says, they took great pleasure to see their Mullets change to several colours, when they were dying. But enough of this, for I doubt I have stayed too long from giving you some observations of the trout, and how to fish for him, which shall take up the next of my spare time.

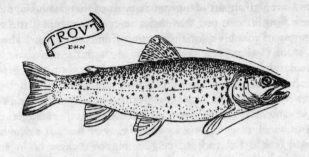

CHAPTER IV

*Observations of the Nature and Breeding
of the Trout, and how to Fish for him;
and the Milkmaid's song*

The Trout is a fish highly valued both in this and foreign nations: he may be justly said (as the old poet said of wine, and we English say of venison) to be a generous fish: a fish that is so like the buck that he also has his seasons; for it is observed, that he comes in and goes out of season with the stag and buck; Gesner says, his name is of a German offspring, and says he is a fish that feeds clean and purely, in the swiftest streams, and on the hardest gravel; and that he may justly contend with all fresh-water fish, as the Mullet may with all sea-fish, for precedency and daintiness of taste, and that being in right season, the most dainty palates have allowed precedency to him.

And before I go further in my discourse, let me tell you, that you are to observe, that as there be some barren does, that are good in summer, so there be some barren trouts that are good in winter; but there are not many that are so, for usually they be in their perfection in the month of May, and decline with the buck. Now you are to take notice, that in several countries, as in Germany and in other parts, compared to ours, fish do differ much in their bigness and shape, and other ways, and so do trouts; it is well known that in the Lake Leman (the Lake of Geneva) there are trouts taken of three cubits long, as is affirmed by Gesner, a writer of good credit; and Mercator says, the trouts that are taken in the Lake of

Geneva, are a great part of the merchandise of that famous city. And you are further to know, that there be certain waters, that breed trouts remarkable both for their number and smallness. I know a little brook in Kent, that breeds them to a number incredible, and you may take them twenty or forty in an hour, but none greater than about the size of a gudgeon: there are also in divers rivers, especially that relate to, or be near to the sea (as Winchester, or the Thames about Windsor) a little trout called samlet, or skegger trout (in both which places I have caught twenty or forty at a standing) that will bite as fast and as freely as minnows: these be by some taken to be young salmon; but in those waters they never grow to be bigger than a herring.

There is also in Kent, near to Canterbury, a trout (called there a Fordidge trout), a trout that bears the name of the town where it is usually caught, that is accounted the rarest of fish; many of them near the bigness of a salmon, but known by their different colour; and in their best season they cut very white; and none of these have been known to be caught with an angle, unless it were one that was caught by Sir George Hastings (an excellent angler, and now with God); and he hath told me, he thought that trout bit not for hunger but wantonness; and it is rather to be believed, because both he, then, and many others before him, have been curious to search into their bellies, what the food was by which they lived; and have found out nothing by which they might satisfy their curiosity.

Concerning which you are to take notice, that it is reported by good authors, that grasshoppers, and some fish, have no mouths, but are nourished and take breath by the porousness of their gills, man knows not how: and this may be believed, if we consider that when the raven hath hatched her eggs, she takes no further care, but leaves her young ones to the care of the God of nature, who is said, in the Psalms, 'to feed the young ravens that call upon him'. And they be kept alive, and fed by dew, or worms that breed in their nests, or some other ways that we mortals know not; and this may be believed of the Fordidge trout, which, as it is said of the Stork that, 'he knows his season,' so he knows his times, I think almost his day, of coming into that river out of the sea, where he lives, and, it is like, feeds nine months of the year, and fasts three in the river of Fordidge. And you are to note that those townsmen are very punctual in observing the time of beginning to fish for them; and boast much that their river affords a trout, that exceeds all others. And just so does Sussex boast of several fish; as namely, a Shelsey cockle, a Chichester lobster, an Arundel mullet, and an Amerly trout.

And now for some confirmation of the Fordidge trout: you are to know that this trout is thought to eat nothing in the fresh water, and it may be better believed, because it is well known that swallows, and bats, and wagtails, which are called half-year birds, and not seen to fly in England for six months in the year, but about Michaelmas leave us for a better climate than this; yet some of them that have been left behind their fellows, have been found (many thousands at a time) in hollow trees, or clay caves; where they have been observed to live and sleep out the whole winter without meat; and so Albertus observes, that there is one kind of frog that hath her mouth naturally shut up about the end of August, and that she lives so all the winter; and though it be strange to some, yet it is known to too many among us to be doubted.

And so much for these Fordidge trouts, which never afford an angler sport, but either live their time of being in the fresh water, by their meat formerly got in the sea (not unlike the swallow or frog), or by the virtue of the fresh water only; or, as the birds of Paradise and the chameleon are said to live, by the sun and the air.

There is also in Northumberland a trout called a bull-trout, of a much greater length and bigness than any in the southern parts. And there are, in many rivers that relate to the sea, salmon-trouts, as much different from others, both in shape and in their spots, as we see sheep in some countries differ one from another in their shape and bigness, and in the fineness of their wool: and, certainly, as some pastures breed larger sheep, so do some rivers, by reason of the ground over which they run, breed larger trouts.

Now the next thing that I will commend to your consideration is, that the trout is of a more sudden growth than other fish. Concerning which, you are also to take notice, that he lives not so long as the perch, and divers other fishes do, as Sir Francis Bacon hath observed in his *History of Life and Death*.

And next you are to take notice, that he is not like the crocodile, which if he lives never so long, yet always thrives till his death; but it is not so with the trout, for after he has come to his full growth, he declines in his body, and keeps his bigness, or thrives only in his head till his death. And you are to know, that he will about, especially before, the time of his spawning, get almost miraculously through weirs and flood-gates against the streams; even through such high and swift places as is almost incredible. Next, that the trout usually spawns about October or November, but in some rivers a little sooner or later: which is the more observable, because most other fish spawn in the spring or summer, when the sun hath warmed both the earth and the water, and made it fit for generation. And you are to note that he continues many months out of season; for it may be observed of the trout, that he is like the buck or the ox, that he will not be fat in many months, though he go in the very same pasture that horses do, which will be fat in one month: and so you may observe that most other fishes recover strength, and grow sooner fat and in season than the trout doth.

And next you are to note, that till the sun gets to such a height as to warm the earth and the water, the trout is sick, and lean, and lousy, and unwholesome: for you shall in winter find him to have a big head, and then to be lank, and thin, and lean: at which time many of them have sticking on them sugs, or trout-lice, which is a kind of worm, in shape like a clove or pin, with a big head, and sticks close to him and sucks his moisture; those, I think, the trout breeds himself, and never thrives till he free himself from them, which is when warm weather comes; and then, as he grows stronger, he gets from the dead, still water, into the sharp streams, and the gravel, and there rubs off these worms or lice; and then, as he grows stronger, so he gets him into swifter and swifter streams, and there lies at the watch for any fly or minnow that comes near to him; and he especially loves the May-fly, which is bred of the codworm or cadis; and these make the trout bold and lusty, and he is usually fatter and better meat at the end of that month than at any time of the year.

The Four Swans
Waltham Cross

E·H·N·

Now you are to know that it is observed, that usually the best trouts are either red or yellow; though some (as the Fordidge trout) be white and yet good; but that is not usual: and it is a note observable, that the female trout hath usually a less head, and a deeper body than the male trout, and is usually the better meat. And note, that a hog-back and a little head to either trout, salmon, or any other fish, is a sign that that fish is in season.

But yet you are to note, that as you see some willows or palm trees bud and blossom sooner than others do, so some trouts be, in rivers, sooner in season: and as some hollies or oaks are longer before they cast their leaves, so are some trouts in rivers longer before they go out of season.

And you are to note, that there are several kinds of trouts: but these several kinds are not considered but by very few men; for they go under the general name of trouts: just as pigeons do, in most places; though, it is certain, there are tame and wild pigeons; and of the tame, there be helmets and runts, and carriers and cropers; and indeed too many to name. Nay, the Royal Society have found and published lately, that there be thirty and three kinds of spiders; and yet all (for aught I know) go under that one general name of spider. And it is so with many kinds of fish, and of trouts especially; which differ in their bigness and shape and spots and colour. The great Kentish hens may be an instance, compared to other hens. And, doubtless, there is a kind of small trout, which will never thrive to be big; that breeds very many more than others do, that be of a larger size: which you may rather believe, if you consider that the little wren and titmouse will have twenty young ones at a time, when usually the noble hawk, or the musical thrassel or blackbird, exceed not four or five.

And now you shall see me try my skill to catch a trout; and at my next walking, either this evening or tomorrow morning, I will give you direction how you yourself shall fish for him.

Ven. Trust me, master, I see now it is a harder matter to catch a trout than a chub: for I have put on patience, and followed you these two hours, and not seen a fish stir, neither at your minnow nor your worm.

Pisc. Well, scholar, you must endure worse luck sometime, or you will never make a good angler. But what say you now? There is a trout now, and a good one too, if I can but hold him, and two or three more turns will tire him. Now you see he lies still, and the sleight is to land him. Reach me that landing net; so, sir, now he is mine own, what say you now? Is not this worth all my labour and your patience?

Ven. On my word, master, this is a gallant trout; what shall we do with him?

Pisc. Marry, e'en eat him to supper; we'll go to my hostess, from whence we came; she told me, as I was going out of door, that my brother Peter, a good angler and a cheerful companion, had sent word that he would lodge there tonight, and bring a friend with him.

My hostess has two beds, and I know you and I may have the best; we'll rejoice with my brother Peter and his friend, tell tales, or sing ballads, or make a catch, or find some harmless sport to content us and pass away a little time, without offence to God or man.

VEN. A match, good master, let's go to that house; for the linen looks white, and smells of lavender, and I love to lie in a pair of sheets that smell so. Let's be going, good master, for I am hungry again with fishing.

PISC. Nay, stay a little, good scholar; I caught my last trout with a worm; now I will put on a minnow, and try a quarter of an hour about yonder trees for another; and so walk towards our lodging. Look you, scholar, thereabout we shall have a bite presently or not at all. Have with you, sir! o' my word I have hold of him. Oh! it is a great logger-headed chub; come hang him upon that willow twig, and let's be going. But turn out of the way a little, good scholar, towards yonder high honeysuckle hedge; there we'll sit and sing, whilst this shower falls so gently upon the teeming earth, and gives yet a sweeter smell to the lovely flowers that adorn these verdant meadows.

Look! under that broad beech tree I sat down when I was last this way a-fishing. And the birds in the adjoining grove seemed to have a friendly contention with an echo, whose dead voice seemed to live in a hollow tree, near to the brow of that primrose hill. There I sat viewing the silver streams glide silently towards their centre, the tempestuous sea; yet sometimes opposed by rugged roots and pebble-stones, which broke their waves and turned them into foam. And sometimes I beguiled time by viewing the harmless lambs; some leaping securely in the cool shade, whilst others sported themselves in the cheerful sun; and saw others craving comfort from the swollen udders of their bleating dams. As I thus sat, these and other sights had so fully possessed my soul with content, that I thought, as the poet hath happily expressed it,

> I was for that time lifted above earth,
> And possess'd joys not promised in my birth.

As I left this place, and entered into the next field, a second pleasure entertained me: 'twas a handsome milkmaid, that had not yet attained so much age and wisdom as to load her mind with any fears of many things that will never be (as too many men too often do); but she cast away all care, and sung like a nightingale; her voice was good, and the ditty fitted for it: 'twas that smooth song which was made by Kit Marlow, now at least fifty years ago; and the milkmaid's mother sung an answer to it, which was made by Sir Walter Raleigh in his younger days.

They were old-fashioned poetry, but choicely good, I think much better than the strong lines that are now in fashion in this critical age. Look yonder! on my word, yonder they both be a-milking again. I will give her the chub, and persuade them to sing those two songs to us.

God speed you, good woman! I have been a-fishing, and am going to Bleak Hall to my bed, and having caught more fish than will sup myself and my friend, I will bestow this upon you and your daughter, for I use to sell none.

MILK-W. Marry, God requite you, sir, and we'll eat it cheerfully; and if you come this way a-fishing two months hence, a grace of God, I'll give you a syllabub of new verjuice in a new-made haycock for it, and my Maudlin shall sing you one of her best ballads; for she and I both love all anglers, they be such honest, civil, quiet men; in the meantime will you drink a draught of red cow's milk? you shall have it freely.

PISC. No, I thank you; but, I pray, do us a courtesy that shall stand you and your daughter in nothing, and yet we will think ourselves still something in your debt; it is but to sing us a song that was sung by your daughter when I last passed over this meadow about eight or nine days since.

MILK-W. What song was it, I pray? Was it *Come shepherds, deck your herds*? or, *As at noon Dulcina rested*? or, *Philida flouts me*? or, *Chevy Chace*? or, *Johnny Armstrong*? or, *Troy Town*?

PISC. No, it is none of those; it is a song that your daughter sung the first part, and you sung the answer to it.

MILK-W. O, I know it now. I learned the first part in my golden age, when I was about the age of my poor daughter; and the latter

near Theobalds
EHN

part, which indeed fits me best now, but two or three years ago, when the cares of the world began to take hold of me: but you shall, God willing, hear them both, and sung as well as we can, for we both love anglers. Come, Maudlin, sing the first part to the gentleman with a merry heart, and I'll sing the second, when you have done.

The Milkmaid's Song

> Come live with me, and be my love,
> And we will all the pleasures prove
> That valleys, groves, or hills, or field,
> Or woods and steepy mountains yield;
>
> Where we will sit upon the rocks,
> And see the shepherds feed our flocks
> By shallow rivers, to whose falls
> Melodious birds sing madrigals.
>
> And I will make thee beds of roses,
> And then a thousand fragrant posies,
> A cap of flowers, and a kirtle
> Embroider'd all with leaves of myrtle;
>
> A gown made of the finest wool
> Which from pretty lambs we pull;

Slippers lined choicely for the cold,
With buckles of the purest gold;

A belt of straw and ivy buds,
With choral clasps and amber studs:
And if these pleasures may thee move,
Come live with me, and be my love.

Thy silver dishes for thy meat,
As precious as the gods do eat,
Shall, on an ivory table, be
Prepared each day for thee and me.

The shepherd swains shall dance and sing,
For thy delight, each May morning,
If these delights thy mind may move,
Then live with me, and be my love.

VEN. Trust me, my master, it is a choice song, and sweetly sung by
honest Maudlin. I now see it was not without cause that our good
Queen Elizabeth did so often wish herself a milkmaid all the month
of May, because they are not troubled with fears and cares, but sing
sweetly all the day, and sleep securely all the night: and without
doubt, honest, innocent, pretty Maudlin does so. I'll bestow Sir
Thomas Overbury's milkmaid's wish upon her, 'That she may die
in the spring, and being dead, may have good store of flowers stuck
round about her winding sheet.'

The Milkmaid's Mother's Answer

If all the world and love were young,
And truth in every shepherd's tongue,
These pretty pleasures might me move
To live with thee, and be thy love.

But Time drives flocks from field to fold,
When rivers rage and rocks grow cold;
Then Philomel becometh dumb,
And age complains of care to come.

The flowers do fade and wanton fields
To wayward winter reckoning yields.
A honey tongue, a heart of gall,
Is fancy's spring, but sorrow's fall.

Thy gowns, thy shoes, thy beds of roses,
Thy cap, thy kirtle, and thy posies,
Soon break, soon wither, soon forgotten;
In folly ripe, in reason rotten.

Thy belt of straw and ivy buds,
Thy coral clasps and amber studs,
All these in me no means can move
To come to thee, and be thy love.

What should we talk of dainties, then,
Of better meat than's fit for men?
These are but vain; that's only good
Which God hath bless'd, and sent for food.

But could youth last and love still breed,
Had joys no date, or age no need,
Then those delights my mind might move
To live with thee, and be thy love.

MOTHER. Well! I have done my song. But stay, honest anglers; for I will make Maudlin to sing you one short song more. Maudlin! sing that song that you sung last night, when young Coridon the shepherd played so purely on his oaten pipe to you and your cousin Betty.

MAUD. I will, mother.

I married a wife of late,
The more's my unhappy fate;
    I married her for love,
    As my fancy did me move,
And not for a worldly estate;
But, oh! the green sickness
Soon changed her likeness
    And all her beauty did fail.
        But 'tis not so
        With those that go
        Through frost and snow,
        As all men know,
And carry the milking-pail.

PISC. Well sung, good woman; I thank you. I'll give you another dish of fish one of these days, and then beg another song of you. Come, scholar, let Maudlin alone; do not you offer to spoil her voice. Look, yonder comes mine hostess, to call us to supper. How now? Is my brother Peter come?

HOST. Yes, and a friend with him; they are both glad to hear that you are in these parts, and long to see you, and long to be at supper, for they be very hungry.

Theobald's Park

CHAPTER V

More Directions how to Fish for, and how to make for the Trout on Artificial Minnow and Flies; with some Merriment

PISC. Well met, brother Peter: I heard you and a friend would lodge here tonight, and that hath made me to bring my friend to lodge here too. My friend is one that would fain be a brother of the angle; he hath been an angler but this day, and I have taught him how to catch a chub by dapping with a grasshopper, and the chub that he caught was a lusty one of nineteen inches long. But pray, brother Peter, who is your companion?

PETER. Brother Piscator, my friend is an honest countryman, and his name is Coridon, and he is a downright witty companion, that met me here purposely to be pleasant and eat a trout, and I have not yet wetted my line since we met together; but I hope to fit him with a trout for his breakfast, for I'll be early up.

PISC. Nay, brother, you shall not stay so long? for, look you, here is a trout will fill six reasonable bellies. Come, hostess, dress it presently, and get us what other meat the house will afford, and give us some of your best barley-wine, the good liquor that our honest forefathers did use to drink of; the drink which preserved their health, and made them live so long, and do so many good deeds.

PETER. O' my word, this trout is perfect in season. Come, I thank you, and here is a hearty draught to you, and to all the brothers of the angle wheresoever they be, and to my young brother's good fortune tomorrow. I will furnish him with a rod if you will furnish him with the rest of the tackling; we will set him up and make him a fisher.

And I will tell him one thing for his encouragement, that his fortune hath made him happy to be scholar to such a master; a master that knows as much, both of the nature and breeding of fish, as any man; and can also tell him as well how to catch and cook them, from the minnow to the salmon, as any that I ever met withal.

PISC. Trust me, brother Peter, I find my scholar to be so suitable to my own humour, which is, to be free and pleasant and civilly merry, that my resolution is to hide nothing that I know from him. Believe me, scholar, this is my resolution; and so here's to you a hearty draught, and to all that love us and the honest art of angling.

VEN. Trust me, good master, you shall not sow your seed in barren ground; for I hope to return you an increase answerable to your hopes: but, however, you shall find me obedient and thankful and serviceable to my best ability.

PISC. 'Tis enough, honest scholar! come, let's to supper. Come, my friend Coridon, this trout looks lovely; it was twenty-two inches when it was taken! and the belly of it looked, some part of it, as yellow as a marigold, and part of it as white as a lily; and yet, methinks, it looks better in this good sauce.

CORIDON. Indeed, honest friend, it looks well, and tastes well: I thank you for it, and so doth my friend Peter, or else he is to blame.

PETER. Yes, and so do I, we all thank you; and when we have supped, I will get my friend Coridon to sing you a song for requital.

COR. I will sing a song, if anybody will sing another; else, to be plain with you, I will sing none: I am none of those that sing for meat, but for company: I say, ' 'Tis merry in hall, when men sing all.'

PISC. I'll promise you I'll sing a song that was lately made at my request by Mr William Basse, one that hath made the choice songs of *The Hunter in his Career*, and of *Tom of Bedlam*, and many others of note; and this that I will sing is in praise of angling.

COR. And then mine shall be, the praise of a countryman's life: what will the rest sing of?

near Amwell

PETER. I will promise you, I will sing another song in praise of angling tomorrow night; for we will not part till then, but fish tomorrow, and sup together, and the next day every man leave fishing, and fall to his business.

VEN. 'Tis a match; and I will provide you a song or a catch against then too, which shall give some addition of mirth to the company; for we will be civil, and as merry as beggars.

PISC. 'Tis a match, my masters; let's e'en say grace, and turn to the fire, drink the other cup to wet our whistles, and so sing away all sad thoughts.

Come on, my masters, who begins? I think it is best to draw cuts, and avoid contention.

PETER. It is a match. Look, the shortest cut falls to Coridon.

COR. Well, then, I will begin, for I hate contention.

Coridon's Song

Oh, the sweet contentment
The countryman doth find!
   Heigh trolollie lollie loe,
   Heigh trolollie lee.
That quiet contemplation
Possesseth all my mind;
   Then care away,
   And wend along with me.

For courts are full of flattery,
As hath too oft been tried;
    Heigh trolollie lollie loe, etc.
The city full of wantoness,
And both are full of pride:
    Then care away, etc.

But, oh! the honest countryman
Speaks truly from his heart;
    Heigh trolollie lollie loe, etc.
His pride is in his tillage,
His horses and his cart:
    Then care away, etc.

Our clothing is good sheepskins,
Gray russet for our wives;
    Heigh trolollie lollie loe, etc.
'Tis warmth, and not gay clothing,
That doth prolong our lives:
    Then care away, etc.

The ploughman, though he labour hard,
Yet on the holiday,
    Heigh trolollie lollie loe, etc.
No emperor so merrily
Doth pass his time away,
    Then care away, etc.

To recompense our tillage,
The heavens afford us showers;
    Heigh trolollie lollie loe, etc.
And for our sweet refreshments
The earth affords us bowers;
    Then care away, etc.

The cuckoo and the nightingale
Full merrily do sing,
    Heigh trolollie lollie loe, etc.
And with their pleasant roundelays
Bid welcome to the spring:
    Then care away, etc.

This is not half the happiness
The countryman enjoys;
    Heigh trolollie lollie loe, etc.
Though others think they have as much,
Yet he that says so lies:
    Then come away, turn
    Countryman with me.

Jo. Chalkhill

Pisc. Well sung, Coridon; this song was sung with mettle, and was choicely fitted to the occasion; I shall love you for it as long as I know you; I would you were a brother of the angle; for a companion that is cheerful, and free from swearing and scurrilous discourse, is worth gold. I love such mirth as does not make friends ashamed to look upon one another next morning; nor men (that cannot well bear it) to repent the money they spent when they be warmed with drink: and take this for a rule, you may pick out such times, and such companions, that you may make yourselves merrier for a little than a great deal of money; for, ' 'Tis the company and not the charge that makes the feast;' and such a companion you prove, I thank you for it.

But I will not compliment you out of the debt that I owe you; and therefore I will begin my song, and wish it may be so well liked.

The Angler's Song

As inward love breeds outward talk,
The hound some praise, and some the hawk;
Some, better pleased with private sport,
Use tennis; some a mistress court;
   But these delights I neither wish
   Nor envy, while I freely fish.

Who hunts, doth oft in danger ride;
Who hawks, lures oft both far and wide;
Who uses games, shall often prove
A loser; but who falls in love
   Is fetter'd in fond Cupid's snare;
   My angle breeds me no such care.

Of recreation there is none
So free as fishing is alone;
All other pastimes do no less
Than mind and body both possess;
   My hand alone my work can do,
   So I can fish and study too.

I care not, I, to fish in seas –
Fresh rivers best my mind do please,
Whose sweet calm course I contemplate,
And seek in life to imitate:
   In civil bounds I fain would keep,
   And for my past offences weep.

And when the timorous trout I wait
To take, and he devours my bait,
How poor a thing, sometimes I find,
Will captivate a greedy mind;
   And when none bite, I praise the wise,
   Whom vain allurements ne'er surprise.

But yet, though while I fish I fast,
I make good fortune my repast;
And thereunto my friend invite,
In whom I more than that delight:
   Who is more welcome to my dish
   Than to my angle was my fish.

As well content no prize to take,
As use of taken prize to make:
For so our Lord was pleased, when
He fishers made fishers of men;
   Where (which is in no other game)
   A man may fish and praise His name.

The first men that our Saviour dear
Did choose to wait upon Him here,
Bless'd fishers were, and fish the last
Food was that He on earth did taste:
   I therefore strive to follow those
   Whom He to follow Him hath chose.

COR. Well sung, brother, you have paid your debt in good coin. We anglers are all beholden to the good man that made this song: come, hostess, give us more ale, and let's drink to him.

And now let's everyone go to bed, that we may rise early: but first let's pay our reckoning, for I will have nothing to hinder me in the morning, for my purpose is to prevent the sunrising.

PETER. A match. Come, Coridon, you are to be my bedfellow. I know, brother, you and your scholar will lie together. But where shall we meet tomorrow night? for my friend Coridon and I will go up the water towards Ware.

PISC. And my scholar and I will go down towards Waltham.

COR. Then let's meet here, for here are fresh sheets that smell of lavender; and I am sure we cannot expect better meat or better usage in any place.

PETER. 'Tis a match. Good-night to everybody.

PISC. And so say I.

VEN. And so say I.

SALMON TROVT

PISC. Good-morrow, good hostess; I see my brother Peter is still in bed: come, give my scholar and me a morning drink, and a bit of meat to breakfast; and be sure to get a good dish of meat or two against supper, for we shall come home as hungry as hawks. Come scholar let's be going.

VEN. Well now, good master, as we walk towards the river give me direction, according to your promise, how I shall fish for a trout.

PISC. My honest scholar, I will take this very convenient opportunity to do it.

The trout is usually caught with a worm or a minnow (which some call a penk) or with a fly, viz., either a natural or an artificial fly: concerning which three I will give you some observations and directions.

And, first, for worms: of these there be very many sorts: some breed only in the earth, as the earthworm; others of or amongst plants, as the dung-worm; and others breed either out of excrements, or in the bodies of living creatures, as in the horns of sheep or deer; or some of dead flesh, as the maggot or gentle, and others.

Now these be most of them particularly good for particular fishes: but for the trout, the dew-worm (which some also call the lob-worm) and the brandling are the chief; and especially the first for a great trout, and the latter for a less. There be also of lob-worms some called squirrel-tails (a worm that has a red head, a streak down the back, and a broad tail) which are noted to be the best, because they are the toughest and most lively, and live longest in the water: for you are to know that a dead worm is but a dead bait, and like to catch nothing, compared to a lively, quick, stirring worm: and for a brandling, he is usually found in an old dunghill, or some very rotten place near to it: but most usually in cow-dung, or hog's dung, rather than horse-dung, which is somewhat too hot and dry for that worm. But the best of them are to be found in the bark of the tanners, which they cast up in heaps after they have used it about their leather.

There are also divers other kinds of worms, which for colour and shape alter even as the ground out of which they are got; as the marsh-worm, the tag-tail, the flag-worm, the dock-worm, the oak-worm, the gilt-tail, the twachel, or lob-worm, which of all others is the most excellent bait for a salmon; and too many to name, even as many sorts as some think there be of several herbs or shrubs, or of several kinds of birds in the air; of which I shall say no more, but tell you that what worms soever you fish with are the better for being well scoured, that is, long kept before they be used: and in case you have not been so provident, then the way to cleanse and scour them quickly is to put them all night in water, if they be lob-worms, and then put them into your bag with fennel. But you must not put your brandlings above an hour in water, and then put them into fennel, for sudden use: but if you have time, and purpose to keep them long, then they be best preserved in an earthen pot, with good store of moss, which is to be fresh every three or four days in summer, and every week or eight days in winter; or, at least, the moss taken from them and clean washed, and wrung betwixt your hands till it be dry, and then put it to them again. And when your worms, especially the brandling, begins to be sick and lose of his bigness, then you may recover him by putting a little milk or cream (about a spoonful in a day) into them, by drops on the moss; and if there be added to the cream an egg beaten and boiled in it, then it will both fatten and preserve them long. And note, that when the knot, which is near to the middle of the brandling, begins to swell, then he is sick; and, if he be not well looked to, is near dying. And for moss, you are to note, that there be divers kinds of it, which I could name to you, but I will only tell you that that which is likest a buck's-horn is the best, except it be soft white moss, which grows on some heaths, and is hard to be found. And note, that in a very dry time, when you are put to an extremity for worms, walnut tree leaves squeezed into water, or salt in water, to make it bitter or salt, and then that water poured on the ground, where you shall see worms are used to rise in the night, will make them to appear above ground presently. And you may take notice, some say that camphor, put into your bag with your moss and worms, gives them a strong and so tempting a smell, that the fish fare the worse and you the better for it.

And now I shall show you how to bait your hook with a worm, so as shall prevent you from much trouble, and the loss of many a hook too, when you fish for a trout with a running-line, that is to say, when you fish for him by hand at the ground: I will direct you in this as plainly as I can, that you may not mistake.

Suppose it be a big lob-worm, put your hook into him somewhat above the middle, and out again a little below the middle; having so done, draw your worm above the arming of your hook: but note that at the entering of your hook it must not be at the head-end of the worm, but at the tail-end of him, that the point of your hook may come out toward the head-end, and having drawn him above the arming of your hook, then put the point of your hook again into the very head of the worm, till it come near to the place where the point of the hook first came out: and then draw back that part of the worm that was above the shank or arming of your hook, and so fish with it. And if you mean to fish with two worms, then put the second on before you turn back the hook's-head of the first worm: you cannot lose above two or three worms before you attain to what I direct you; and having attained it, you will find it very useful, and thank me for it, for you will run on the ground without tangling.

Now for the Minnow or Penk: he is not easily found and caught till March, or in April, for then he appears first in the river; nature having taught him to shelter and hide himself, in the winter, in ditches that be near to the river; and there both to hide, and keep himself warm, in the mud, or in the weeds, which rot not so soon as in a running river, in which place if he were in winter, the distempered floods that are usually in that season would suffer him to take no rest, but carry him headlong to mills and weirs, to his confusion. And of these minnows; first you are to know that the biggest size is not the best; and next, that the middle size and the

Theobald's
Palace

whitest are the best; and then you are to know, that your minnow
must be so put on your hook, that it must turn round when 'tis
drawn against the stream; and, that it may turn nimbly, you must put
it on a big-sized hook, as I shall now direct you, which is thus: put
your hook in at his mouth, and out at his gill; then, having drawn
your hook two or three inches beyond or through his gill, put it
again into his mouth, and the point and beard out at his tail; and
then tie the hook and his tail about, very neatly, with a white thread,
which will make it the apter to turn quick in the water: that done,
pull back that part of your line which was slack when you did put
your hook into the minnow the second time; I say, pull that part of
your line back, so that it shall fasten the head, so that the body of the
minnow shall be almost straight on your hook: this done, try how it
will turn, by drawing it across the water or against the stream; and if
it do not turn nimbly, then turn the tail a little to the right or left
hand, and try again, till it turn quick; for if not, you are in danger to
catch nothing: for know, that it is impossible that it should turn too
quick; and you are yet to know, that in case you want a minnow,
then a small loach or a stickle-bag, or any other small fish that will
turn quick, will serve as well: and you are yet to know, that you may
salt them, and by that means keep them ready and fit for use three or
four days or longer; and that of salt, bay-salt is the best.

And here let me tell you, what many old anglers know right well,
that at some times, and in some waters, a minnow is not to be got;
and therefore let me tell you, I have (which I will show you) an
artificial minnow, that will catch a trout as well as an artificial fly,

and it was made by a handsome woman that had a fine hand, and a live minnow lying by her: the mould or body of the minnow was cloth, and wrought upon or over it thus with a needle: the back of it with very sad French green silk, the paler green silk towards the belly, shadowed as perfectly as you can imagine, just as you see a minnow; the belly was wrought also with a needle, and it was a part of it white silk, and another part of it with silver thread; the tail and fins were of a quill which was shaven thin; the eyes were of two little black beads, and the head was so shadowed, and all of it so curiously wrought, and so exactly dissembled that it would beguile any sharp-sighted trout in a swift stream. And this minnow I will now show you; look, here it is, and, if you like it, lend it you, to have two or three made by it; for they be easily carried about an angler, and be of excellent use; for note, that a large trout will come as fiercely at a minnow as the highest mettled hawk doth seize on a partridge, or a greyhound on a hare. I have been told that a hundred and sixty minnows have been found in a trout's belly; either the trout had devoured so many, or the miller that gave it to a friend of mine had forced them down his throat after he had taken him.

Now for flies, which is the third bait wherewith trouts are usually taken. You are to know that there are so many sorts of flies as there be of fruits: I will name you but some of them; as the dun-fly, the stone-fly, the red-fly, the moor-fly, the tawny-fly, the shell-fly, the cloudy or blackish-fly, the flag-fly, the vine-fly; there be of flies, caterpillars, and canker-flies, and bear-flies; and indeed too many either for me to name, or for you to remember: and their breeding is so various and wonderful, that I might easily amaze myself, and tire you in a relation of them.

And, yet, I will exercise your promised patience by saying a little of the caterpillar, or the palmer-fly or worm; that by them you may guess what a work it were, in a discourse, but to run over those very many flies, worms, and little living creatures with which the sun and summer adorn and beautify the river-banks and meadows, both for the recreation and contemplation of us anglers; pleasures which, I think, I myself enjoy more than any other man that is not of my profession.

Pliny holds an opinion that many have their birth or being from a dew that in the spring falls from the leaves of trees; and that some kinds of them are from a dew left upon herbs or flowers; and others, from a dew left upon coleworts or cabbages: all which kinds of dews being thickened and condensed, are by the sun's generative heat

The Bull's He at Turnford

most of them hatched, and in three days made living creatures; and these of several shapes and colours; some being hard and tough, some smooth and soft; some are horned in their head, some in their tail, some have none; some have hair, some none; some have sixteen feet, some less, and some have none; but (as our Topsel hath with great diligence observed) those which have none move upon the earth, or upon broad leaves, their motion being not unlike to the waves of the sea. Some of them, he also observes, to be bred of the eggs of other caterpillars, and that those in their time turn to be butterflies; and again, that their eggs turn the following year to be caterpillars. And some affirm that every plant has his particular fly or caterpillar, which it breeds and feeds. I have seen, and may therefore affirm it, a green caterpillar or worm, as big as a small peascod, which had fourteen legs, eight on the belly, four under the neck, and two near the tail. It was found on a hedge of privet, and was taken thence and put into a large box, and a little branch or two of privet put to it, on which I saw it feed as sharply as a dog gnaws a bone; it lived thus five or six days, and thrived and changed the colour two or three times; but by some neglect in the keeper of it, it then died, and did not turn to a fly: but if it had lived, it had doubtless turned to one of those flies that some call flies of prey, which those that walk by the rivers may, in summer, see fasten on smaller flies, and, I think, make them their food. And 'tis observable, that as there be these flies of prey, which be very large, so there be others, very little, created, I think, only to feed them, and breed out of I know not what; whose life, they say, nature intended not to exceed an hour: and yet that life is thus made shorter by other flies, or by accident.

It is needless to tell you what the curious searchers into nature's productions have observed of these worms and flies: but yet I shall tell you what Aldrovandus, our Topsel, and others say of the palmer-worm, or caterpillar, that whereas others content them-selves to feed on particular herbs or leaves (for most think those very leaves that gave them life and shape give them a particular feeding and nourishment, and that upon them they usually abide) yet he observes that this is called a pilgrim, or palmer-worm, for his very wandering life and various food: not contenting himself, as others do, with any one certain place for his abode, nor any certain kind of herb or flower for his feeding, but will boldly and disorderly wander up and down, and not endure to be kept to a diet, or fixed to a particular place.

Nay, the very colours of caterpillars are, as one has observed, very elegant and beautiful. I shall (for a taste of the rest) describe one of them; which I will, sometime the next month, show you feeding on a willow tree; and you shall find him punctually to answer this very description: his lips and mouth somewhat yellow; his eyes black as jet; his forehead purple; his feet and hinder parts green; his tail two-forked and black; the whole body stained with a kind of red spots, which run along the neck and shoulder-blade, not unlike the form of St Andrew's cross, or the letter **X**, made thus cross-wise, and a white line drawn down his back to his tail; all which add much beauty to his whole body. And it is to me observable, that at a fixed age this caterpillar gives over to eat, and towards winter comes to be covered over with a strange shell or crust, called an aurelia: and so lives a kind of dead life, without eating, all the winter; and, as others of several kinds turn to be several kinds of flies and vermin the spring following, so this caterpillar then turns to be a painted butterfly.

Come, come, my scholar, you see the river stops our morning walk, and I will also here stop my discourse; only as we sit down under this honeysuckle hedge, whilst I look a line to fit the rod that our brother Peter hath lent you, I shall for a little confirmation of what I have said, repeat the observation of Du Bartas.

On the site of
Theobald's
Palace

God, not contented to each kind to give,
And to infuse the virtue generative,
By His wise power made many creatures breed
Of lifeless bodies, without Venus' deed.

So the cold humour breeds the salamander,
Who, in effect like to her birth's commander,
With child with hundred winters, with her touch
Quencheth the fire, though glowing ne'er so much.

So in the fire, in burning furnace springs
The fly Perausta, with the flaming wings;
Without the fire it dies, in it it joys,
Living in that which all things else destroys.

So slow Boötes underneath him sees,
In th' icy islands, goslings hatch'd of trees,
Whose fruitful leaves, falling into the water,
Are turn'd ('tis known) to living fowls soon after.

So rotten planks of broken ships do change
To barnacles. O transformation strange!
'Twas first a green tree, then a broken hull,
Lately a mushroom, now a flying gull.

VEN. O my good master, this morning-walk has been spent to my great pleasure and wonder: but I pray, when shall I have your direction how to make artificial flies, like to those that the trout loves best, and also how to use them?

PISC. My honest scholar, it is now past five of the clock, we will fish till nine, and then go to breakfast. Go you to yon sycamore tree and hide your bottle of drink under the hollow root of it; for about that time, and in that place, we will make a brave breakfast with a piece of powdered beef, and a radish or two that I have in my fish-bag; we shall, I warrant you, make a good, honest, wholesome, hungry breakfast, and I will then give you direction for the making and using of your flies; and in the meantime there is your rod, and line, and my advice is, that you fish as you see me do, and let's try which can catch the first fish.

VEN. I thank you, master, I will observe and practise your direction as far as I am able.

PISC. Look you, scholar, you see I have hold of a good fish: I now see it is a trout, I pray put that net under him, and touch not my line, for if you do, then we break all. Well done, scholar, I thank you.

Now for another. Trust me, I have another bite: come, scholar, come lay down your rod, and help me to land this as you did the other. So now we shall be sure to have a good dish of fish for supper.

VEN. I am glad of that; but I have no fortune: sure, master, yours is a better rod and better tackling.

PISC. Nay, then, take mine, and I will fish with yours. Look you, scholar, I have another. Come, do as you did before. And now I have a bite at another. Oh me! he has broke all: there's half a line and a good hook lost.

VEN. Ay, and a good trout too.

PISC. Nay, the trout is not lost; for pray take notice, no man can lose what he never had.

VEN. Master, I can neither catch with the first nor second angle: I have no fortune.

PISC. Look you, scholar, I have yet another. And now, having caught three brace of trouts, I will tell you a short tale as we walk towards our breakfast. A scholar (a preacher I should say) that was to preach to procure the approbation of a parish, that he might be

The Cock Waltham

E.H.N.

their lecturer, had got from his fellow pupil the copy of a sermon that was first preached with great commendation by him that composed it: and though the borrower of it preached it, word for word, as it was at first, yet it was utterly disliked as it was preached by the second to his congregation: which the sermon-borrower complained of to the lender of it; and thus was answered: 'I lent you, indeed, my fiddle, but not my fiddlestick; for you are to know that everyone cannot make music with my words, which are fitted to my own mouth.' And so, my scholar, you are to know, that as the ill pronunciation or ill accenting of words in a sermon spoils it, so the ill carriage of your line, or not fishing even to a foot in a right place, makes you lose your labour: and you are to know, that though you have my fiddle, that is, my very rod and tacklings with which you see I catch fish, yet you have not my fiddlestick, that is, you yet have not skill to know how to carry your hand and line, or how to guide it to a right place: and this must be taught you (for you are to remember, I told you angling is an art) either by practice or a long observation, or both. But take this for a rule, when you fish for a trout with a worm, let your line have so much, and not more lead than will fit the stream in which you fish; that is to say, more in a great troublesome stream than in a smaller that is quieter; as near as may be, so much as will sink the bait to the bottom, and keep it still in motion, and not more.

But now let's say grace and fall to breakfast: what say you, scholar, to the providence of an old angler? Does not this meat taste well? and was not this place well chosen to eat it? for this sycamore tree will shade us from the sun's heat.

VEN. All excellent good, and my stomach excellent good too. And now I remember and find that true which devout Lessius says: 'That poor men, and those that fast often, have much more pleasure in eating than rich men and gluttons, that always feed before their stomachs are empty of their last meat, and call for more: for by that means they rob themselves of that pleasure that hunger brings to poor men.' And I do seriously approve of that saying of yours, 'that you would rather be a civil, well-governed, well-grounded, temperate, poor angler than a drunken lord'. But I hope there is none such; however, I am certain of this, that I have been at very many costly dinners that have not afforded me half the content that this has done, for which I thank God and you.

And now, good master, proceed to your promised direction for making and ordering my artificial fly.

PISC. My honest scholar, I will do it; for it is a debt due unto you by my promise: and because you shall not think yourself more engaged to me than indeed you really are, I will freely give you such directions as were lately given to me by an ingenious brother of the angle, an honest man and a most excellent fly-fisher.

You are to note, that there are twelve kinds of artificially made flies to angle with on the top of the water. Note, by the way, that the fittest season of using these is in a blustering windy day, when the waters are so troubled that the natural fly cannot be seen, or rest upon them. The first is the dun-fly, in March: the body is made of dun wool; the wings, of the partridge's feathers. The second is another dun-fly: the body of black wool; and the wings made of the black drake's feathers, and of the feathers under his tail. The third is the stone-fly, in April: the body is made of black wool; made yellow under the wings and under the tail, and so made with the wings of the drake. The fourth is the ruddy-fly, in the beginning of May: the body made of red wool, wrapt about with black silk; and the feathers are the wings of the drake, with the feathers of a red capon also, which hang dangling on his sides next to the tail. The fifth is the yellow or greenish fly (in May likewise): the body made of yellow wool: and the wings made of the red cock's hackle or tail. The sixth is the black-fly, in May also: the body made of black wool, and lapped about with the herle of a peacock's tail; the wings are made

Cheshunt Church

E·H·N

of the wings of a brown capon, with his blue feathers in his head. The seventh is the sad yellow-fly, in June: the body is made of black wool, with a yellow list on either side; and the wings taken off the wings of a buzzard, bound with black braked hemp. The eighth is the moorish-fly: made with the body of duskish wool; and the wings made of the blackish mail of the drake. The ninth is the tawny-fly, good until the middle of June: the body made of tawny wool, the wings made contrary, one against the other, made of the whitish mail of the wild drake. The tenth is the wasp-fly, in July: the body made of black wool, lapped about with yellow silk; the wings made of the feathers of the drake, or of the buzzard. The eleventh is the shell-fly, good in mid-July: the body made of greenish wool, lapped about with the herle of a peacock's tail, and the wings made of the wings of the buzzard. The twelfth is the dark drake-fly, good in August: the body made with black wool, lapped about with black silk; his wings are made with the mail of the black drake, with a black head. Thus have you a jury of flies, likely to betray and condemn all the trouts in the river.

I shall next give you some other directions for fly fishing, such as are given by Mr Thomas Barker, a gentleman that hath spent much time in fishing; but I shall do it with a little variation.

First, let your rod be light, and very gentle; I take the best to be of two pieces: and let not your line exceed, (especially for three or four links next to the hook,) I say, not exceed three or four hairs at the most, though you may fish a little stronger above, in the upper part of your line; but if you can attain to angle with one hair, you shall have more rises, and catch more fish. Now you must be sure not to cumber yourself with too long a line, as most do. And before you begin to angle, cast to have the wind on your back; and the sun, if it shines, to be before you; and to fish down the stream; and carry the point or top of your rod downward, by which means, the shadow of yourself and rod too will be least offensive to the fish; for the sight of any shade amazes the fish, and spoils your sport – of which you must take a great care.

In the middle of March (till which time a man should not, in honesty, catch a trout), or in April, if the weather be dark, or a little windy or cloudy, the best fishing is with the palmer-worm, of which I last spoke to you; but of these there be divers kinds, or at least of divers colours; these and the May-fly are the ground of all fly-angling, which are to be thus made:

First, you must arm your hook with the line in the inside of it, then take your scissors, and cut so much of a brown mallard's feather, as in your own reason will make the wings of it, you having withal regard to the bigness or littleness of your hook, then the point of your feather next the shank of your hook; and having done so, whip it three or four times about the hook with the same silk with which your hook was armed; and, having made the silk fast, take the hackle of a cock or capon's neck, or a plover's top, which is usually better; take off the one side of the feather, and then take the hackle, silk, or crewel, gold or silver thread, make these fast at the bent of the hook, that is to say, below your arming; then you must take the hackle, the silver or gold thread, and work it up to the wings, shifting or still removing your finger, as you turn the silk about the hook; and still looking at every stop or turn, that your gold, or what materials soever you make your fly of, do lie right and neatly; and if you find they do so, then, when you have made the head, make all fast and then work your hackle up to the head, and make that fast: and then with a needle or pin divide the wing into two, and then with the arming silk whip it about crossways betwixt the wings, and then with your thumb you must turn the point of the feather towards the bent of the hook, and then work three or four times about the shank of the hook, and then view the proportion, and if all be neat and to your liking, fasten.

Cheshunt
Great House

I confess, no direction can be given to make a man of a dull
capacity able to make a fly well: and yet I know this with a little
practice, will help an ingenious angler in a good degree; but to see a
fly made by an artist in that kind is the best teaching to make it. And
then an ingenious angler may walk by the river and mark what flies
fall on the water that day, and catch one of them, if he sees the trouts
leap at a fly of that kind; and then having always hooks ready hung
with him, and having a bag always with him, with bear's hair, or the
hair of a brown or sad-coloured heifer, hackles of a cock or capon,
several coloured silk and crewel to make the body of the fly, the
feathers of a drake's head, black or brown sheep's wool, or hog's
wool or hair, thread of gold and of silver; silk of several colours
(especially a smoking shower; and therefore sit close; this sycamore
tree will shelter us: and I will tell you, as they shall come into my
mind, more observations of fly-fishing for a trout.

But first, for the wind; you are to take notice, that of the winds,
the south wind is said to be the best. One observes that

> . . . when the wind is south,
> It blows your bait into a fish's mouth.

Next to that, the west wind is believed to be the best; and having
told you that the east wind is the worst I need not tell you which

wind is the best in the third degree: and yet (as Solomon observes), that 'he that considers the wind shall never sow', so he that busies his head too much about them (if the weather be not made extreme cold by an east wind) shall be a little superstitious: for as it is observed by some that 'there is no good horse of a bad colour', so I have observed, that if it be a cloudy day, and not extreme cold, let the wind set in what corner it will and do its worst, I heed it not. And yet take this for a rule, that I would willingly fish standing on the lee-shore: and you are to take notice, that the fish lies or swims nearer the bottom, and in deeper water, in winter than in summer; and also nearer the bottom in any cold day, and then gets nearest the lee-side of the water.

But I promised to tell you more of the flying-fish for a trout, which I may have time enough to do, for you see it rains May-butter. First, for a May-fly, you may make his body with greenish-coloured crewel or willowish colour, darkening it in most places with waxed silk, or ribbed with black hair, or some of them ribbed with silver thread; and such wings for the colour as you see the fly to have at that season, nay, at that very day on the water. Or you may make the oak-fly with an orange tawny, and black ground, and the brown of a mallard's feather for the wings; and you are to know, that these two are most excellent flies, that is, the May-fly and the oak-fly. And let me again tell you that you keep as far from the water as you can possibly, whether you fish with a fly or worm, and fish down the stream: and when you fish with a fly, if it be possible, let no part of your line touch the water, but your fly only; and be still moving your fly upon the water, or casting it into the water, you yourself being also always moving down the stream. Mr Barker commends several sorts of the palmer-flies, not only those ribbed with silver and gold, but others that have their bodies all made of black, or some with red, and a red hackle; you may also make the hawthorn-fly, which is all black, and not big, but very small, the smaller the better; or the oak-fly, the body of which is orange colour and black crewel, with a brown wing; or a fly made with a peacock's feather is excellent in a bright day. You must be sure you want not in your magazine-bag the peacock's feather, and grounds of such wool and crewel as will make the grasshopper; and note, that usually the smallest flies are the best; and note also, that the light fly does usually make most sport in a dark day, and the darkest and least fly in a bright or clear day; and lastly, note, that you are to repair upon any occasion to your magazine-bag, and upon any occasion vary and make them lighter or sadder, according to your fancy, or the day.

And now I shall tell you that the fishing with a natural fly is excellent, and affords much pleasure. They may be found thus: the May-fly, usually in and about that month, near to the river-side, especially against rain: the oak-fly, on the butt or body of an oak or ash, from the beginning of May to the end of August; it is a brownish fly and easy to be so found, and stands usually with his head downward, that is to say, towards the root of the tree: the small black-fly, or hawthorn-fly, is to be had on any hawthorn bush after the leaves be come forth. With these and a short line (as I showed, to angle for a chub), you may dape or dop, and also with a grasshopper, behind a tree, or in any deep hole; still making it to move on the top of the water, as if it were alive, and still keeping yourself out of sight, you shall certainly have sport if there be trouts; yea, in a hot day, but especially in the evening of a hot day, you will have sport.

And now, scholar, my direction for fly-fishing is ended with this shower, for it has done raining; and now look about you, and see how pleasantly that meadow looks; nay, and the earth smells as sweetly too. Come, let me tell you what holy Mr Herbert says of such days and flowers as these; and then we will thank God that we enjoy them, and walk to the river and sit down quietly, and try to catch the other brace of trouts.

Sweet day, so cool, so calm, so bright,
The bridal of the earth and sky,
Sweet dews shall weep thy fall tonight –
      For thou must die.

Sweet rose, whose hue, angry and brave,
Bids the rash gazer wipe his eye,
Thy root is ever in its grave –
      And thou must die.

Sweet spring, full of sweet days and roses,
A box where sweets compacted lie;
My music shows you have your closes –
      And all must die.

Only a sweet and virtuous soul,
Like season'd timber, never gives;
But when the whole world turns to coal,
      Then chiefly lives.

VEN. I thank you, good master, for your good direction for fly-fishing, and for the sweet enjoyment of the pleasant day, which is so far spent without offence to God or man: and I thank you for the sweet close of your discourse with Mr Herbert's verses, who, I have heard, loved angling; and I do the rather believe it, because he had a spirit suitable to anglers, and to those primitive Christians that you love, and have so much commended.

PISC. Well, my loving scholar, and I am pleased to know that you are so well pleased with my direction and discourse.

And since you like these verses of Mr Herbert's so well, let me tell you what a reverend and learned divine that professes to imitate him (and has indeed done so most excellently) hath writ of our *Book of Common Prayer*; which I know you will like the better, because he is a friend of mine, and I am sure no enemy to angling.

What! Prayer by the Book? and Common? Yes! why not?
The spirit of grace
And supplication
Is not left free alone
For time and place,
But manner too: to read, or speak, by rote,
Is all alike to him that prays
In's heart, what with his mouth he says.

They that in private, by themselves alone,
Do pray, may take
What liberty they please,
In choosing of the ways
Wherein to make
Their soul's most intimate affections known
To him that sees in secret, when
They're most conceal'd from other men.

But he that unto others leads the way
In public prayer,
Should do it so
As all that hear may know
They need not fear
To tune their hearts unto his tongue, and say,
Amen; not doubt they were betrayed
To blaspheme, when they meant to have pray'd

Devotion will add life unto the letter:
And why should not
That which authority
Prescribes, esteemed be
Advantage got?
If the prayer be good, the commoner the better;
Prayer in the Church's words as well
As sense, of all prayers bears the bell.

CH. HARVIE

And now, scholar, I think it will be time to repair to our angle-rods, which we left in the water to fish for themselves; and you shall choose which shall be yours; and it is an even lay, one of them catches.

And, let me tell you, this kind of fishing with a dead rod, and laying night-hooks, are like putting money to use; for they both work for the owners, when they do nothing but sleep, or eat, or rejoice; as you know we have done this last hour, and sat as quietly and as free from cares under this sycamore as Virgil's Tityrus and his Meliboeus did under their broad beech tree. No life, my honest scholar, no life so happy and so pleasant as the life of a well-governed angler, for when the lawyer is swallowed up with business, and the statesman is preventing or contriving plots, then we sit on cowslip banks, hear the birds sing, and possess ourselves in as much quietness as these silent silver streams, which we now see glide so quietly by us. Indeed, my good scholar, we may say of angling, as Dr Boteler said of strawberries, 'Doubtless God could have made a better berry, but doubtless God never did;' and so (if I might be judge) 'God never did make a more calm, quiet, innocent recreation than angling.'

I'll tell you, scholar, when I sat last on this primrose bank, and looked down these meadows, I thought of them, as Charles the emperor did of the city of Florence, 'That they were too pleasant to be looked on, but only on holidays.' As I then sat on this very grass, I turned my present thoughts into verse: 'twas a wish, which I'll repeat to you.

The Angler's Song

I in these flowery meads will be:
These crystal streams should solace me;
To whose harmonious bubbling noise
I with my angle would rejoice,
  Sit here, and see the turtle dove
  Court his chaste mate to acts of love:

Or, on that bank, feel the west wind
Breathe health and plenty: please my mind,
To see sweet dewdrops kiss these flowers,
And then wash'd off by April showers,
  Here, hear my Kenna sing a song;*
  There, see a blackbird feed her young,

Or a leverock build her nest:
Here, give my weary spirits rest,
And raise my low-pitch'd thoughts above
Earth, or what poor mortals move:
  Thus, free from lawsuits and the noise
  Of princes' courts, I would rejoice;

Or, with my Bryan and a book,
Loiter long days near Shawford brook;
There sit by him, and eat my meat;
There see the sun both rise and set;
There bid good-morning to next day;
There meditate my time away;
  And angle on, and beg to have
  A quiet passage to a welcome grave.

* Like Hermit Poor.

Shawford
Brook

B·H·N·

When I had ended this composure, I left this place, and saw a brother of the angle sit under that honeysuckle hedge (one that will prove worth your acquaintance): I sat down by him, and presently we met with an accidental piece of merriment, which I will relate to you; for it rains still.

On the other side of this very hedge sat a gang of gypsies, and near to them sat a gang of beggars. The gypsies were then to divide all the money that had been got that week, either by stealing linen or poultry, or by fortune-telling, or legerdemain, or indeed by any other sleights and secrets belonging to their mysterious government. And the sum that was got that week proved to be but twenty and some odd shillings. The odd money was agreed to be distributed amongst the poor of their own corporation; and for the remaining twenty shillings, that was to be divided unto four gentlemen gypsies, according to their several degrees in their commonwealth.

And the first or chiefest gypsy was, by consent, to have a third part of the 20s., which all men know is 6s. 8d.

The second was to have a fourth part of the 20s., which all men know to be 5s.

The third was to have a fifth part of the 20s., which all men know to be 4s.

The fourth and last gypsy was to have a sixth part of the 20s., which all men know to be 3s. 4d.

As for example,   3 times 6s. 8d. is . . 20s.
            And so is 4 times 5s . . . . 20s.
            And so is 5 times 4s . . . . 20s.
            And so is 6 times 3s. 4d . . . . 20s.

And yet he that divided the money was so very a gypsy, that though he gave to everyone these said sums, yet he kept 1s. of it for himself.

As for example,   *s.*   *d.*
                            6   8
                            5   0
                            4   0
                            3   4
                            _____
        make but . . .   19   0

But now you shall know, that when the four gypsies saw that he had got 1s. by dividing the money, though not one of them knew any reason to demand more, yet, like lords and courtiers, every gypsy envied him that was the gainer, and wrangled with him, and everyone said the remaining shilling belonged to him: and so they fell to so high a contest about it, as none that knows the faithfulness of one gypsy to another will easily believe; and only we that have lived these last twenty years are certain that money has been able to do much mischief. However, the gypsies were too wise to go to law, and did therefore choose their choice friends Rook and Shark, and our late English Gusman, to be their arbitrators and umpires; and so they left this honeysuckle hedge, and went to tell fortunes, and cheat, and get more money and lodging in the next village.

Cheshunt
Great
House

When these were gone, we heard a high contention amongst the beggars, whether it was easiest to rip a cloak or to unrip a cloak. One beggar affirmed it was all one. But that was denied by asking her if doing and undoing were all one. Then another said 'twas easiest to unrip a cloak, for that was to let it alone. But she was answered by asking her how she unripped it, if she let it alone: and she confessed herself mistaken. These and twenty suchlike questions were proposed, and answered with as much beggarly logic and earnestness as was ever heard to proceed from the mouth of the most pertinacious schismatic: and sometimes all the beggars (whose number was neither more nor less than the poet's nine muses) talked altogether about this ripping and unripping, and so loud that not one heard what the other said: but at last one beggar craved audience, and told them that old father Clause, whom Ben Jonson in his *Beggar's Bush* created king of their corporation, was to lodge at an alehouse called 'Catch-her-by-the-way', not far from Waltham Cross, and in the high road towards London; and he therefore desired them to spend no more time about that and suchlike questions, but refer all to father Clause at night, for he was an upright judge, and in the meantime draw cuts what song should be next sung, and who should sing it. They all agreed to the motion; and the lot fell to her that was the youngest and veriest virgin of the company; and she sung Frank Davison's song, which he made forty years ago; and all the others of the company joined to sing the burden with her. The ditty was this: but first the burden:

> Bright shines the sun; play, beggars, play!
> Here's scraps enough to serve today.

What noise of viols is so sweet
  As when our merry clappers ring?
What mirth doth want when beggars meet?
  A beggar's life is for a king,
Eat, drink, and play, sleep when we list,
Go where we will – so stocks be miss'd.
  Bright shines the sun; play, beggars, play!
  Here's scraps enough to serve today.

The world is ours, and ours alone;
  For we alone have world at will.
We purchase not – all is our own;
  Both fields and streets we beggars fill.
  Bright shines the sun; play, beggars, play!
  Here's scraps enough to serve today.

A hundred herds of black and white
  Upon our gowns securely feed;
And yet if any dare us bite,
  He dies, therefore, as sure as creed.
Thus beggars lord it as they please,
And only beggars live at ease.
  Bright shines the sun; play, beggars, play!
  Here's scraps enough to serve today.

VEN. I thank you, good master, for this piece of merriment, and this song, which was well humoured by the maker, and well remembered by you.

PISC. But, I pray, forget not the catch which you promised to make against night; for our countryman, honest Coridon, will expect your catch, and my song, which I must be forced to patch up, for it is so long since I learnt it, that I have forgotten a part of it. But come, now it hath done raining, let's stretch our legs a little in a gentle walk to the river, and try what interest our angles will pay us for lending them so long to be used by the trouts; lent them, indeed, like usurers, for our profit and their destruction.

VEN. Oh me! look you, master, a fish! a fish! Oh, alas, master, I have lost her!

PISC. Ay, marry, sir, that was a good fish indeed: if I had had the luck to have taken up that rod, then 'tis twenty to one he should not have broke my line by running to the rod's end, as you suffered him. I would have held him within the bent of my rod (unless he had been fellow to the great trout that is near an ell long, which was of such a length and depth that he had his picture drawn, and now is to be seen at mine host Rickabie's, at the George, in Ware), and it may be by giving that very great trout the rod, that is, by casting it to him into the water, I might have caught him at the long run; for so I use always to do when I meet with an overgrown fish; and you will learn to do so too hereafter: for I tell you, scholar, fishing is an art; or, at least, it is an art to catch fish.

VEN. But, master, I have heard that the great trout you speak of is a salmon.

PISC. Trust me, scholar, I know not what to say to it. There are many country people that believe hares change sexes every year: and there be very many learned men think so too, for in their dissecting them they find many reasons to incline them to that belief. And to make the wonder seem yet less, that hares change sexes, note, that Doctor Mer. Casaubon affirms in his book of credible and incredible things, that Gaspar Peucerus, a learned physician, tells us of a people that once a year turn wolves, partly in shape and partly in conditions. And so, whether this were a salmon when he came into the fresh water, and his not returning into the sea hath altered him to another colour or kind, I am not able to say; but I am certain he hath all the signs of being a trout both for his shape, colour, and spots; and yet many think he is not.

Rawdon Ho: Hoddesdon

VEN. But, master, will this trout which I had hold of die? for it is like he hath the hook in his belly.

PISC. I will tell you, scholar, that unless the hook be fast in his very gorge, 'tis more than probable he will live; and a little time, with the help of the water, will rust the hook, and it will in time wear away; as the gravel doth in the horse-hoof, which only leaves a false quarter.

And now, scholar, let's go to my rod. Look you, scholar, I have a fish too, but it proves a logger-headed chub; and this is not much amiss, for this will pleasure some poor body, as we go to our lodging to meet our brother Peter and honest Coridon. Come, now bait your hook again, and lay it into the water, for it rains again: and we will even retire to the sycamore tree, and there I will give you more directions concerning fishing; for I would fain make you an artist.

VEN. Yes, good master, I pray let it be so.

PISC. Well, scholar, now we are sat down and are at ease, I shall tell you a little more of trout-fishing, before I speak of salmon (which I purpose shall be next) and then of the pike or luce. You are to know there is night as well as day-fishing for a trout, and that in the night the best trouts come out of their holes: and the manner of taking them is on the top of the water, with a great lob or garden-worm, or rather two, which you are to fish within a place where the waters run somewhat quietly, for in a stream the bait will not be so well discerned. I say, in a quiet or dead place, near to some swift: there draw your bait over the top of the water, to and fro; and if there be a good trout in the hole he will take it, especially if the night be dark; for then he is bold, and lies near the top of the water, watching the motion of any frog, or water-rat, or mouse that swims between him and the sky: these he hunts after if he sees the water but wrinkle or move in one of these dead holes, where these great old trouts usually lie near to their holds; for you are to note, that the great old trout is both subtle and fearful, and lies close all day, and does not usually stir out of his hold, but lies in it as close in the day as the timorous hare does in her form, for the chief feeding of either is seldom in the day, but usually in the night, and then the great trout feeds very boldly.

And you must fish for him with a strong line, and not a little hook; and let him have time to gorge your hook, for he does not usually forsake it, as he oft will in the day-fishing. And if the night be not dark, then fish so with an artificial fly of a light colour, and at the snap: nay, he will sometimes rise at a dead mouse, or a piece of cloth, or anything that seems to swim across the water, or to be in motion. That is a choice way, but I have not often used it, because it is void of the pleasures that such days as these, that we two now enjoy, afford an angler.

And you are to know that in Hampshire, which I think exceeds all England for swift, shallow, clear, pleasant brooks, and store of trouts, they used to catch trouts in the night, by the light of a torch or straw, which, when they have discovered, they strike with a trout-spear, or

Broxbourne

other ways. This kind of way they catch very many; but I would not
believe it till I was an eye-witness of it, nor do I like it now I have
seen it.

VEN. But, master, do not trouts see us in the night?

PISC. Yes, and hear and smell too, both then and in the daytime; for
Gesner observes, the otter smells a fish forty furlongs off him in the
water: and that it may be true, seems to be affirmed by Sir Francis
Bacon, in the eighth century of his *Natural History*, who there
proves that water may be the medium of sounds, by demonstrating
it thus: 'that if you knock two stones together very deep under the
water, those that stand on a bank near to that place may hear the
noise without any diminution of it by the water'. He also offers the
like experiment concerning the letting an anchor fall, by a very long
cable or rope, on a rock, or the sand within the sea. And this being
so well observed and demonstrated as it is by that learned man, has
made me to believe that eels unbed themselves and stir at the noise
of thunder; and not only, as some think, by the motion or stirring of
the earth, which is occasioned by that thunder.

And this reason of Sir Francis Bacon (Exper. 792) has made me
crave pardon of one that I laughed at, for affirming that he knew
carps come to a certain place in a pond, to be fed, at the ringing of a
bell, or the beating of a drum; and however, it shall be a rule for me
to make as little noise as I can when I am fishing, until Sir Francis
Bacon be confuted, which I shall give any man leave to do.

And, lest you may think him singular in his opinion, I will tell
you, this seems to be believed by our learned Dr Hakewill, who (in
his *Apology of God's Power and Providence*, fol. 360) quotes Pliny to

report that one of the emperors had particular fishponds, and in them several fish that appeared and came when they were called by their particular names; and St James tells us (chap. 3. 7) that all things in the sea have been tamed by mankind. And Pliny tells us (lib. 9. 35) that Antonia, the wife of Darsus, had a lamprey, at whose gills she hung jewels or earrings; and that others have been so tender-hearted as to shed tears at the death of fishes which they have kept and loved. And these observations, which will to most hearers seem wonderful, seem to have a further confirmation from Martial (lib. 4., Epigr. 30), who writes thus:

Piscator, Fuge; Ne Nocens, etc.

Angler! wouldst thou be guiltless? then forbear;
For these are sacred fishes that swim here,
Who know their sovereign, and will lick his hand;
Than which none's greater in the world's command:
Nay more, they've names, and, when they called are,
Do to their several owners' call repair.

All the further use that I shall make of this shall be, to advise anglers to be patient and forbear swearing, lest they be heard, and catch no fish.

And so I shall proceed next to tell you, it is certain, that certain fields near Leominster, a town in Herefordshire, are observed to make the sheep that graze upon them more fat than the next, and also to bear finer wool; that is to say that that year in which they feed in such a particular pasture, they shall yield finer wool than they did that year before they came to feed in it, and coarser again if they shall return to their former pasture; and again return to a finer wool, being fed in the fine-wool ground. Which I tell you, that you may the better believe that I am certain, if I catch a trout in one meadow he shall be white and faint, and very like to be lousy; and as certainly, if I catch a trout in the next meadow, he shall be strong, and red, and lusty, and much better meat. Trust me, scholar, I have caught many a trout in a particular meadow, that the very shape and the enamelled colour of him hath been such as have joyed me to look on him; and I have then with much pleasure concluded with Solomon, 'Everything is beautiful in his season.'

I should by promise speak next of the salmon; but I will by your favour say a little of the umber or grayling, which is so like a trout for his shape and feeding, that I desire I may exercise your patience with a short discourse of him, and then the next shall be of the salmon.

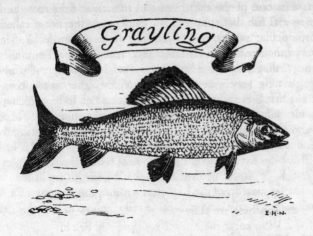

CHAPTER VI

Observations of the Umber or Grayling, and Directions how to Fish for them

Pisc. The umber and grayling are thought by some to differ, as the herring and pilchard do. But though they may do so in other nations, I think those in England differ in nothing but their names. Aldrovandus says they be of a trout kind; and Gesner says, that in his country (which is in Switzerland) he is accounted the choicest of all fish. And in Italy, he is in the month of May so highly valued, that he is sold at a much higher rate than any other fish. The French (which call the chub *un vilain*) call the umber of the lake Leman *un umble chevalier*; and they value the umber or grayling so highly, that they say he feeds on gold, and say that many have been caught out of their famous river Loire, and of whose bellies grains of gold have been often taken. And some think that he feeds on water-thyme, and smells of it at his first taking out of the water; and they may think so with as good reason as we do that our smelts smell like violets at their first being caught, which I think is a truth. Aldrovandus says, the salmon, the grayling, and trout, and all fish that live in clear and sharp streams, are made by their mother nature of such exact shape and pleasant colours purposely to invite us to a joy and contentedness in feasting with her. Whether this is a truth or not it is not my purpose to dispute; but 'tis certain, all that write of the umber declare him to be very medicinable. And Gesner says, that the fat of an umber or grayling, being set, with a little honey, a day or two in the sun, in a little glass, is very excellent against redness, or swarthiness, or anything that breeds in the eyes. Salvian takes him to be called umber from his swift swimming, or gliding out of sight, more like a shadow or a ghost than a fish. Much more might be said both of his smell and taste; but I shall only tell you, that St Ambrose, the glorious bishop of Milan (who lived when the church kept fasting days) calls him the flower-fish, or flower of fishes: and that he was so far in love with him that he would not let him pass without the honour of a long discourse; but I must, and pass on to tell you how to take this dainty fish.

First, note, that he grows not to the bigness of a trout; for the biggest of them do not usually exceed eighteen inches. He lives in such rivers as the trout does, and is usually taken with the same baits as the trout is, and after the same manner; for he will bite both at the minnow, or worm, or fly; though he bites not often at the minnow, and is very gamesome at the fly, and much simpler, and therefore bolder than a trout; for he will rise twenty times at a fly, if you miss him, and yet rise again. He has been taken with a fly made of the red feathers of a parakita, a strange outlandish bird; and he will rise at a fly not unlike a gnat or a small moth, or indeed at most flies that are not too big. He is a fish that lurks close all winter, but is very pleasant and jolly after mid-April, and in May, and in the hot months: he is of a very fine shape, his flesh is white; his teeth, those little ones that he has, are in his

Broxbourne

throat, yet he has so tender a mouth, that he is oftener lost after an
angler has hooked him, than any other fish. Though there be many
of these fishes in the delicate river Dove and in Trent, and some
other small rivers, as that which runs by Salisbury, yet he is not so
general a fish as the trout, nor to me so good to eat or to angle for.
And so I shall take my leave of him; and now come to some
observations of the salmon, and how to catch him.

CHAPTER VII

Observations of the Salmon; with Directions how to Fish for him

PISC. The salmon is accounted the king of fresh-water fish; and is ever bred in rivers relating to the sea, yet so high or far from it as admits of no tincture of salt or brackishness. He is said to breed, or cast his spawn, in most rivers, in the month of August: some say that then they dig a hole or grave in a safe place in the gravel, and there place their eggs or spawn (after the melter has done his natural office), and then hide it most cunningly, and cover it over with gravel and stones, and then leave it to their Creator's protection, who, by a gentle heat which He infuses into that cold element, makes it brood and beget life in the spawn, and to become samlets early in the spring next following.

The salmons having spent their appointed time, and done this natural duty in the fresh waters, they then haste to the sea before winter, both the melter and spawner; but if they be stopped by floodgates or weirs or lost in the fresh waters, then those so left behind by degrees grow sick, and lean, and unseasonable, and kipper; that is to say, have bony gristles grow out of their lower chaps (not unlike a hawk's beak) which hinders their feeding; and in time such fish, so left behind, pine away and die. 'Tis observed that he may live thus one year from the sea; but he then grows insipid and tasteless, and loses both his blood and strength, and pines and dies the second year. And 'tis noted that those little salmons called skeggers, which abound in many rivers relating to the sea, are bred by such sick salmons that might not go to the sea; and that though they abound, yet they never thrive to any considerable bigness.

But if the old salmon gets to the sea, then that gristle, which shows him to be kipper, wears away, or is cast off (as the eagle is said to cast his bill) and he recovers his strength, and comes next summer to the same river, if it be possible, to enjoy the former pleasures that there possessed him; for (as one has wittily observed) he has, like some persons of honour and riches, which have both their winter and summer houses, the fresh rivers for summer, and the salt water for winter, to spend his life in; which is not (as Sir Francis Bacon hath observed in his *History of Life and Death*) above ten years. And it is to be observed that though the salmon does grow big in the sea, yet he grows not fat but in fresh rivers; and it is observed that the farther they get from the sea, they be both the fatter and better.

Next I shall tell you, that though they make very hard shift to get out of the fresh rivers into the sea, yet they will make a harder shift to get out of the salt into the fresh rivers, to spawn, or possess the pleasures that they have formerly found in them: to which end they will force themselves through flood-gates, or over weirs or hedges, or stops in the water, even to a height beyond common belief. Gesner speaks of such places as are known to be above eight feet high above water. And our Camden mentions (in his *Britannia*) the like wonder to be in Pembrokeshire, where the river Tivy falls into the sea; and that the fall is so downright, and so high, that the people stand and wonder at the strength and sleight by which they see the salmon use to get out of the sea into the said river; and the manner and height of the place is so notable, that it is known, far, by the name of the 'Salmon-leap'. Concerning which, take this also out of Michael Drayton, my honest old friend, as he tells it you in his *Polyolbion* –

> And when the salmon seeks a fresher stream to find,
> Which hither from the sea comes yearly by his kind;
> As he tow'rds season grows, and stems the wat'ry tract
> Where Tivy falling down, makes a high cataract,
> Forced by the rising rocks that there her course oppose,

As though within her bounds they meant her to enclose;
Here, when the labouring fish does at the foot arrive,
And finds that by his strength he does but vainly strive,
His tail takes in his mouth, and, bending, like a bow,
That's to full compass drawn, aloft himself doth throw;
Then springing at his height, as doth a little wand
That, bended end to end, and started from man's hand,
Far oft itself doth cast; so does the salmon vault;
And if at first he fail, his second somersault
He instantly essays; and from his nimble ring,
Still yerking, never leaves until himself he fling
Above the opposing stream –

This Michael Drayton tells you of this leap or somersault of the salmon.

And next I shall tell you, that it is observed by Gesner and others, that there is no better salmon than in England; and that though some of our northern counties have as fat and as large as the river Thames, yet none are of so excellent a taste.

And as I have told you that Sir Francis Bacon observes, the age of a salmon exceeds not ten years; so let me next tell you, that his growth is very sudden; it is said, that after he is got into the sea, he becomes from a samlet not so big as a gudgeon, to be a salmon, in as short a time as a gosling becomes to be a goose. Much of this has been observed by tying a ribbon, or some known tape or thread, in the tail of some young salmons, which have been taken in weirs as they have swimmed towards the salt water, and then by taking a part of them again with the known mark at the same place at their return from the sea, which is usually about six months after; and the like experiment hath been tried upon young swallows, who have, after six months' absence, been observed to return to the same chimney, there to make their nests and habitations for the summer following: which has inclined many to think, that every salmon usually returns to the same river in which it was bred, as young pigeons taken out of the same dovecote have also been observed to do.

And you are yet to observe farther, that the he-salmon is usually bigger than the spawner; and that he is more kipper, and less able to endure a winter in the fresh water than she is: yet she is, at that time of looking less kipper and better, as watery, and as bad meat.

And yet you are to observe that as there is no general rule without an exception, so there are some few rivers in this nation that have trouts and salmons in season in winter, as it is certain there be in the river Wye, in Monmouthshire, where they be in season (as Camden

Market Hall
E·H·N·
Hoddesdon

observes) from September till April. But, my scholar, the observation of this and many other things, I must in manners omit, because they will prove too large for our narrow compass of time, and therefore I shall next fall upon my directions how to fish for this salmon.

And for that, first you shall observe, that usually he stays not long in a place (as trouts will), but (as I said) covets still to go nearer the spring head; and that he does not (as the trout and many other fish) lie near the waterside, or bank, or roots of trees, but swims in the deep and broad parts of the water, and usually in the middle, and near the ground; and that there you are to fish for him, and that he is to be caught as the trout is, with a worm, a minnow (which some call a penk), or with a fly.

And you are to observe that he is very seldom observed to bite at a minnow (yet sometimes he will) and not usually at a fly; but more usually at a worm, and then most usually at a lob or garden-worm, which should be well scoured, that is to say, kept seven or eight days in moss before you fish with them: and if you double your time of eight into sixteen, twenty, or more days, it is still the better; for the worms will still be clearer, tougher, and more lively, and continue so longer upon your hook; and they may be kept longer by keeping them cool and in fresh moss, and some advise to put camphor into it.

Note also, that many used to fish for a salmon with a ring of wire on the top of their rod, through which the line may run to as great a length as is needful when he is hooked. And to that end, some use a wheel about the middle of their rod, or near their hand; which is to be observed better by seeing one of them, than by a large demonstration of words.

And now I shall tell you that which may be called a secret: I have been a-fishing with old Oliver Henley (now with God), a noted fisher both for trout and salmon, and have observed that he would usually take three or four worms out of his bag, and put them into a little box in his pocket, where he would usually let them continue half an hour or more before he would bait his hook with them. I have asked him his reason, and he has replied: 'He did but pick the best out to be in readiness against he baited his hook the next time;' but he has been observed, both by others and myself, to catch more fish than I or any other body that has ever gone a-fishing with him could do, and especially salmons; and I have been told lately by one of his most intimate and secret friends, that the box in which he put those worms was anointed with a drop, or two or three, of the oil of ivy-berries, made by expression or infusion; and told, that by the worms remaining in that box an hour, or a like time, they had incorporated a kind of smell that was irresistibly attractive, enough to force any fish within the smell of them to bite. This I heard not long since from a friend, but have not tried it; yet I grant it probable, and refer my reader to Sir Francis Bacon's *Natural History*, where he proves fishes may hear, and doubtless can more probably smell; and I am certain Gesner says the otter can smell in the water, and I know not but that fish may do so too; 'tis left for a lover of angling, or any that desires to improve that art, to try this conclusion.

I shall also impart two other experiments (but not tried by myself), which I will deliver in the same words that they were given me, by an excellent angler, and a very friend, in writing: he told me the latter was too good to be told but in a learned language, lest it should be made common.

'Take the stinking oil drawn out of the polybody of the oak by a retort, mixed with turpentine and hive-honey, and anoint your bait therewith, and it will doubtless draw the fish to it.'

The other is this: '*Vulnera hederae grandissimae inflicta sudant balsamum oleo gelato, albicantique persimile, odoris vero longe suavissimi.*'

'Tis supremely sweet to any fish, and yet asafoetida may do the like.

But in these things I have no great faith, yet grant it probable, and have had from some chemical men (namely, from Sir George Hastings and others) an affirmation of them to be very advantageous:

but no more of these, especially not in this place.

I might here, before I take my leave of the salmon, tell you that there is more than one sort of them; as, namely, a tecon, and another called in some places a samlet, or by some a skegger; but these and others, which I forbear to name, may be fish of another kind, and differ as we know a herring and a pilchard do, which, I think, are as different as the rivers in which they breed, and must by me be left to the disquisitions of men of more leisure, and of greater abilities, than I profess myself to have.

And lastly, I am to borrow so much of your promised patience as to tell you that the trout or salmon, being in season, have, at their first taking out of the water (which continues during life) their bodies adorned, the one with such red spots, and the other with such black or blackish spots, as give them such an addition of natural beauty, as I think was never given to any woman by the artificial paint or patches in which they so much pride themselves in this age. And so I shall leave them both, and proceed to some observations on pike.

CHAPTER VIII

Observations of the Luce, or Pike; with Directions how to Fish for him

Pisc. The mighty Luce, or Pike, is taken to be the tyrant (as the salmon is the king) of the fresh waters. 'Tis not to be doubted but that they are bred, some by generation, and some not, as namely, of a weed called pickerel weed, unless learned Gesner be much mistaken, for he says this weed and other glutinous matter, with the help of the sun's heat, in some particular months, and some ponds apted for it by nature, do become pikes. But, doubtless, divers pikes are bred after this manner, or are brought into some ponds some such other ways as is past man's finding out, of which we have daily testimonies.

Sir Francis Bacon, in his *History of Life and Death*, observes the pike to be the longest lived of any fresh-water fish; and yet he computes it to be not usually above forty years; and others think it to be not above ten years; and yet Gesner mentions a pike taken in Swedeland, in the year 1449, with a ring about his neck, declaring he was put into that pond by Frederick the Second more than two hundred years before he was last taken, as by the inscription in that ring (being Greek) was interpreted by the then Bishop of Worms. But of this no more but that it is observed that the old or very great pikes have in them more of state than goodness; the smaller or middle-sized pikes being, by the most and choicest palates, observed to be the best meat; and, contrary, the eel is observed to be the better for age and bigness.

All pikes that live long prove chargeable to their keepers, because their life is maintained by the death of so many other fish, even those of their own kind; which has made him by some writers to be called the tyrant of the rivers, or the fresh-water wolf, by reason of his bold, greedy, devouring disposition; which is so keen, as Gesner relates a man going to a pond (where it seems a pike had devoured all the fish) to water his mule, had a pike bit his mule by the lips; to which the pike hung so fast that the mule drew him out of the water, and by that accident the owner of the mule angled out the pike. And the same Gesner observes, that a maid in Poland had a pike bit her by the foot, as she was washing clothes in a pond. And I have heard the like of a woman in Killingworth pond, not far from Coventry. But I have been assured by my friend Mr Seagrave (of whom I spake to you formerly) that keeps tame otters, that he hath known a pike in extreme hunger fight with one of his otters for a carp that the otter had caught, and was then bringing out of the water. I have told you who relate these things, and tell you they are persons of credit; and shall conclude this observation, by telling you what a wise man has observed, 'It is a hard thing to persuade the belly, because it has no ears.'

But if these relations be disbelieved, it is too evident to be doubted, that a pike will devour a fish of his own kind that shall be bigger than his belly or throat will receive, and swallow a part of him, and let the other part remain in his mouth till the swallowed part be digested, and then swallow that other part that was in his mouth, and so put it over by degrees; which is not unlike the ox and some other beasts, taking their meat, not out of their mouth immediately into their belly, but first into some place betwixt, and then chew it, or digest it by degrees after, which is called chewing the cud. And, doubtless, pikes will bite when they are not hungry; but, as some think, even for very anger, when a tempting bait comes near to them.

And it is observed that the pike will eat venomous things (as some kind of frogs are) and yet live without being harmed by them; for, as some say, he has in him a natural balsam, or antidote against all poison: and he has a strange heat, that though it appears to us to be cold, can yet digest or put over any fish-flesh, by degrees, without being sick. And others observe that he never eats the venomous frog till he have first killed her, and then (as ducks are observed to do to frogs in spawning time, at which time some frogs are observed to be venomous) so thoroughly washed her, by tumbling her up and down in the water, that he may devour her without danger. And Gesner affirms that a Polonian gentleman did faithfully assure him, he had seen two young geese at one time in the belly of a pike. And doubtless a pike, in his height of hunger, will bite at and devour a dog that swims in a pond; and there have been examples of it, or the like; for, as I told you, 'The belly has no ears when hunger comes upon it.'

The pike is also observed to be a solitary, melancholy, and a bold fish: melancholy because he always swims or rests himself alone, and never swims in shoals or with company, as roach and dace and most other fish do: and bold, because he fears not a shadow, or to see or be seen of anybody, as the trout and chub and all other fish do.

And it is observed by Gesner, that the jaw-bones, and hearts and galls of pikes are very medicinable for several diseases; or to stop blood, to abate fevers, to cure agues, to oppose or expel the infection of the plague, and to be many ways medicinable and useful for the good of mankind; but he observes that the biting of a pike is venomous, and hard to be cured.

And it is observed that the pike is a fish that breeds but once a year, and that other fish (as namely loaches) do breed oftener, as we are certain tame pigeons do almost every month; and yet the hawk (a bird of prey, as the pike is of fish) breeds but once in twelve months. And you are to note, that his time of breeding, or spawning, is usually about the end of February, or somewhat later, in March, as the weather proves colder or warmer; and to note, that his manner of breeding is thus: a he and a she pike will usually go together out of a river into some ditch or creek, and that there the spawner casts her eggs, and the melter hovers over her all that time that she is casting her spawn, but touches her not.

I might say more of this, but it might be thought curiosity or worse, and shall therefore forbear it; and take up so much of your attention as to tell you, that the best of pikes are noted to be in rivers; next, those in great ponds or meres; and the worst, in small ponds.

But before I proceed further, I am to tell you, that there is a great antipathy betwixt the pike and some frogs; and this may appear to the reader of Dubravius (a bishop in Bohemia) who, in his book *Of Fish and Fishponds*, relates what, he says, he saw with his own eyes, and could not forbear to tell the reader, which was:

'As he and the Bishop Thurzo were walking by a large pond in Bohemia they saw a frog, when the pike lay very sleepily and quiet by the shore side, leap upon his head; and the frog having expressed malice or anger by his swollen cheeks and staring eyes, did stretch out his legs and embraced the pike's head, and presently reached them to his eyes, tearing with them and his teeth those tender parts: the pike, moved with anguish, moves up and down the water, and rubs himself against weeds and whatever he thought might quit him of his enemy; but all in vain, for the frog did continue to ride triumphantly, and to bite and torment the pike till his strength failed, and then the frog sunk with the pike to the bottom of the water; then presently the frog appeared again at the top and croaked, and seemed to rejoice like a conqueror; after which he presently retired to his secret hole. The bishop that had beheld the battle called his fisherman to fetch his nets, and by all means to get the pike that they might declare what had happened; and the pike was drawn forth, and both his eyes eaten out; at which when they began to wonder, the fisherman wished them to forbear, and assured them he was certain that pikes were often so served.'

I told this, which is to be read in the sixth chapter of the first book of Dubravius, unto a friend, who replied, 'It was as improbable as to have the mouse scratch out the cat's eyes.' But he did not consider that there be fishing frogs (which the Dalmatians call the water-devil) of which I might tell you as wonderful a story; but I shall tell you, that 'tis not to be doubted, but that there be some frogs so fearful of the water-snake, that, when they swim in a place in which they fear to meet with him, they then get a reed across into their mouths, which, if they two meet by accident, secures the frog from the strength and malice of the snake; and note, that the frog usually swims the fastest of the two.

And let me tell you, that as there be water and land frogs, so there be land and water-snakes. Concerning which, take this observation, that the land-snake breeds and hatches her eggs, which become young snakes, in some old dunghill, or a like hot place; but the water-snake, which is not venomous (and, as I have been assured by a great observer of such secrets) does not hatch, but breed her young alive, which she does not then forsake, but bides with them, and in case of danger will take them into her mouth and swim away from any apprehended danger, and then let them out again when she thinks all danger to be passed; these be accidents that we anglers sometimes see, and often talk of.

But whither am I going? I had almost lost myself, by remembering the discourse of Dubravius. I will therefore stop here, and tell you, according to my promise, how to catch the pike.

His feeding is usually of fish or frogs, and sometimes a weed of his own called pickerel-weed, of which I told you some think pikes are bred; for they have observed that where none have been put into ponds, yet they have there found many, and that there has been plenty of that weed in those ponds, and that that weed both breeds and feeds them; but whether those pikes so bred will ever breed by generation as the others do, I shall leave to the disquisitions of men of more curiosity and leisure than I profess myself to have; and shall proceed to tell you that you may fish for a pike either with a ledger or a walking-bait; and you are to note, that I call that a ledger-bait which is fixed or made to rest in one certain place when you shall be absent from it; and I call that a walking-bait which you take with you, and have ever in motion. Concerning which two, I shall give you this direction, that your ledger-bait is best to be a living bait, though a dead one may catch, whether it be a fish or a frog; and that you may make them live the longer, you may, or indeed you must, take this course:

First, for your live-bait of fish, a roach or dace is, I think, best and most tempting and a perch is the longest lived on a hook; and having cut off his fin on his back, which may be done without hurting him, you must take your knife (which cannot be too sharp) and betwixt the head and the fin on the back, cut or make an incision, or such a scar, as you may put the arming-wire of your hook into it, with as little bruising or hurting the fish as art and diligence will enable you to do; and so carrying your arming-wire along his back, unto or near the tail of your fish, betwixt the skin and the body of it, draw out that wire or arming of your hook at another scar near to his tail: then tie him about with thread, but no harder than of necessity to prevent hurting the fish; and the better to avoid hurting the fish, some have a kind of probe to open the way, for the more easy entrance and passage of your wire or arming; but as for these, time and a little experience will teach you better than I can by words; therefore I will for the present say no more of this, but come next to give you some directions how to bait your hook with a frog.

VEN. But, good master, did you not say even now that some frogs are venomous, and is it not dangerous to touch them?

PISC. Yes; but I will give you some rules or cautions concerning them. And first, you are to note, that there are two kinds of frogs; that is to say (if I may so express myself) a flesh and a fish-frog: by flesh-frogs, I mean frogs that breed and live on the land; and of these there be several sorts also, and of several colours, some being speckled, some greenish, some blackish or brown: the green frog, which is a small one, is by Topsel taken to be venomous, and so is the paddock or frog paddock, which usually keeps or breeds on the land, and is very large and bony and big, especially the she-frog of that kind; yet these will sometimes come into the water, but it is not often; and the land-frogs are some of them observed by him to breed by laying eggs, and others to breed of the slime and dust of the earth, and that in winter they turn to slime again, and that the next summer that very slime returns to be a living creature; this is the opinion of Pliny, and Cardanus (in his tenth book *De Subtilitate*) undertakes to give a reason for the raining of frogs: but if it were in my power, it should rain none but water-frogs, for those I think are not venomous, especially the right water-frog, which about February or March breeds in ditches by slime, and blackish eggs in that slime: about which time of breeding the he and she-frogs are observed to use divers somersaults, and to croak and make a noise, which the land-frog, or paddock-frog, never does. Now of these water-frogs, if you intend to fish with a frog for a pike, you are to choose the yellowest that you can get, for that the pike ever likes best. And thus use your frog, that he may continue long alive:

Put your hook into his mouth, which you may easily do from the middle of April till August, and then the frog's mouth grows up, and he continues so for at least six months without eating, but is sustained none but He whose name is Wonderful knows how: I say, put your hook, I mean the arming-wire, through his mouth and out at his gills; and then with a fine needle and silk sew the upper part of his leg, with only one stitch, to the arming-wire of your hook; or tie the frog's leg, above the upper joint, to the arming-wire; and, in so doing, use him as though you loved him, that is, harm him as little as you may possibly, that he may live the longer.

And now, having given you this direction for the baiting your ledger-hook with a live fish or frog, my next must be to tell you how your hook thus baited must or may be used, and it is thus: Having fastened your hook to a line, which, if it be not fourteen yards long, should not be less than twelve, you are to fasten that line to any bough near to a hole where a pike is, or is likely to lie, or to have a haunt, and then wind your line on any forked stick, all your line, except half a yard of it, or rather more, and split that forked stick with such a nick or notch at one end of it as may keep the line from any more of it ravelling from about the stick than so much of it as you intend; and choose your forked stick to be of that bigness as may keep the fish or frog from pulling the forked stick under the water till the pike bites; and then the pike having pulled the line forth of the cleft or nick of that stick in which it was gently fastened, he will have line enough to go to his hold and pouch the bait; and if you would have this ledger-bait to keep at a fixed place, undisturbed by wind or other accidents, which may drive it to the shore side (for you are to note, that it is likeliest to catch a pike in the midst of the water), then hang a small plummet of lead, a stone, or piece of tile, or a turf in a string, and cast it into the water with the forked stick, to hang upon the ground, to be a kind of anchor to keep the forked stick from moving out of your intended place till the pike come. This I take to be a very good way, to use so many ledger-baits as you intend to make trial of.

Or if you bait your hooks thus with live fish or frogs, and in a windy day, fasten them thus to a bough or bundle of straw, and by the help of that wind can get them to move across a pond or mere, you are like to stand still on the shore and see sport presently if there be any store of pikes; or these live baits may make sport, being tied about the body or wings of a goose or duck, and she chased over a pond; and the like may be done with turning three or four live baits thus fastened to bladders, or boughs, or bottles of hay or flags, to swim down a river, whilst you walk quietly alone on the shore, and are still in expectation of sport. The rest must be taught you by practice, for time will not allow me to say more of this kind of fishing with live baits.

And for your dead bait for a pike, for that you may be taught by one day's going a-fishing with me, or any other body that fishes for him, for the baiting your hook with a dead gudgeon or a roach, and moving it up and down the water, is too easy a thing to take up any time to direct you to do it; and yet, because I cut you short in that, I will commute for it by telling you that that was told me for a secret: it is this:

'Dissolve gum of ivy in oil of spike, and therewith anoint your dead bait for a pike, and then cast it into a likely place, and when it has lain a short time at the bottom, draw it towards the top of the water, and so up the stream, and it is more than likely that you have a pike follow with more than common eagerness.'

And some affirm, that any bait anointed with the marrow of the thigh-bone of an hern is a great temptation to any fish.

These have not been tried by me, but told me by a friend of note, that pretended to do me a courtesy; but if this direction to catch a

The Great
Bed of Ware

pike thus do you no good, yet I am certain this direction how to roast him when he is caught is choicely good, for I have tried it, and it is somewhat the better for not being common; but with my direction you must take this caution, that your pike must not be a small one, that is, it must be more than half a yard, and should be bigger.

First, open your pike at the gills, and if need be, cut also a little slit towards the belly; out of these take his guts and keep his liver, which you are to shred very small with thyme, sweet marjoram, and a little winter-savory; to these put some pickled oysters, and some anchovies, two or three, both these last whole (for the anchovies will melt, and the oysters should not); to these you must add also a pound of sweet butter, which you are to mix with the herbs that are shred, and let them all be well salted (if the pike be more than a yard long, then you may put into these herbs more than a pound, or if he be less, then less butter will suffice): these being thus mixed with a blade or two of mace, must be put into the pike's belly, and then his belly so sewed up as to keep all the butter in his belly, if it be possible, if not, then as much of it as you possibly can; but take not off the scales: then you are to thrust the spit through his mouth out at his tail; and then take four, or five, or six split sticks or very thin laths, and a convenient quantity of tape or filleting: these laths are to be tied round about the pike's body from his head to his tail, and the tape tied somewhat thick to prevent his breaking or falling off from the spit: let him be roasted very leisurely, and often basted with claret wine and anchovies and butter mixed together, and also with what moisture falls from him into the pan: when you have roasted him sufficiently, you are to hold under him (when you unwind or cut the tape that ties him) such a dish as you purpose to eat him out of; and let him fall into it with the sauce that is roasted in his belly; and by this means the pike will be kept unbroken and complete: then, to the sauce which was within, and also that sauce in the pan, you are to add a fit quantity of the best butter, and to squeeze the juice of three or four oranges: lastly, you may either put into the pike with the oysters two cloves of garlic, and take it whole out, when the pike is cut off the spit; or to give the sauce a *haut-gout* let the dish (into which you let the pike fall) be rubbed with it: the using or not using of this garlic is left to your discretion. – M. B.

This dish of meat is too good for any but anglers, or very honest men; and I trust you will prove both, and therefore I have trusted you with this secret.

Let me next tell you that Gesner tells us there are no pikes in Spain; and that the largest are in the lake Thrasymene in Italy; and the next, if not equal to them, are the pikes of England; and that in England, Lincolnshire boasteth to have the biggest. Just so doth Sussex boast of four sorts of fish; namely, an Arundel Mullet, a Chichester Lobster, a Shelsey Cockle, and an Amerley Trout.

But I will take up no more of your time with this relation, but proceed to give you some observations of the Carp, and how to angle for him, and to dress him, but not till he is caught.

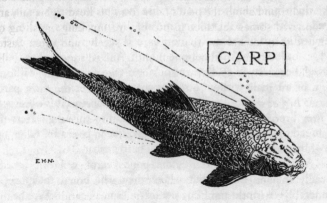

CARP

CHAPTER IX

Observations of the Carp; with Directions how to Fish for him

PISC. The Carp is the queen of rivers; a stately, a good, and a very subtle fish; that was not at first bred, nor hath been long in England, but is now naturalised. It is said they were brought hither by one Mr Mascal, a gentleman that then lived at Plumstead, in Sussex, a county that abounds more with fish than any in this nation.

You may remember that I told you Gesner says there are no pikes in Spain; and doubtless there was a time, about a hundred or a few more years ago, when there were no carps in England, as may seem to be affirmed by Sir Richard Baker, in whose *Chronicle* you may find these verses:

> Hops and turkeys, carps and beer,
> Came into England all in a year.

And doubtless, as of sea-fish the herring dies soonest out of the water, and of fresh-water fish, the trout, so (except the eel) the carp endures most hardness, and lives longest out of his own proper element. And, therefore, the report of the carp's being brought out of a foreign country into this nation is the more probable.

Carps and loaches are observed to breed several months in one year, which pikes and most other fish do not. And this is partly proved by tame and wild rabbits; and also by some ducks, which will lay eggs nine out of the twelve months; and yet there be other ducks that lay not longer than about one month. And it is the rather to be believed, because you shall scarce or never take a male carp without a melt, or a female without a roe or spawn, and for the most part, very much, and especially all the summer season. And it is observed that they breed more naturally in ponds than in running waters (if they breed there at all); and that those that live in rivers are taken by men of the best palates to be much the better meat.

And it is observed that in some ponds carps will not breed, especially in cold ponds; but where they will breed they breed innumerably: Aristotle and Pliny say six times in a year, if there be no pikes or perch to devour their spawn, when it is cast upon grass, or flags, or weeds, where it lies ten or twelve days before it is enlivened.

The carp, if he have water room and good feed, will grow to a very great bigness and length; I have heard, to be much above a yard long. 'Tis said (by Jovius, who hath writ of fishes) that in the lake Lurian in Italy carps have thriven to be more than fifty pounds weight; which is the more probable, for as the bear is conceived and born suddenly, and being born, is but short-lived, so, on the contrary, the elephant is said to be two years in his dam's belly (some think he is ten years in it), and being born, grows in bigness twenty years; and 'tis observed, too, that he lives to the age of a hundred years. And 'tis also observed that the crocodile is very long-lived, and more than that, that all that long life he thrives in bigness; and so I think some carps do, especially in some places; though I never saw one above twenty-three inches, which was a great and a goodly fish; but have been assured they are of a far greater size, and in England too.

Now, as the increase of carps is wonderful for their number, so there is not a reason found out, I think, by any, why they should breed in some ponds, and not in others of the same nature for soil and all other circumstances. And as their breeding, so are their decays also very mysterious: I have both read it, and been told by a gentleman of tried honesty, that he has known sixty or more large carps put into several ponds near to a house, where, by reason of the stakes in the ponds, and the owner's constant being near to them, it was impossible they should be stole away from him; and that when he has, after three or four years, emptied the pond, and expected an increase from them by breeding young ones (for that they might do

so, he had, as the rule is, put in three melters for one spawner), he has, I say, after three or four years, found neither a young nor old carp remaining. And the like I have known of one that had almost watched the pond, and at a like distance of time, at the fishing of the pond, found, of seventy or eighty large carps, not above five or six; and that he had foreborne longer to fish the said pond, but that he saw, in a hot day in summer, a large carp swim near the top of the water with a frog upon his head; and that he, upon that occasion, caused his pond to be let dry: and I say, of seventy or eighty carps, only found five or six in the said pond, and those very sick and lean, and with every one a frog sticking so fast on the head of the said carps, that the frog would not be got off without extreme force or killing. And the gentleman that did affirm this to me, told me he saw it; and did declare his belief to be (and I also believe the same) that he thought the other carps, that were so strangely lost, were so killed by the frogs, and then devoured.

And a person of honour, now living in Worcestershire, assured me he had seen a necklace or collar of tadpoles, hang like a chain or necklace of beads about a pike's neck, and to kill him; whether it be for meat or malice must be to me a question.

But I am fallen into this discourse by accident, of which I might say more, but it has proved longer than I intended, and possibly

WaterFrog
E·H·N·

may not to you be considerable; I shall therefore give you three or four more short observations of the carp, and then fall upon some directions how you shall fish for him.

The age of carps is by Sir Francis Bacon, in his *History of Life and Death*, observed to be but ten years; yet others think they live longer. Gesner says a carp has been known to live in the Palatinate above a hundred years; but most conclude, that (contrary to the pike or luce) all carps are the better for age and bigness. The tongues of carps are noted to be choice and costly meat, especially to them that buy them: but Gesner says carps have no tongue like other fish, but a piece of flesh-like fish in their mouth like to a tongue, and should be called a palate: but it is certain it is choicely good; and that the carp is to be reckoned amongst those leather-mouthed fish, which I told you have their teeth in their throat, and for that reason he is very seldom lost by breaking his hold, if your hook be once stuck into his chaps.

I told you that Sir Francis Bacon thinks that the carp lives but ten years; but Janus Dubravius has writ a book, *Of Fish and Fishponds*; in which he says, that carps begin to spawn at the age of three years, and continue to do so till thirty: he says also, that in the time of their breeding, which is in summer, when the sun hath warmed both the earth and water, and so apted them also for generation, that then three or four male carps will follow a female; and that then, she putting on a seeming coyness, they force her through weeds and flags, where she lets fall her eggs or spawn, which sticks fast to the weeds; and then they let fall their melt upon it, and so it becomes in a short time to be a living fish: and, as I told you, it is thought that the carp does this several months in the year. And most believe that most fish breed after this manner except the eel. And it has been observed, that when the spawner has weakened herself by doing that natural office, that two or three melters have helped her from off the weeds, by bearing her up on both sides, and guarding her into the deep. And you may note, that though this may seem a curiosity not worth observing, yet *others* have judged it worth their time and cost to make glass hives, and order them in such a manner as to see how bees have bred and make their honeycombs, and how they have obeyed their king, and governed their commonwealth. But it is thought that all carps are not bred by generation; but that some breed other ways, as some pikes do.

The physicians make the galls and stones in the heads of carps to be very medicinable. But 'tis not to be doubted but that in Italy they make great profit of the spawn of carps, by selling it to the Jews, who make it into red caviare; the Jews not being by their law admitted to eat of caviare made of the sturgeon, that being a fish that wants scales, and (as may appear in Lev. 11.) by them reputed to be unclean.

Much more might be said out of him, and out of Aristotle, which Dubravius often quotes in his Discourse of Fishes; but it might rather perplex than satisfy you; and therefore I shall rather choose to direct you how to catch, than spend more time in discoursing either of the nature or the breeding of this carp, or of any more circumstances concerning him; but yet I shall remember you of what I told you before, that he is a very subtle fish, and hard to be caught.

And my first direction is, that if you will fish for a carp, you must put on a very large measure of patience; especially to fish for a river carp: I have know a very good fisher angle diligently four or six hours in a day, for three or four days together, for a river carp, and not have a bite: and you are to note that in some ponds it is as hard to catch a carp as in a river; that is to say, where they have store of feed, and the water is of a clayish colour; but you are to remember that I have told you there is no rule without an exception; and therefore being possessed with that hope and patience which I wish to all fishers, especially to the carp-angler, I shall tell you with what bait to fish for him. But first, you are to know that it must be either early or late; and let me tell you that in hot weather (for he will seldom bite in cold) you cannot be too early or too late at it. And some have been so curious as to say the tenth of April is a fatal day for carps.

The carp bites either at worms or at paste; and of worms I think the bluish marsh or meadow worm is best; but possibly another worm not too big may do as well, and so may a green gentle: and as for pastes, there are almost as many sorts as there are medicines for the toothache; but doubtless sweet pastes are the best; I mean pastes made with honey or with sugar; which, that you may the better beguile this crafty fish, should be thrown in the pond or place in which you fish for him some hours, or longer, before you undertake your trial of skill with the angle-rod; and doubtless if it be thrown into the water a day or two before, at several times, and in small pellets, you are the likelier, when you fish for the carp, to obtain your desired sport. Or, in a large pond, to draw them to a certain place, that they may the better and with more hope be fished for, you are to throw into it, in some certain place, either grains or blood mixed with cow-dung, or with bran; or any garbage, as chickens' guts or the like; and then some of your small sweet pellets with which you purpose to angle: and these small pellets being a few of them also thrown in as you are angling, will be the better.

And your paste must be thus made: take the flesh of a rabbit or cat cut small; and bean flour; and if that may not be easily got, get other flour; and then mix these together, and put to them either sugar, or honey, which I think better; and then beat these together in a mortar, or sometimes work them in your hands (your hands being very clean); and then make it into a ball, or two, or three, as you like best, for your use; but you must work or pound it so long in the mortar as to make it so tough as to hang upon your hook, without washing from it, yet not too hard; or, that you may the better keep it on your hook, you may knead with your paste a little (and not much) white or yellowish wool.

And if you would have this paste keep all the year, for any other fish, then mix with it virgin wax, and clarified honey, and work them together with your hands before the fire; then make these into balls, and they will keep all the year.

And if you fish for a carp with gentles, then put upon your hook a little piece of scarlet about this bigness □, it being soaked in or anointed with oil of peter, called by some oil of the rock; and if your gentles be put two or three days before into a box or horn anointed with honey, and so put upon your hook as to preserve them to be living, you are as like to kill this crafty fish this way as any other; but still, as you are fishing, chew a little white or brown bread in your mouth, and cast it into the pond about the place where your float swims. Other baits there be; but these, with diligence and patient watchfulness, will do it better than any that I have ever practised, or heard of: and yet I shall tell you that the crumb of white bread and honey, made into a paste, is a good bait for a carp; and you know it is more easily made. And having said thus much of a carp, my next discourse shall be of the bream; which shall not prove so tedious, and therefore I desire the continuance of your attention.

But, first, I will tell you how to make this carp, that is so curious to be caught, so curious a dish of meat, as shall make him worth all your labour and patience; and though it is not without some trouble and charges, yet it will recompense both.

Take a carp (alive if possible), scour him, and rub him clean with water and salt, but scale him not; then open him, and put him, with his blood, and his liver (which you must save when you open him) into a small pot or kettle; then take sweet marjoram, thyme, and parsley, of each half a handful, a sprig of rosemary, and another of savory, bind them into two or three small bundles, and put them to your carp, with four or five whole onions, twenty pickled oysters, and three anchovies. Then pour upon your carp as much claret wine as will only cover him, and season your claret well with salt, cloves, and mace, and the rinds of oranges and lemons; that done, cover your pot and set it on a quick fire till it be sufficiently boiled; then take out the carp and lay it with the broth into the dish, and pour upon it a quarter of a pound of the best fresh butter, melted and beaten with half a dozen spoonfuls of the broth, the yolks of two or three eggs, and some of the herbs shred; garnish your dish with lemons, and so serve it up, and much good do you.

The RYE HOVSE Inn

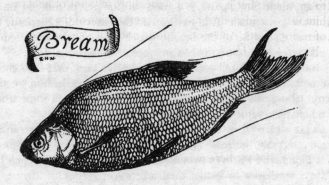

CHAPTER X

Observations of the Bream, and Directions to Catch him

PISC. The Bream, being at a full growth, is a large and stately fish: he will breed both in rivers and ponds; but loves best to live in ponds, and where, if he likes the water and air, he will grow not only to be very large, but as fat as a hog: he is by Gesner taken to be more pleasant or sweet than wholesome: this fish is long in growing, but breeds exceedingly in a water that pleases him: yea, in many ponds so fast as to overstore them, and starve the other fish.

He is very broad, with a forked tail, and his scales set in excellent order; he hath large eyes, and a narrow sucking mouth; he hath two sets of teeth, and a lozenge-like bone, a bone to help his grinding. The melter is observed to have two large melts; and the female two large bags of eggs or spawn.

Gesner reports, that in Poland a certain and a great number of large breams were put into a pond, which in the next following winter were frozen up into one entire ice, and not one drop of water remaining, nor one of these fish to be found, though they were diligently searched for; and yet the next spring, when the ice was thawed, and the weather warm, and fresh water got into the pond, he affirms they all appeared again. This Gesner affirms, and I quote my author because it seems almost as incredible as the resurrection to an atheist: but it may win something, in point of believing it, to him that considers the breeding or renovation of the silk-worm, and of many insects. And that is considerable, which Sir Francis Bacon observes in his *History of Life and Death* (fol. 20), that there be some herbs that die and spring every year, and some endure longer.

But though some do not, yet the French esteem this fish highly, and to that end have this proverb, 'He that hath breams in his pond is able to bid his friend welcome.' And it is noted that the best part of a bream is his belly and head.

Some say that breams and roaches will mix their eggs and melt together, and so there is in many places a bastard breed of breams, that never come to be either large or good, but very numerous.

The baits good to catch this Bream are many. 1. Paste made of brown bread and honey, gentles, or the brood of wasps that be young (and then not unlike gentles), and should be hardened in an oven, or dried on a tile before the fire, to make them tough; or there is at the root of docks or flags, or rushes in watery places, a worm not unlike a maggot, at which tench will bite freely. Or he will bite at a grasshopper with his legs nipped off, in June or July, or at several flies under water, which may be found on flags that grow near to the waterside. I doubt not but that there be many other baits that are good; but I will turn them all into this excellent one, either for a carp or bream, in any river or mere: it was given to me by a most honest and excellent angler; and hoping you will prove both, I will impart it to you.

1. Let your bait be as big a red worm as you can find, without a knot; get a pint or quart of them in an evening in garden walks, or chalky common, after a shower of rain, and put them with clean moss well washed and picked, and the water squeezed out of the moss as dry as you can, into an earthen pot or pipkin set dry, and change the moss fresh every three or four days, for three weeks or a month together; then your bait will be at the best, for it will be clear and lively.

2. Having thus prepared your baits, get your tackling ready and fitted for this sport. Take three long angling rods, and as many and more silk, or silk and hair lines, and as many large swan or goose-quill floats. Then take a piece of lead, made after this manner, and fasten them to the low ends of your lines; then fasten your link-hook also to the lead, and

Hoddesdon

let there be about a foot or ten inches between the lead and the hook; but be sure the lead be heavy enough to sink the float or quill a little under the water, and not the quill to bear up the lead, for the lead must lie on the ground. Note, that your link next the hook may be smaller than the rest of your line, if you dare adventure, for fear of taking the pike or perch, who will assuredly visit your hooks, till they be taken out (as I will show you afterward), before either carp or bream will come near to bite. Note also, that when the worm is well baited, it will crawl up and down as far as the lead will give leave, which much enticeth the fish to bite without suspicion.

3. Having thus prepared your baits, and fitted your tackling, repair to the river, where you have seen them swim in skulls or shoals, in the summer time, in a hot afternoon, about three or four of the clock, and watch their going forth of their deep holes and returning (which you may well discern), for they return about four of the clock, most of them seeking food at the bottom, yet one or two will lie on the top of the water, rolling and tumbling themselves whilst the rest are under him at the bottom, and so you shall perceive him to keep sentinel; then mark where he plays most, and stays longest (which commonly is in the broadest and deepest place of the river), and there, or near thereabouts, at a clear bottom and a convenient

landing-place, take one of your angles ready fitted as aforesaid, and sound the bottom, which should be about eight or ten feet deep (two yards from the bank is the best). Then consider with yourself whether that water will rise or fall by the next morning, by reason of any water-mills near, and according to your discretion take the depth of the place, where you mean after to cast your ground-bait, and to fish, to half an inch, that the lead lying on near the ground-bait, the top of the float may only appear upright half an inch above the water.

Thus you having found and fitted for the place and depth thereof, then go home and prepare your ground-bait, which is, next to the fruit of your labours, to be regarded.

THE GROUND BAIT

You shall take a peck, or a peck and a half (according to the greatness of the stream and deepness of the water where you mean to angle) of sweet gross-ground barley malt, and boil it in a kettle (one or two warms is enough), then strain it through a bag into a tub (the liquor whereof hath often done my horse much good), and when the bag and malt is near cold, take it down to the waterside about eight or nine of the clock in the evening, and not before; cast in two parts of your ground-bait, squeezed hard between both your hands; it will sink presently to the bottom, and be sure it may rest in the very place where you mean to angle; if the stream run hard or move a little, cast your malt in handfuls a little the higher, upwards the stream. You may, between your hands, close the malt so fast in handfuls, that the water will hardly part it with the fall.

Your ground thus baited and tackling fitted, leave your bag with the rest of your tackling and ground-bait near the sporting-place all night, and in the morning about three or four of the clock visit the waterside, but not too near, for they have a cunning watchman, and are watchful themselves too.

Then gently take one of your three rods, and bait your hook; casting it over your ground-bait, and gently and secretly draw it to you, till the lead rests about the middle of the ground-bait.

Then take a second rod, and cast in about a yard above, and your third a yard below the first rod: and stay the rods in the ground; but go yourself so far from the waterside, that you perceive nothing but the top of the floats, which you must watch most diligently. Then when you have a bite, you shall perceive the top of your float to sink suddenly into the water; yet, nevertheless, be not too hasty to run to

EHN

your rods, until you see that the line goes clear away, then creep to the waterside, and give as much line as you possibly can: if it be a good carp or bream, they will go to the farther side of the river: then strike gently, and hold your rod at a bent a little while; but if you both pull together, you are sure to lose your game, for either your line, or hook, or hold will break; and after you have overcome them, they will make noble sport, and are very shy to be landed. The carp is far stronger and more mettlesome than the bream.

Much more is to be observed in this kind of fish and fishing, but it is far better for experience and discourse than paper. Only, thus much is necessary for you to know, and to be mindful and careful of, that if the pike or perch do breed in that river, they will be sure to bite first, and must first be taken. And for the most part they are very large; and will repair to your ground-bait, not that they will eat of it, but will feed and sport themselves amongst the young fry that gather about and hover over the bait.

The way to discern the pike and to take him, if you mistrust your bream-hook (for I have taken a pike a yard long several times at my bream-hooks, and sometimes he hath had the luck to share my line), may be thus:

Take a small bleak, or roach, or gudgeon, and bait it, and set it alive among your rods, two feet deep from the cork, with a little red worm on the point of the hook; then take a few crumbs of white bread, or some of the ground-bait, and sprinkle it gently amongst your rods. If Mr Pike be there, then the little fish will skip out of the water at his appearance, but the live-set bait is sure to be taken.

Thus continue your sport from four in the morning till eight, and if it be a gloomy windy day, they will bite all day long. But this is too long to stand to your rods at one place, and it will spoil your evening sport that day, which is this:

About four of the clock in the afternoon repair to your baited place; and as soon as you come to the waterside, cast in one half of the rest of your ground-bait, and stand off: then whilst the fish are gathering together (for there they will most certainly come for their supper) you may take a pipe of tobacco; and then in with your three rods, as in the morning: you will find excellent sport that evening till eight of the clock; then cast in the residue of your ground-bait, and next morning by four of the clock visit them again for four hours, which is the best sport of all; and after that, let them rest till you and your friends have a mind to more sport

From St James's-tide until Bartholomew-tide is the best; when they have had all the summer's food, they are the fattest.

Observe lastly, that after three or four days' fishing together, your game will be very shy and wary, and you shall hardly get above a bite or two at a baiting; then your only way is to desist from your sport about two or three days; and in the meantime (on the place you late baited, and again intend to bait) you shall take a tuft of green, but short grass, as big or bigger than a round trencher; to the top of this turf, on the green side, you shall with a needle and green thread, fasten one by one as many little red worms as will near cover all the turf; then take a round board or trencher, make a hole in the middle thereof, and through the turf, placed on the board or trencher, with a string or cord as long as is fitting, tied to a pole, let it down to the bottom of the water, for the fish to feed upon without disturbance about two or three days; and after that you have drawn it away, you may fall to and enjoy your former recreation.

CHAPTER XI

Observations of the Tench, and Advice how to Angle for him

PISC. The Tench, the physician of fishes, is observed to love ponds better than rivers, and to love pits better than either; yet Camden observes, there is a river in Dorsetshire that abounds with tenches, but doubtless they retire to the most deep and quiet places in it.

This fish hath very large fins, very small and smooth scales, a red circle about his eyes, which are big and of a gold colour, and from either angle of his mouth there hangs down a little barb. In every tench's head there are two little stones, which foreign physicians make great use of, but he is not commended for wholesome meat, though there be very much use made of them for outward applications. Rondeletius says, that at his being at Rome, he saw a great cure done by applying a tench to the feet of a very sick man. This, he says, was done after an unusual manner, by certain Jews. And it is observed, that many of those people have many secrets yet unknown to Christians; secrets that have never yet been written, but have been since the days of their Solomon (who knew the nature of all things, even from the cedar to the shrub) delivered by tradition, from the father to the son, and so from generation to generation, without writing, or (unless it were casually) without the least communicating them to any other nation or tribe; for to do that they account a profanation. And yet it is thought that they, or some spirit worse than they, first told us that lice swallowed alive were a certain cure for the yellow-jaundice. This, and many other medicines, were discovered by them, or by revelation; for, doubtless, we attained them not by study.

Well, this fish, besides his eating, is very useful both dead and alive for the good of mankind. But I will meddle no more with that; my honest humble art teaches no such boldness; there are too many foolish meddlers in physic and divinity, that think themselves fit to meddle with hidden secrets, and so bring destruction to their followers. But I'll not meddle with them any further than to wish them wiser; and shall tell you next (for I hope I may be so bold) that the tench is the physician of fishes, for the pike especially; and that the pike, being either sick or hurt, is cured by the touch of the Tench. And it is observed that the tyrant pike will not be a wolf to his physician, but forbears to devour him though he be never so hungry.

This fish, that carries a natural balsam in him to cure himself and others, loves yet to feed in very foul water, and amongst weeds. And yet I am sure he eats pleasantly, and doubtless you will think so too, if you taste him. And I shall therefore proceed to give you some few, and but a few, directions how to catch this Tench, of which I have given you these observations.

He will bite a paste made of brown bread and honey, or at a marsh-worm, or a lob-worm; he inclines very much to any paste with which tar is mixed; and he will bite also at a smaller worm, with his head nipped off, and a cod-worm put on the hook before that worm; and I doubt not but that he will also in the three hot months (for in the nine colder he stirs not much) bite at a flag-worm, or at a green gentle; but I can positively say no more of the tench, he being a fish I have not often angled for; but I wish my honest scholar may, and be ever fortunate when he fishes.

The Rye House

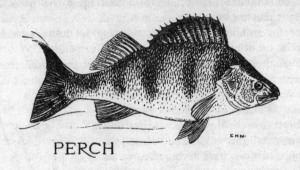

PERCH

CHAPTER XII

Observations of the Perch, and Directions how to Fish for him

Pisc. The Perch is a very good and a very bold-biting fish. He is one of the fishes of prey that, like the pike and trout, carries his teeth in his mouth, which is very large; and he dare venture to kill and devour several other kinds of fish. He has a hooked or hog back, which is armed with sharp and stiff bristles, and all his skin armed or covered over with thick dry hard scales, and hath (which few other fish have) two fins on his back. He is so bold that he will invade one of his own kind, which the pike will not do willingly, and you may therefore easily believe him to be a bold biter.

The perch is of great esteem in Italy, saith Aldrovandus, and especially the least are there esteemed a dainty dish. And Gesner prefers the perch and pike above the trout, or any fresh-water fish: he says the Germans have this proverb, 'More wholesome than a perch of Rhine;' and he says the river perch is so wholesome that physicians allow him to be eaten by wounded men, or by men in fevers, or by women in child-bed.

He spawns but once a year, and is, by physicians, held very nutritive; yet, by many, to be hard of digestion. They abound more in the river Po, and in England (says Rondeletius) than other parts, and have in their brain a stone which is in foreign parts sold by apothecaries, being there noted to be very medicinable against the stone in the reins. These be a part of the commendations which some philosophical brains have bestowed upon the fresh-water perch; yet they commend the sea-perch, which is known by having but one fin on his back (of which, they say, we English see but a few) to be a much better fish.

The perch grows slowly, yet will grow, as I have been credibly informed, to be almost two feet long; for an honest informer told me such a one was not long since taken by Sir Abraham Williams, a gentleman of worth, and a brother of the angle (that yet lives, and I wish he may): this was a deep bodied fish, and doubtless durst have devoured a pike of half his own length; for I have told you he is a bold fish, such a one as, but for extreme hunger, the pike will not devour; for to affright the pike, and save himself, the perch will set up his fins, much like as a turkey-cock will sometimes set up his tail.

But, my scholar, the perch is not only valiant to defend himself, but he is (as I said) a bold-biting fish, yet he will not bite at all seasons of the year; he is very abstemious in winter, yet will bite then in the midst of the day, if it be warm: and note, that all fish bite best about the midst of a warm day in winter, and he hath been observed by some not usually to bite till the mulberry tree buds, that is to say, till extreme frosts be past the spring, for when the mulberry tree blossoms, many gardeners observe their forward fruit to be past the danger of frosts, and some have made the like observation on the perch's biting.

But bite the perch will, and that very boldly: and as one has wittily observed, if there be twenty or forty in a hole, they may be at one standing all catched one after another, they being, as he says, like the wicked of the world, not afraid, though their fellows and companions perish in their sight. And you may observe, that they are not like the solitary pike, but love to accompany one another, and march together in troops.

And the baits for this bold fish are not many: I mean, he will bite as well at some or at any of these three, as at any or all others whatsoever: a worm, a minnow, or a little frog (of which you may find many in hay-time); and of worms, the dunghill-worm, called a brandling, I take to be best, being well scoured in moss or fennel; or he will bite at a worm that lies under a cow-turd, with a bluish head. And if you rove for a perch with a minnow, then it is best to be alive, you sticking your hook through his back fin, or a minnow with the hook in his upper lip, and letting him swim up and down about midwater, or a little lower, and you still keeping him to about that depth by a cork, which ought not to be a very little one; and the like way you are to fish for the perch, with a small frog, your hook being fastened through the skin of his leg, towards the upper part of it; and lastly, I will give you but this advice, that you give the perch time enough when he bites, for there was scarce ever any angler that has given him too much. And now I think best to rest myself, for I have almost spent my spirits with talking so long.

VEN. Nay, good master, one fish more, for you see it rains still, and you know our angles are like money put to usury, they may thrive, though we sit still and do nothing but talk and enjoy one another. Come, come, the other fish, good master.

PISC. But, scholar, have you nothing to mix with this discourse, which now grows both tedious and tiresome? Shall I have nothing from you, that seem to have both a good memory and a cheerful spirit?

VEN. Yes, master, I will speak you a copy of verses that were made by Doctor Donne, and made to show the world that he could make soft and smooth verses when he thought smoothness worth his

Amwellch from the river · E·K

labour; and I love them the better because they allude to rivers, and
fish and fishing. They be these –

> Come live with me, and be my love,
> And we will some new pleasures prove,
> Of golden sands and crystal brooks,
> With silken lines and silver hooks.
>
> There will the river whisp'ring run,
> Warm'd by thy eyes more than the sun,
> And there th' enamell'd fish will stay,
> Begging themselves they may betray.
>
> When thou wilt swim in that live bath,
> Each fish, which every channel hath,
> Most amorously to thee will swim,
> Gladder to catch thee, than thou him.
>
> If thou to be seen be'st loath,
> By sun or moon, thou darkenest both;
> And if mine eyes have leave to see,
> I need not their light, having thee.
>
> Let others freeze with angling-reeds,
> And cut their legs with shells and weeds,
> Or treacherously poor fish beset,
> With strangling snares, or windowy net:
>
> Let coarse bold bands, from slimy nest,
> The bedded fish in banks outwrest;
> Let curious traitors sleave silk flies,
> To witch poor wandering fishes' eyes:
>
> For thee thou need'st no such deceit,
> For thou thyself art thine own bait:
> That fish that is not catch'd thereby
> Is wiser far, alas! than I.

   Pisc. Well remembered, honest scholar; I thank thee for these
choice verses, which I have heard formerly, but had quite forgot till
they were recovered by your happy memory. Well, being I have
now rested myself a little, I will make you some requital, by telling
you some observations of the eel, for it rains still, and because (as
you say) our angles are as money put to use, that thrives when we
play, therefore we'll sit still and enjoy ourselves a little longer under
this honeysuckle hedge.

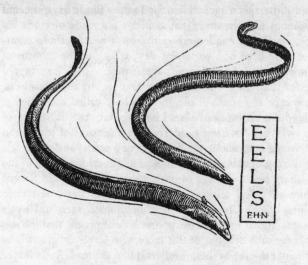

EELS
F·H·N·

CHAPTER XIII

Observations of the Eel, and other Fish that want Scales, and how to Fish for them

PISC. It is agreed by most men, that the eel is a most dainty fish; the Romans have esteemed her the Helena of their feasts, and some the queen of palate-pleasure. But most men differ about their breeding: some say they breed by generation as other fish do, and others, that they breed (as some worms do) of mud; as rats and mice, and many other living creatures are bred in Egypt, by the sun's heat, when it shines upon the overflowing of the river Nilus; or out of the putrefaction of the earth, and divers other ways. Those that deny them to breed by generation as other fish do, ask, if any man ever saw an eel to have a spawn or melt? and they are answered, that they may be as certain of their breeding as if they had seen spawn: for they say, that they are certain that eels have all parts, fit for generation, like other fish, but so small as not to be easily discerned, by reason of their fatness; but that discerned they may be; and that the he and the she-eel may be distinguished by their fins. And Rondeletius says he has seen eels cling together like dew-worms.

And others say that eels, growing old, breed other eels out of the corruption of their own age; which, Sir Francis Bacon says, exceeds not ten years. And others say, that as pearls are made of glutinous dew-drops, which are condensed by the sun's heat in those countries, so eels are bred of a particular dew, falling in the months of May or June on the banks of some particular ponds or rivers (apted by nature for that end), which in a few days are, by the sun's heat, turned into eels; and some of the ancients have called the eels that are thus bred the offspring of Jove. I have seen, in the beginning of July, in a river not far from Canterbury, some parts of it covered over with young eels, about the thickness of a straw; and these eels did lie on the top of that water, as thick as motes are said to be in the sun; and I have heard the like of other rivers, as namely, in Severn (where they are called yelvers), and in a pond, or mere, near unto Staffordshire, where, about a set time in summer, such small eels abound so much that many of the poorer sort of people that inhabit near to it, take such eels out of this mere with sieves or sheets; and make a kind of eel-cake of them, and eat it like as bread. And Gesner quotes venerable Bede, to say, that in England there is an island called Ely, by reason of the innumerable number of eels that breed in it. But that eels may be bred as some worms, and some kind of bees and wasps are, either of dew, or out of the corruption of the earth, seems to be made probable by the barnacles and young goslings bred by the sun's heat and the rotten planks of an old ship, and hatched of trees; both which are related for truths by Du Bartas and Lobel, and also by our learned Camden, and laborious Gerard, in his *Herbal*.

It is said by Rondeletius, that those eels that are bred in rivers that relate to or be nearer to the sea, never return to the fresh waters (as the salmon does always desire to do), when they have once tasted the salt water; and I do the more easily believe this, because I am certain that powdered beef is a most excellent bait to catch an eel. And though Sir Francis Bacon will allow the eel's life to be but ten years, yet he, in his *History of Life and Death*, mentions a lamprey belonging to the Roman emperor, to be made tame, and so kept for almost threescore years; and that such useful and pleasant observations were made of this lamprey, that Crassus the orator (who kept her) lamented her death. And we read (in Dr Hakewill) that Hortensius was seen to weep at the death of a lamprey that he had kept long and loved exceedingly.

It is granted by all, or most men, that eels, for about six months (that is to say, the six cold months of the year) stir not up and down, neither in the rivers, nor in the pools in which they usually are, but

Stanstead old church

get into the soft earth or mud; and there many of them together bed
themselves, and live without feeding upon anything (as I have told
you some swallows have been observed to do in hollow trees, for
those cold six months); and this the eel and swallow do, as not being
able to endure winter weather: for Gesner quotes Albertus to say,
that in the year 1125 (that year's winter being more cold than
usually) eels did by nature's instinct get out of the water into a stack
of hay in a meadow upon dry ground, and there bedded themselves,
but yet at last a frost killed them. And our Camden relates, that in

Great Amwell

Lancashire fishes were digged out of the earth with spades, where no water was near to the place. I shall say little more of the eel, but that, as it is observed, he is impatient of cold; so it hath been observed, that in warm weather an eel has been known to live five days out of the water.

And lastly, let me tell you that some curious searchers into the natures of fish observe, that there be several sorts or kinds of eels, as the silver eel, and green or greenish eel (with which the river of Thames abounds, and those are called grigs); and a blackish eel, whose head is more flat and bigger than ordinary eels; and also an eel whose fins are reddish, and but seldom taken in this nation, and yet taken sometimes: these several kinds of eels are (say some) diversely bred; as namely, out of the corruption of the earth, and some by dew, and other ways (as I have said to you): and yet it is affirmed by some for certain, that the silver eel is bred by generation, but not by spawning as other fish do, but that her brood come alive from her, being then little live eels, no bigger nor longer than a pin; and I have had too many testimonies of this to doubt the truth of it myself; and if I thought it needful I might prove it, but I think it is needless.

And this eel, of which I have said so much to you, may be caught with divers kinds of baits; as namely, with powdered beef, with a lob or garden-worm, with a minnow, or gut of a hen, chicken, or the guts of any fish, or with almost anything, for he is a greedy fish; but the eel may be caught especially with a little, a very little lamprey,

Amwell Magna Fishery

which some call a pride, and may in the hot months be found many of them in the river Thames, and in many mud-heaps in other rivers, yea, almost as usually as one finds worms in a dunghill.

Next note, that the eel seldom stirs in the day, but then hides himself; and therefore he is usually caught by night, with one of these baits of which I have spoken; and may be then caught by laying hooks, which you are to fasten to the bank, or twigs of a tree; or by throwing a string across the stream with many hooks at it, and those baited with the aforesaid baits, and a clod, or plummet, or stone, thrown into the river with this line, that so you may in the morning find it near to some fixed place; and then take it up with a draghook, or otherwise: but these things are, indeed, too common to be spoken of; and an hour's fishing with an angler will teach you better, both for these and many other common things, in the practical part of angling, than a week's discourse. I shall therefore conclude this direction for taking the eel by telling you, that in a warm day in summer I have taken many a good eel by sniggling, and have been much pleased with that sport.

And because you, that are but a young angler, know not what sniggling is, I will now teach it to you. You remember I told you that eels do not usually stir in the daytime; for then they hide themselves under some covert; or under boards or planks about flood-gates, or weirs, or mills; or in holes on the river banks: so that you, observing your time in a warm day, when the water is lowest,

may take a strong small hook, tied to a strong line, or to a string about a yard long; and then into one of these holes, or between any boards about a mill, or under any great stone or plank or any place where you think an eel may hide or shelter herself, you may, with the help of a short stick, put in your bait, but leisurely, and as far as you may conveniently; and it is scarce to be doubted, but if there be an eel, within the sight of it, the eel will bite instantly, and as certainly gorge it; and you need not doubt to have him if you pull him not out of the hole too quickly, but pull him out by degrees; for he, laying folded double in his hole, will, with the help of his tail, break all, unless you give him time to be wearied with pulling; and so get him out by degrees, not pulling too hard.

And to commute for your patient hearing this long discourse, I shall next tell you how to make this eel a most excellent dish of meat.

First, wash him in water and salt, then pull off his skin below his vent or navel, and not much further: having done that, take out his guts as clean as you can, but wash him not; then give him three or four scotches with a knife, and then put into his belly and those scotches, sweet herbs, an anchovy, and a little nutmeg grated, or cut very small; and your herbs and anchovies must also be cut very small, and mixed with good butter and salt: having done this, then pull his skin over him all but his head, which you are to cut off, to the end you may tie his skin about that part where his head grew; and it must be so tied as to keep all his moisture within his skin: and having done this, tie him with tape or packthread to a spit, and roast him leisurely, and baste him with water and salt till his skin breaks, and then with butter; and having roasted him enough, let what was put into his belly and what he drips be his sauce. – S.F.

When I go to dress an eel thus, I wish he were as long and big as that which was caught in Peterborough river in the year 1367, which was a yard and three-quarters long. If you will not believe me, then go and see at one of the coffee-houses in King Street, in Westminster.

But now let me tell you, that though the eel thus dressed be not only excellent good, but more harmless than any other way; yet it is certain, that physicians account the eel dangerous meat: I will advise you, therefore, as Solomon says of honey (Prov. 25), 'Hast thou found it, eat no more than is sufficient, lest thou surfeit; for it is not good to eat much honey.' And let me add this, that the uncharitable Italian bids us 'give eels and no wine to our enemies.'

And I will beg a little more of your attention to tell you Aldrovandus, and divers physicians, commend the eel very much for medicine, though not for meat. But let me tell you one observation, that the eel is never out of season, as trouts, and most other fish are at set times: at least most eels are not.

I might here speak of many other fish, whose shape and nature are much like the eel, and frequent both the sea and fresh rivers; as namely, the lamprel, the lamprey, and the lamperne: as also of the mighty conger, taken often in Severn, about Gloucester; and might also tell in what high esteem many of them are for the curiosity of their taste; but these are not so proper to be talked of by me, because they make us anglers no sport; therefore I will let them alone, as the Jews do, to whom they are forbidden by their law.

And, scholar, there is also a flounder, a sea-fish, which will wander very far into fresh rivers, and there lose himself and dwell; and thrive to a hand's breadth, and almost twice so long: a fish without scales, and most excellent meat; and a fish that affords much sport to the angler, with any small worm, but especially a little bluish worm gotten out of marsh-ground or meadows, which should be well scoured: but this, though it be most excellent meat, yet it wants scales, and is, as I told you, therefore an abomination to the Jews.

But, scholar, there is a fish that they in Lancashire boast very much of, called a char; taken there (and I think there only), in a mere called Winander Mere: a mere, says Camden, that is the largest in this nation, being ten miles in length, and some say as smooth in the bottom as if it were paved with polished marble. This fish never exceeds fifteen or sixteen inches in length; and 'tis spotted like a trout; and has scarce a bone but on the back. But this, though I do not know whether it make the angler sport, yet I would have you take notice of it, because it is a rarity, and of so high esteem with persons of great note.

Nor would I have you ignorant of a rare fish called a guiniad; of which I shall tell you of what Camden and others speak. The river Dee (which runs by Chester) springs in Merionethshire; and, as it runs towards Chester, it runs through Pemble-Mere, which is a large water: and it is observed, that though the river Dee abounds with salmon, and Pemble-Mere with the guiniad, yet there is never any salmon caught in the mere, nor a guiniad in the river. And now my next observation shall be of the Barbel.

CHAPTER XIV

Observations of the Barbel, and Directions how to Fish for him

PISC. The Barbel is so called (says Gesner) by reason of his barb or wattles at his mouth, which are under his nose or chaps. He is one of those leather-mouthed fishes, that I told you of, that does very seldom break his hold if he be once hooked: but he is so strong that he will often break both rod and line, if he proves to be a big one.

But the barbel, though he be of a fine shape, and looks big, yet he is not accounted the best fish to eat, neither for his wholesomeness nor his taste: but the male is reputed much better than the female, whose spawn is very hurtful, as I will presently declare to you.

They flock together, like sheep, and are at the worst in April, about which time they spawn, but quickly grow to be in season. He is able to live in the strongest swifts of the water, and in summer they love the shallowest and sharpest streams; and love to lurk under weeds, and to feed on gravel against a rising ground, and will root and dig in the sands with his nose like a hog, and there nest himself: yet sometimes he retires to deep and swift bridges, or floodgates, or weirs, where he will nest himself amongst piles, or in hollow places, and take such hold of moss or weeds, that be the water never so swift, it is not able to force him from the place that he contends for. This is his constant custom in summer, when he and most living creatures sport themselves in the sun; but at the approach of winter, then he forsakes the swift streams and shallow waters, and by degrees retires to those parts of the river that are quieter and deeper; in which places (and I think about that time) he spawns, and, as I have formerly told you, with the help of the melter, hides his spawn or eggs in holes, which they both dig in the gravel, and then they mutually labour to cover it with the same sand, to prevent it from being devoured by other fish.

There be such store of this fish in the river Danube, that Rondeletius says, they may in some places of it, and in some months of the year, be taken by those that dwell near to the river, with their hands, eight or ten load at a time: he says, they begin to be good in May, and that they cease to be so in August; but it is found to be otherwise in this nation: but thus far we agree with him, that the spawn of a barbel, if it be not poison, as he says, yet that it is dangerous meat, and especially in the month of May; which is so certain, that Gesner and Gasius declare it had an ill effect upon them, even to the endangering of their lives.

This fish is of a fine cast and handsome shape, with small scales, which are placed after a most exact and curious manner, and, as I told you, may be rather said not to be ill, than to be good meat: the chub and he have (I think) both lost part of their credit by ill cookery, they being reputed the worst or coarsest of fresh-water fish. But the barbel affords an angler choice sport, being a lusty and a cunning fish; so lusty and cunning as to endanger the breaking of the angler's line, by running his head forcibly towards any covert, or hole, or bank, and then striking at the line, to break it off with his tail (as is observed by Plutarch in his book, *De Industriâ Animalium*); and also so cunning to nibble and suck off your worm close to the hook, and yet avoid the letting the hook come into his mouth.

The barbel is also curious for his baits; that is to say, that they be clean and sweet; that is to say, to have your worms well scoured, and not kept in sour and musty moss, for he is a curious feeder; but at a well scoured lob-worm he will bite as boldly as at any bait, and especially if, the night or two before you fish for him, you shall bait the places where you intend to fish for him with big worms cut into pieces; and note, that none did ever overbait the place, nor fish too early or too late for a barbel. And the barbel will bite also at gentles, which (not being too much scoured, but green) are a choice bait for him; and so is cheese, which is not to be too hard, but kept a day or two in a wet linen cloth to make it tough: with this you may also bait the water a day or two before you fish for the barbel, and be much the likelier to catch store; and if the cheese were laid in clarified honey a short time before (as namely, an hour or two) you are still the likelier to catch fish; some have directed to cut the

Netherhall

cheese into thin pieces, and toast it, and then tie it on the hook with
fine silk: and some advise to fish for the barbel with sheep's tallow
and soft cheese beaten or worked into a paste, and that it is choicely
good in August, and I believe it; but doubtless the lob-worm well
scoured, and the gentle not too much scoured, and cheese ordered
as I have directed, are baits enough, and I think will serve in any
month, though I shall commend any angler that tries conclusions,
and is industrious to improve the art. And now, my honest scholar,

the long shower, and my tedious discourse are both ended together; and I shall give you but this observation, that when you fish for barbel, your rod and line be both long and of good strength, for (as I told you) you will find him a heavy and a dogged fish to be dealt withal, yet he seldom or never breaks his hold if he be once strucken. And if you would know more of fishing for the umber or barbel, get into favour with Dr Sheldon, whose skill is above others; and of that the poor that dwell about him have a comfortable experience.

And now let us go and see what interest the trouts will pay us for letting our angle-rods lie so long, and so quietly in the water, for their use. Come, scholar, which will you take up?

VEN. Which you think fit, master.

PISC. Why, you shall take up that, for I am certain, by viewing the line, it has a fish at it. Look you, scholar! well done! Come, now take up the other too: well! now you may tell my brother Peter, at night, that you have caught a leash of trouts this day. And now let's move towards our lodging, and drink a draught of red cow's milk as we go; and give pretty Maudlin and her honest mother a brace of trouts for their supper.

VEN. Master, I like your motion very well; and I think it is now about milking-time; and yonder they be at it.

PISC. God speed you, good woman! I thank you both for our songs last night: I and my companion have had such fortune a-fishing this day, that we resolve to give you and Maudlin a brace of trouts for supper; and we will now taste a draught of your red cow's milk.

MILK-W. Marry, and that you shall with all my heart; and I will still be your debtor when you come this way. If you will but speak the word, I will make you a good syllabub of new verjuice; and then you may sit down in a haycock and eat it; and Maudlin shall sit by and sing you the good old song of the *Hunting in Chevy Chase*, or some other good ballad, for she hath store of them; Maudlin, my honest Maudlin, hath a notable memory, and she thinks nothing too good for you, because you be such honest men.

VEN. We thank you; and intend once in a month to call upon you again, and give you a little warning; and so, good-night; good-night, Maudlin. And now, good master, let's lose no time; but tell me somewhat more of fishing; and, if you please, first, something of fishing for a gudgeon.

PISC. I will, honest scholar.

CHAPTER XV

Observations of the Gudgeon, the Ruffle and the Bleak, and how to Fish for them

PISC. The Gudgeon is reputed a fish of excellent taste, and to be very wholesome: he is of fine shape, of a silver colour, and beautified with black spots both on his body and tail. He breeds two or three times a year, and always in summer. He is commended for a fish of excellent nourishment: the Germans call him groundling, by reason of his feeding on the ground; and he there feasts himself in sharp streams, and on the gravel. He and the barbel both feed so, and do not hunt for flies at any time, as most other fishes do: he is a most excellent fish to enter a young angler, being easy to be taken with a small red-worm, on or near to the ground. He is one of those leather-mouthed fish that has his teeth in his throat, and will hardly be lost off from the hook if he be once stricken. They be usually scattered up and down every river in the shallows, in the heat of summer; but in autumn, when the weeds begin to grow sour and rot, and the weather colder, then they gather together, and get into the deep parts of the water, and are to be fished for there, with your hook always touching the ground, if you fish for him with a float, or with a cork; but many will fish for the gudgeon by hand, with a running line upon the ground, without a cork, as a trout is fished for; and it is an excellent way, if you have a gentle rod and as gentle a hand.

There is also another fish called a pope, and by some a ruffe, a fish that is not known to be in some rivers: he is much like the perch

for his shape, and taken to be better than the perch, but will not grow to be bigger than a gudgeon. He is an excellent fish, no fish that swims is of a pleasanter taste, and he is also excellent to enter a young angler, for he is a greedy biter; and they will usually lie abundance of them together, in one reserved place, where the water is deep, and runs quietly; and an easy angler, if he has found where they lie, may catch forty or fifty, or sometimes twice as many, at a standing.

You must fish for him with a small red-worm; and if you bait the ground with earth, it is excellent.

There is also a bleak, or fresh-water sprat, a fish that is ever in motion, and therefore called by some the river swallow; for just as you shall observe the swallow to be most evenings in summer ever in motion, making short and quick turns when he flies to catch flies in the air (by which he lives) so does the bleak at the top of the water. Ausonius would have him called bleak

SⁱʳHENRY WOTTON

from his whitish colour: his back is of a pleasant sad or sea-water green, his belly white and shining as the mountain snow; and doubtless, though he have the fortune (which virtue has in poor people) to be neglected, yet the bleak ought to be much valued, though we want Allamot salt, and the skill that the Italians have to turn them into anchovies. This fish may be caught with a Paternoster line; that is, six or eight very small hooks tied along the line, one half a foot above the other: I have seen five caught thus at one time, and the bait has been gentles, than which none is better.

Or this fish may be caught with a fine small artificial fly, which is to be of a very sad brown colour, and very small, and the hook answerable. There is no better sport than whipping for bleaks in a boat, or on a bank, in the swift water, in a summer's evening, with a hazel top about five or six foot long, and a line twice the length of the rod. I have heard Sir Henry Wotton say, that there be many that in Italy will catch swallows so, or especially martins (this bird-angler standing on the top of a steeple to do it, and with a line twice so long as I have spoken of). And let me tell you, scholar, that both martins and bleaks be most excellent meat.

And let me tell you, that I have known a hern, that did constantly frequent one place, caught with a hook baited with a big minnow or small gudgeon. The line and hook must be strong, and tied to some loose staff, so big as she cannot fly away with it, a line not exceeding two yards.

CHAPTER XVI

Is of nothing, or that which is nothing worth

PISC. My purpose was to give you some directions concerning roach and dace, and some other inferior fish, which make the angler excellent sport, for you know there is more pleasure in hunting the hare than in eating her; but I will forbear at this time to say any more, because you see yonder come our brother Peter and honest Coridon: but I will promise you, that as you and I fish, and walk tomorrow towards London, if I have now forgotten anything that I can then remember, I will not keep it from you.

Well met, gentlemen: this is lucky that we meet so just together at this very door. Come, hostess, where are you? Is supper ready? Come, first give us drink, and be as quick as you can, for I believe we are all very hungry. Well, brother Peter, and Coridon, to you both; come drink, and then tell me what luck of fish: we two have caught but ten trouts, of which my scholar caught three; look, here's eight, and a brace we gave away: we have had a most pleasant day for fishing and talking, and are returned home both weary and hungry, and now meat and rest will be pleasant.

PET. And Coridon and I have had not an unpleasant day, and yet I have caught but five trouts: for indeed we went to a good honest ale-house, and there we played at shovel-board half the day; all the time that it rained we were there, and as merry as they that fished;

and I am glad we are now with a dry house over our heads, for hark how it rains and blows. Come, hostess, give us more ale, and our supper with what haste you may; and when we have supped, let us have your song, Piscator, and the catch that your scholar promised us; or else Coridon will be dogged.

PISC. Nay, I will not be worse than my word; you shall not want my song, and I hope I shall be perfect in it.

VEN. And I hope the like for my catch, which I have ready too; and therefore let's go merrily to supper, and then have a gentle touch at singing and drinking; but the last with moderation.

COR. Come, now for your song; for we have fed heartily. Come, hostess, lay a few more sticks on the fire. And now sing when you will.

PISC. Well, then, here's to you, Coridon; and now for my song.

> O the gallant fisher's life,
>   It is the best of any!
> 'Tis full of pleasure, void of strife,
>   And 'tis beloved by many:
>   Other joys
>   Are but toys;
>   Lawful is;
>   For our skill
>   Breeds no ill,
> But contest and pleasure.
>
> In a morning up we rise
>   Ere Aurora's peeping;
> Drink a cup to wash our eyes;
>   Leave the sluggard sleeping.
>   Then we go
>   To and fro
>   With our knacks
>   At our backs
>   To such streams
>   As the Thames,
> If we have the leisure.
>
> When we please to walk abroad
>   For our recreation,
> In the fields is our abode,
>   Full of delectation:
>   Where in a brook,

    With a hook,
    Or a lake,
    Fish we take;
    There we sit
    For a bit,
Till we fish entangle.

We have gentles in a horn,
 We have paste and worms too;
We can watch both night and morn,
 Suffer rain and storms too.
    None do here
    Use to swear;
    Oaths do fray
    Fish away:
    We sit still
    And watch our quill;
Fishers must not wrangle.

If the sun's excessive heat
 Make our bodies swelter,
To an osier-hedge we get
 For a friendly shelter;
    Where in a dike,
    Perch or pike,
    Roach or dace,
    We do chase;
    Bleak or gudgeon,
    Without grudging:
We are still contented.

Or we sometimes pass an hour
 Under a green willow,
That defends us from a shower –
 Making earth our pillow:
    Where we may
    Think and pray,
    Before death
    Stops our breath:
    Other joys
    Are but toys,
And to be lamented.

          Jo. Chalkhill

Church
E.H.N.
Amwell

VEN. Well sung, master: this day's fortune and pleasure, and this night's company and song, do all make me more and more in love with angling. Gentlemen, my master left me alone for an hour this day; and I verily believe he retired himself from talking with me, that he might be so perfect in this song: was it not, master?

PISC. Yes, indeed; for it is many years since I learned it, and having forgotten a part of it, I was forced to patch it up by the help of mine own invention, who am not excellent at poetry, as my part of the song may testify: but of that I will say no more, lest you should think I mean by discommending it to beg your commendations of it. And therefore, without replications, let us hear your catch, scholar, which I hope will be a good one; for you are both musical, and have a good fancy to boot.

VEN. Marry, and that you shall; and as freely as I would have my honest master tell me some more secrets of fish and fishing as we walk and fish towards London tomorrow. But, master, first let me tell you, that, that very hour which you were absent from me, I sat down under a willow tree by the waterside, and considered what you had told me of the owner of that pleasant meadow in which you had then left me; that he had a plentiful estate, and not a heart to think so; that he had at this time many law-suits depending, and that they both damped his mirth and took up so much of his time and thoughts, that he himself had not leisure to take the sweet content that I (who pretended no title to them) took in his fields: for I could sit there quietly, and looking on the water, see some fishes sport themselves in the silver streams, others leaping at flies of several shapes and colours; looking on the hills, I could behold them spotted with woods and groves; looking down the meadows, could see, here a boy gathering lilies and lady-smocks, and there a girl cropping culverkeys and cowslips, all to make garlands suitable to this present month of May: these, and many other field-flowers, so perfumed the air, that I thought that very meadow like that field in Sicily (of which Diodorus speaks) where the perfumes arising from the place make all dogs that hunt in it to fall off, and to lose their hottest scent. I say, as I thus sat, joying in my own happy condition, and pitying this poor rich man that owned this and many other pleasant groves and meadows about me, I did thankfully remember what my Saviour said, that the meek possess the earth; or rather, they enjoy what the others possess and enjoy not; for anglers and meek quiet-spirited men are free from those high, those restless thoughts which corrode the sweets of life; and they, and they only, can say, as the poet has happily expressed it:

> Hail blest estate of lowliness!
>   Happy enjoyments of such minds
> As, rich in self-contentedness,
>   Can, like the reeds in roughest winds,
> By yielding make that blow but small,
> At which proud oaks and cedars fall.

There came also into my mind, at that time, certain verses in praise of a mean estate and an humble mind; they were written by Phineas Fletcher, an excellent divine, and an excellent angler, and the author of excellent piscatory eclogues, in which you shall see the picture of this good man's mind, and I wish mine to be like it.

> No empty hopes, no courtly fears from fright;
> No begging wants his middle fortune bite;
> But sweet content exiles both misery and spite.
>
> His certain life, that never can deceive him,
>   Is full of thousand sweets and rich content;
> The smooth-leaved beeches in the field receive him,
>   With coolest shade till noontide's heat be spent.
> His life is neither toss'd in boisterous seas
> Or the vexatious world, or lost in slothful ease;
> Pleased and full bless'd he lives, when he his God can
>   please.
>
> His bed, more safe than soft, yields quiet sleeps,
>   While by his side his faithful spouse hath place;
> His little son into his bosom creeps,
>   The lively picture of his father's face;
> His humble house or poor state ne'er torment him –
> Less he could like, if less his God had lent him;
> And when he dies, green turfs do for a tomb content him.

Gentlemen, these were a part of the thoughts that then possessed me. And I there made a conversion of a piece of an old catch, and added more to it, fitting them to be sung by anglers. Come, master, you can sing well; you must sing a part of it as it is in this paper.

> Man's life is but vain, for 'tis subject to pain
> And sorrow, and short as a bubble;
> 'Tis a hodgepodge of business, and money, and care,
> And care, and money, and trouble.
> But we'll take no care when the weather proves fair;
> Nor will we vex now, though it rain;
> We'll banish all sorrow and sing till tomorrow
> And angle, and angle again.

PETER. Ay, marry, sir, this is music indeed: this has cheered my heart, and made me to remember six verses in praise of music, which I will speak to you instantly.

Music! miraculous rhetoric, that speakest sense
Without a tongue, excelling eloquence;
With what ease might thy errors be excused,
Wert thou as truly loved as thou'rt abused!
But though dull souls neglect, and some reprove thee,
I cannot hate thee 'cause the angels love thee.

VEN. And the repetition of these last verses of music has called to my memory what Mr Ed. Waller (a lover of the angle) says of love and music.

Whilst I listen to thy voice,
    Chloris, I feel my heart decay:
        That powerful voice
    Calls my fleeting soul away:
O suppress that magic sound,
Which destroys without a wound!

Peace, Chloris, peace, or singing die,
    That together you and I
        To heaven may go;
        For all we know
Of what the blessed do above
Is – that they sing, and that they love.

PISC. Well remembered, brother Peter: these verses came seasonably, and we thank you heartily. Come, we will all join together, my host and all, and sing my scholar's catch over again, and then each man drink the other cup, and to bed, and thank God we have a dry house over our heads.

PISC. Well now, good-night to everybody.

PETER. And so say I.

VEN. And so say I.

COR. Good-night to you all, and I thank you.

PISC. Good-morrow, brother Peter, and the like to you, honest Coridon: come, my hostess says there is seven shillings to pay: let us each man drink a pot for his morning's draught, and lay down his two shillings; that so my hostess may not have occasion to repent herself of being so diligent, and using us so kindly.

PETER. The motion is liked by everybody; and so, hostess, here's your money: we anglers are all beholding to you, it will not be long ere I'll see you again. And now, brother Piscator, I wish you and my brother your scholar a fair day and good fortune. Come, Coridon, this is our way.

The GEORGE THE FOVRTH Inn Amwell

CHAPTER XVII

Of Roach and Dace, and how to
Fish for them; and of Cadis

VEN. Good master, as we go now towards London, be still so
courteous as to give me more instructions; for I have several boxes
in my memory, in which I will keep them all very safe, there shall
not one of them be lost.

PISC. Well, scholar, that I will and I will hide nothing from you that
I can remember, and can think may help you forward towards a
perfection in this art. And because we have so much time, and I have
said so little of roach and dace, I will give you some directions
concerning them.

Some say the roach is so called from *rutilus*, which they say
signifies red fins. He is a fish of no great reputation for his dainty
taste; and his spawn is accounted much better than any other part of
him. And you may take notice, that as the carp is accounted the
water-fox, for his cunning; so the roach is accounted the water-
sheep, for his simplicity or foolishness. It is noted, that the roach
and dace recover strength, and grow in season, in a fortnight after
spawning; the barbel and chub in a month; the trout in four months;
and the salmon in the like time, if he gets into the sea, and after into
fresh water.

Roaches be accounted much better in the river than in a pond,
though ponds usually breed the biggest. But there is a kind of

bastard small roach, that breeds in ponds, with a very forked tail, and of a very small size, which some say is bred by the bream and right roach; and some ponds are stored with these beyond belief; and knowing-men, that know their difference, call them ruds; they differ from the true roach as much as a herring from a pilchard. And these bastard breed of roach are now scattered in many rivers; but I think not in the Thames, which I believe affords the largest and fattest in this nation, especially below London Bridge. The roach is a leather-mouthed fish, and has a kind of saw-like teeth in his throat. And lastly, let me tell you, the roach makes an angler capital sport, especially the great roaches about London, where I think there be the best roach anglers. And I think the best trout anglers be in Derbyshire; for the waters there are clear to an extremity.

Next, let me tell you, you shall fish for this roach in winter with paste or gentles; in April, with worms or cadis; in the very hot months with little white snails, or with flies under water, for he seldom takes them at the top, though the dace will. In many of the hot months roaches may also be caught thus: take a May-fly or ant-fly, sink him with a little lead to the bottom, near to the piles or posts of a bridge, or near to any posts of a weir, I mean any deep place where roaches lie quietly, and then pull your fly up very leisurely, and usually a roach will follow your bait to the very top of the water, and gaze on it there, and run at it and take it, lest the fly should fly away from him.

I have seen this done at Windsor and Henley-bridge, and great store of roach taken, and sometimes a dace or chub; and in August you may fish for them with a paste made only of the crumbs of bread, which should be of pure fine manchet; and that paste must be so tempered betwixt your hands till it be both soft and tough too; a very little water, and time and labour, and clean hands, will make it a most excellent paste: but when you fish with it, you must have a small hook, a quick eye, and a nimble hand, or the bait is lost, and the fish too (if one may lose that which he never had). With this paste you may, as I said, take both the roach and the dace or dare, for they be much of a kind in matter of feeding, cunning, goodness, and usually in size. And therefore, take this general direction for some other baits which may concern you to take notice of. They will bite almost at any fly, but especially at ant-flies; concerning which, take this direction, for it is very good:

Take the blackish ant-fly out of the mole-hill or ant-hill, in which place you shall find them in the month of June, or if that be too early in the year, then doubtless you may find them in July, August,

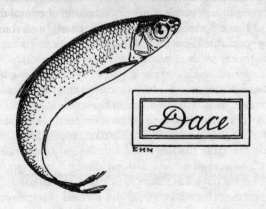

and most of September; gather them alive with both their wings, and then put them into a glass that will hold a quart or a pottle; but first put into the glass a handful or more of the moist earth out of which you gather them, and as much of the roots of the grass of the said hillock, and then put in the flies gently, that they lose not their wings; lay a clod of earth over it, and then so many as are put into the glass without bruising will live there a month or more, and be always in a readiness for you to fish with; but if you would have them keep longer, then get any great earthen pot, or barrel of three or four gallons (which is better) then wash your barrel with water and honey, and having put into it a quantity of earth and grass roots, then put in your flies, and cover it, and they will live a quarter of a year: these in any stream and clear water are a deadly bait for roach or dace, or for a chub; and your rule is to fish not less than a handful from the bottom.

I shall next tell you a winter bait for a roach, a dace, or chub, and it is choicely good. About All-hallowtide and so till frost comes, when you see men ploughing up heath ground, or sandy ground, or greenswards, then follow the plough, and you shall find a white worm as big as two maggots, and it hath a red head (you may observe in what ground most are, for there the crows will be very watchful and follow the plough very close); it is all soft, and full of whitish guts; a worm, that is, in Norfolk and some other counties, called a grub; and is bred of the spawn or eggs of a beetle, which she leaves in holes that she digs in the ground under cow or horse-dung, and there rests all winter, and in March or April comes to be first a red, and then a black beetle. Gather a thousand or two of these, and put them with a peck or two of their own earth into some tub or firkin, and cover and keep them so warm that the frost or cold air or winds kill them not: these you may keep all winter, and kill fish with them at any time; and if you put some of them into a little earth and honey, a day before you use them, you will find them an excellent bait for bream, carp, or indeed for almost any fish.

And after this manner you may also keep gentles all winter; which are a good bait then, and much the better for being lively and tough. Or you may breed and keep gentles thus: take a piece of beast's liver, and with a cross stick hang it in some corner, over a pot or barrel half full of dry clay: and as the gentles grow big they will fall into the barrel and scour themselves, and be always ready for use whensoever you incline to fish; and these gentles may be thus created till after Michaelmas. But if you desire to keep gentles to fish with all the year, then get a dead cat or a kite, and let it be fly-blown; and when the gentles begin to be alive and to stir, then bury it and them in soft moist earth, but as free from frost as you can; and these you may dig up at any time when you intend to use them: these will last till March, and about that time turn to be flies.

But if you will be nice to foul your fingers (which good anglers seldom are), then take this bait: get a handful of well-made malt, and put into a dish of water; and then wash and rub it betwixt your hands till you make it clean, and as free from husks as you can; then put that water from it, and put a small quantity of fresh water to it, and set it in something that is fit for that purpose, over the fire, where it is not to boil apace, but leisurely and very softly, until it become somewhat soft, which you may try by feeling it betwixt your finger and thumb; and when it is soft, then put your water from it, and then take a sharp knife, and turning the sprout end of the corn upward, with the point of your knife take the back part of the husk off from it, and yet leaving a kind of inward husk on the corn, or else it is marred; and then cut off that sprouted end (I mean a little of it) that the white may appear, and so pull off the husk on the cloven side (as I directed you) and then cutting off a very little of the other end, that so your hook may enter; and if your hook be small and good, you will find this to be a very choice bait either for winter or summer, you sometimes casting a little of it into the place where your float swims.

And to take the roach and dace, a good bait is the young brood of wasps or bees, if you dip their heads in blood; especially good for bream, if they be baked or hardened in their husks in an oven, after the bread is taken out of it, or hardened on a fire shovel; and so also is the thick blood of sheep, being half dried on a trencher, that so you may cut it into such pieces as may best fit the size of your hook, and a little salt keeps it from growing black, and makes it not the worse but better: this is taken to be a choice bait if rightly ordered.

There be several oils of a strong smell that I have been told of, and to be excellent to tempt fish to bite, of which I could say much; but I remember I once carried a small bottle from Sir George Hastings to Sir Henry Wotton (they were both chymical men) as a great present; it was sent and received, and used with great confidence; and yet upon enquiry, I found it did not answer the expectation of Sir Henry, which, with the help of this and other circumstances, makes me have little belief in such things as many men talk of: not but that I think fishes both smell and hear (as I have expressed in my former discourse); but there is a mysterious knack, which, though it be much easier than the philosopher's stone, yet it is not attainable by common capacities, or else lies locked up in the brain or breast of some chymical man, that, like the Rosicrucians, will not yet reveal it. But let me nevertheless tell you, that camphor, put with moss into your worm-bag with your worms, makes them (if many anglers be not very much mistaken) a tempting bait, and the angler more fortunate. But I stepped by chance into this discourse of oils and fishes smelling; and though there might be more said, both of it and of baits for roach and dace and other float fish, yet I will forbear it at this time, and tell you in the next place how you are to prepare your tackling; concerning which I will, for sport's sake, give you an old rhyme out of an old fish-book, which will prove a part, and but a part, of what you are to provide.

> My rod and my line, my float and my lead,
>   My hook and my plummet, my whetstone and knife,
> My basket, my baits both living and dead,
>   My net, and my meat, for that is the chief:
> Then I must have thread, and hairs green and small,
> With mine angling-purse – and so you have all.

But you must have all these tackling, and twice so many more, with which, if you mean to be a fisher, you must store yourself; and to that purpose I will go with you either to Mr Margrave, who dwells amongst the booksellers in St Paul's Churchyard, or to Mr John Stubs, near to the Swan in Golden Lane; they be both honest men, and will fit an angler with what tackling he lacks.

Great Amwell

VEN. Then, good master, let it be at —, for he is nearest to my dwelling; and I pray let us meet there the ninth of May next, about two of the clock, and I'll want nothing that a fisher should be furnished with.

PISC. Well, and I'll not fail you (God willing) at the time and place appointed.

VEN. I thank you, good master, and I will not fail you: and, good master, tell me what baits more you remember, for it will not now be long ere we shall be at Tottenham High Cross, and when we come thither I will make you some requital of your pains, by repeating as choice a copy of verses as any we have heard since we met together; and that is a proud word, for we have heard very good ones.

PISC. Well, scholar, and I shall be then right glad to hear them; and I will, as we walk, tell you whatsoever comes in my mind, that I think may be worth your hearing. You may make another choice bait thus: take a handful or two of the best and biggest wheat you can get, boil it in a little milk (like as frumity is boiled); boil it so till it be soft, and then fry it very leisurely with honey, and a little beaten saffron dissolved in milk; and you will find this a choice bait, and good, I think, for any fish, especially for roach, dace, chub, or grayling: I know not but that it may be as good for a river carp, and especially if the ground be a little baited with it.

And you may also note, that the spawn of most fish is a very tempting bait, being a little hardened on a warm tile, and cut into fit pieces. Nay, mulberries, and those blackberries which grow upon briars, be good baits for chubs or carps; with these many have been taken in ponds, and in some rivers where such trees have grown near the water, and the fruits customarily dropped into it. And there be a hundred other baits, more than can be well named, which, by constant baiting the water, will become a tempting bait to any fish in it.

You are also to know that there be divers kinds of cadis, or case-worms, that are to be found in this nation, in several distinct counties, and in several little brooks that relate to bigger rivers; as namely, one cadis called a piper, whose husk or case is a piece of reed about an inch long, or longer, as big about as the compass of a twopence. These worms being kept three or four days in a woollen bag, with sand at the bottom of it, and the bag wet once a day, will in three or four days turn to be yellow: and these be a choice bait for the chub or chavender, or indeed for any great fish, for it is a large bait.

There is also a lesser cadis-worm, called a cock-spur, being in fashion like the spur of a cock, sharp at one end; and the case or house, in which this dwells, is made of small husks, and gravel, and slime, most curiously made of these, even so as to be wondered at, but not to be made by man no more than a kingfisher's nest can, which is made of little fishes' bones, and have such a geometrical interweaving and connection, as the like is not to be done by the art of man: this kind of cadis is a choice bait for any float-fish; it is much less than the piper-cadis, and to be so ordered; and these may be so preserved, ten, fifteen, or twenty days, or it may be longer.

There is also another cadis, called by some a straw-worm, and by some a ruff-coat, whose house or case is made of little pieces of bents, and rushes, and straws, and water-weeds, and I know not what, which are so knit together with condensed slime, that they stick about her husk or case, not unlike the bristles of a hedgehog; these three cadises are commonly taken in the beginning of summer, and are good indeed to take any kind of fish, with float or otherwise. I might tell you of many more, which as these do early, so those have their time also of turning to be flies later in summer; but I might lose myself and tire you by such a discourse: I shall therefore but remember you, that to know these, and their several kinds, and to what flies every particular cadis turns, and then how to

At Ware

use them, first as they be cadis, and after as they be flies, is an art that everyone that professes to be an angler has not leisure to search after and, if he had, is not capable of learning.

I will tell you, scholar, several countries have several kinds of cadises, that indeed differ as much as dogs do; that is to say, as much as a very cur and a greyhound do. These be usually bred in the very little rills, or ditches, that run into bigger rivers: and I think, a more proper bait for those very rivers than any other. I know not how or of what, this cadis receives life, or what coloured

At Ware

fly it turns to; but doubtless they are the death of many trouts; and this is one killing way:

Take one (or more if need be) of these large yellow cadis: pull off his head, and with it pull out his black gut: put the body (as little bruised as is possible) on a very little hook, armed on with a red hair (which will show like the cadis head) and a very little thin lead, so put upon the shank of the hook that it may sink presently: throw this bait, thus ordered (which will look very yellow) into any great still hole where a trout is, and he will presently venture his life for it, 'tis not to be doubted, if you be not espied; and that the bait first touch the water before the line. And this will do best in the deepest, stillest water.

Next let me tell you, I have been much pleased to walk quietly by a brook with a little stick in my hand, with which I might easily take these, and consider the curiosity of their composure; and if you shall ever like to do so, then note, that your stick must be a little hazel or willow, cleft, or have a nick at one end of it; by which means you may with ease take many of them in that nick out of the water, before you have any occasion to use them. These, my honest scholar, are some observations told to you as they now come suddenly into my memory, of which you may make some use; but for the practical part, it is that that makes an angler: it is diligence, and observation, and practice, and an ambition to be the best in the art, that must do it. I will tell you, scholar, I once heard one say, 'I envy not him that eats better meat than I do, nor him that is richer, or that wears better clothes than I do; I envy nobody but him, and him only, that catches more fish than I do.' And such a man is like to prove an angler; and this noble emulation I wish to you and all young anglers.

CHAPTER XVIII

Of the Minnow or Penk, of the Loach,
and of the Bull-head or Miller's Thumb

PISC. There be also three or four other little fish that I had almost forgot, that are all without scales, and may for excellency or meat be compared to any fish of greatest value and largest size. They be usually full of eggs or spawn all the months of summer: for they breed often, as it is observed mice, and many of the smaller four-footed creatures of the earth do; and as those, so these, come quickly to their full growth and perfection. And it is needful that they breed both often and numerously, for they be (besides other accidents of ruin) both a prey and baits for other fish. And first, I shall tell you of the minnow or penk.

The minnow hath, when he is in perfect season, and not sick (which is only presently after spawning), a kind of dappled or waved colour, like to a panther, on his sides, inclining to a greenish and sky-colour, his belly being milk-white, and his back almost black or blackish. He is a sharp biter at a small worm, and in hot weather makes excellent sport for young anglers, or boys, or women that love that recreation, and in the spring they make of them excellent minnow-tansies; for being washed well in salt, and their heads and tails cut off, and their guts taken out, and not washed after, they prove excellent for that use; that is, being fried with yolks of eggs,

THE COMPLEAT ANGLER

the flowers of cowslips, and of primroses, and a little tansy; thus used they make a dainty dish of meat.

The loach is, as I told you, a most dainty fish; he breeds and feeds in little and clear swift brooks or rills, and lives there upon the gravel, and in the sharpest streams: he grows not to be above a finger long, and no thicker than is suitable to that length. This loach is not unlike the shape of the eel: he has a beard or wattles like a barbel. He has two fins at his sides, four at his belly, and one at his tail; he is dappled with many black or brown spots, his mouth is barbel-like under his nose. This fish is usually full of eggs or spawn; and is by Gesner, and other learned physicians, commended for great nourishment, and to be very grateful both to the palate and stomach of sick persons: he is to be fished for with a very small worm at the bottom, for he very seldom or never rises above the gravel, on which I told you he usually gets his living.

The miller's thumb, or bull-head, is a fish of no pleasing shape. He is by Gesner compared to the sea-toad-fish, for his similitude and shape. It has a head big and flat, much greater than suitable to his body; a mouth very wide, and usually gaping. He is without teeth, but his lips are very rough, much like to a file. He hath two fins near to his gills, which be roundish or crested; two fins also under the belly; two on the back; one below the vent; and the fin of his tail is round. Nature hath painted the body of this fish with whitish, blackish and brownish spots. They be usually full of eggs or spawn all the summer (I mean the females); and those eggs swell their vents almost into the form of a dug. They begin to spawn about April, and (as I told you) spawn several months in the summer; and in the winter, the minnow, and loach, and bull-head dwell in the mud, as the eel doth; or we know not where, no more than we know where the cuckoo and swallow, and other half-year birds (which first appear to us in April) spend their six cold, winter, melancholy months. This bull-head does usually dwell, and hide himself, in holes, or amongst stones in clear water; and in very hot days will lie a long time very still, and sun himself, and will be easy to be seen upon any flat stone, or any gravel; at which time he will suffer an angler to put a hook, baited with a small worm, very near unto his very mouth; and he never refuses to bite, nor indeed to be caught with the worst of anglers. Matthiolus commends him much more for his taste and nourishment, than for his shape or beauty.

There is also a fish called a sticklebag: a fish without scales, but hath his body fenced with several prickles. I know not where he dwells in winter, nor what he is good for in summer, but only to make sport for boys and women-anglers, and to feed other fish that be fish of prey, as trout in particular, who will bite at him as at a penk, and better, if your hook be rightly baited with him; for he may be so baited as, his tail turning like the sail of a windmill, will make him turn more quick than any penk or minnow can. For note, that the nimble turning of that, or the minnow, is the perfection of minnow fishing. To which end, if you put your hook into his mouth, and out at his tail, and then, having first tied him with white thread a little above his tail, and placed him after such a manner on your hook, as he is like to turn, then sew up his mouth to your line, and he is like to turn quick, and tempt any trout; but if he do not turn quick, then turn his tail a little more or less towards the inner part, or towards the side of the hook, or put the minnow, or

sticklebag, a little more crooked or more straight on your hook, until it will turn both true and fast; and then doubt not but to tempt any great trout that lies in a swift stream. And the loach that I told you of will do the like: no bait is more tempting, provided the loach be not too big.

And now, scholar, with the help of this fine morning, and your patient attention, I have said all that my present memory will afford me concerning most of the several fish that are usually fished for in fresh waters.

VEN. But, master, you have, by your former civility, made me hope that you will make good your promise, and say something of the several rivers that be of most note in this nation; and also of fish-ponds and the ordering of them; and do it, I pray, good master, for I love any discourse of rivers, and fish and fishing; the time spent in such discourse passes away very pleasantly.

CHAPTER XIX

Of several Rivers,
and some Observations of Fish

Pisc. Well, scholar, since the ways and weather do both favour us, and that we yet see not Tottenham Cross, you shall see my willingness to satisfy your desire. And first, for the rivers of this nation, there be (as you may note out of Doctor Heylin's *Geography*, and others) in number 325, but those of chiefest note he reckons and describes as followeth:

1. The chief is Thamesis, compounded of two rivers, Thame and Isis, whereof the former, rising somewhat beyond Thame in Buckinghamshire, and the latter in Cirencester in Gloucestershire, meet together about Dorchester in Oxfordshire; the issue of which happy conjunction is the Thamesis, or Thames; hence it flieth betwixt Berks, Buckinghamshire, Middlesex, Surrey, Kent, and Essex; and so weddeth himself to the Kentish Medway, in the very jaws of the ocean. This glorious river feeleth the violence and benefit of the sea more than any river in Europe, ebbing and flowing twice a day, more than sixty miles: about whose banks are so many fair towns and princely palaces that a German poet thus truly spake:

Tot campos, etc.

> We saw so many woods and princely bowers,
> Sweet fields, brave palaces, and stately towers,
> So many gardens dress'd with curious care,
> That Thames with royal Tiber may compare.

2. The second river of note is Sabrina, or Severn: it hath its beginning in Plynlimmon Hill in Montgomeryshire, and his end seven miles from Bristol, washing, in the mean space, the walls of Shrewsbury, Worcester, and Gloucester, and divers other places and palaces of note.

3. Trent, so called from thirty kind of fishes that are found in it, or for that it receiveth thirty lesser rivers; who, having his fountain in Staffordshire, and gliding through the counties of Nottingham, Lincoln, Leicester, and York, augmenteth the turbulent current of Humber, the most violent stream of all the isle. This Humber is not, to say truth, a distinct river, having a spring-head of his own, but it is rather the mouth or aestuarium of divers rivers here confluent, and meeting together, namely, your Derwent, and especially of Ouse and Trent; and (as the Danow, having received into its channel the river Dravus, Savus, Tibiscus, and divers others) changeth his name into this of Humberabus, as the old geographers call it.

4. Medway, a Kentish river, famous for harbouring the royal navy.

5. Tweed, the north-east bound of England; on whose northern banks is seated the strong and impregnable town of Berwick.

6. Tyne, famous for Newcastle, and her inexhaustible coal-pits. These and the rest of principal note, are thus comprehended in one of Mr Drayton's sonnets.

> The floods' queen, Thames, for ships and swans is crown'd;
>   And stately Severn for her shore is praised;
> The crystal Trent, for fords and fish renown'd;
>   And Avon's fame to Albion's cliffs is raised.
> Carlegion Chester vaunts her holy Dee;
>   York many wonders of her Ouse can tell;
> The Peak, her Dove, whose banks so fertile be;
>   And Kent will say, her Medway doth excel.
> Cotswold commends her Isis to the Thame;
>   Our northern borders boast of Tweed's fair flood;
> Our western parts extol their Willy's fame;
>   And the Old Lea brags of the Danish blood.

On the Lea at Ware.

These observations are out of learned Dr Heylin, and my old deceased friend, Michael Drayton; and because you say you love such discourses as these, of rivers and fish and fishing, I love you the better, and love the more to impart them to you: nevertheless, scholar, if I should begin but to name the several sorts of strange fish that are usually taken in many of those rivers that run into the sea, I might beget wonder in you, or unbelief, or both; and yet I will venture to tell you a real truth concerning one lately dissected by Dr Wharton, a man of great learning and experience, and of equal freedom to communicate it; one that loves me and my art; one to whom I have been beholden for many of the choicest observations that I have imparted to you. This good man, that dares to do anything rather than tell an untruth, did (I say) tell me he had lately dissected one strange fish, and he thus described it to me:

'The fish was almost a yard broad, and twice that length; his mouth wide enough to receive, or take into it, the head of a man; his stomach seven or eight inches broad: he is of a slow motion, and usually lies or lurks close in the mud, and has a movable string on his head, about a span or near unto a quarter of a yard long, by the moving of which (which is his natural bait) when he lies close and unseen in the mud, he draws other smaller fish so close to him that he can suck them into his mouth, and so devours and digests them.'

And scholar, do not wonder at this, for besides the credit of the relater, you are to note, many of these, and fishes that are of the like and more unusual shapes, are very often taken on the mouths of our sea-rivers, and on the sea-shore; and this will be no wonder to any that have travelled Egypt; where 'tis known the famous river Nilus does not only breed fishes that yet want names, but by the overflowing of that river, and the help of the sun's heat on the fat slime which that river leaves on the banks (when it falls back into its natural channel) such strange fish and beasts are also bred, that no man can give a name to, as Grotius (in his *Sophom*) and others, have observed.

But whither am I strayed in this discourse? I will end it by telling you, that at the mouth of some of these rivers of ours herrings are so plentiful, as namely, near to Yarmouth, in Norfolk, and in the west country, pilchers so very plentiful, as you will wonder to read what our learned Camden relates of them in his *Britannia* (pp. 178, 186),

Well, scholar, I will stop here, and tell you what by reading and conference I have observed concerning fishponds.

On the Avon

CHAPTER XX

Of Fishponds, and how to order them

PISC. Doctor Lebault, the learned Frenchman, in his large discourse of *Maison Rustique*, gives this direction for making of fishponds; I shall refer you to him to read at large, but I think I shall contract it, and yet make it as useful.

He adviseth, that when you have drained the ground, and made the earth firm where the head of the pond must be, that you must then, in that place, drive in two or three rows of oak or elm piles, which should be scorched in the fire, or half-burnt, before they be driven into the earth (for being thus used, it preserves them much longer from rotting); and having done so, lay faggots or bavins of smaller wood betwixt them, and then earth betwixt and above them, and then having first very well rammed them and the earth, use another pile in like manner as the first were: and note, that the second pile is to be of or about the height that you intend to make your sluice or flood-gate, or the vent that you intend shall convey the overflowings of your pond in any flood that shall endanger the breaking of the pond-dam.

Then he advises, that you plant willows or owlers about it, or both, and then cast in bavins in some places, not far from the side, and in the most sandy places, for fish both to spawn upon, and to defend them and the young fry from the many fish, and also from vermin that lie at watch to destroy them, especially the spawn of the carp and tench, when 'tis left to the mercy of ducks or vermin.

He and Dubravius, and all others advise, that you make choice of such a place for your pond, that it may be refreshed with a little rill, or with rain-water, running or falling into it; by which, fish are more inclined both to breed, and are also refreshed and fed the better, and do prove to be of a much sweeter and more pleasant taste.

To which end it is observed, that such pools as be large, and have most gravel and shallows where fish may sport themselves, do afford fish of the purest taste. And note, that in all pools, it is best for fish to have some retiring place; as namely, hollow banks, or shelves, or roots of trees, to keep them from danger; and when they think fit, from the extreme heat of the summer; as also, from the extremity of cold in winter. And note, that if many trees be growing about your pond, the leaves thereof, falling into the water, make it nauseous to the fish, and the fish to be so to the eater of it.

'Tis noted that the tench and eel love mud, and the carp loves gravelly ground, and in the hot months to feed on grass. You are to cleanse your pond, if you intend either profit or pleasure, once every three or four years (especially some ponds), and then let it lie dry six or twelve months, both to kill the water-weeds, as water-lilies, candocks, reate, and bulrushes, that breed there; and also that as these die for want of water, so grass may grow in the pond's bottom, which carps will eat greedily in all the hot months, if the pond be clean. The letting your pond dry, and sowing oats in the bottom, is also good, for the fish feed the faster: and being sometimes let dry, you may observe what kind of fish either increases or thrives best in that water; for they differ much, both in their breeding and feeding.

Lebault also advises, that if your ponds be not very large and roomy, that you often feed your fish by throwing into them chippings of bread, curds, grains, or the entrails of chickens or of any fowl or beast that you kill to feed yourselves; for these afford fish a great relief. He says that frogs and ducks do much harm, and devour both the spawn and the young fry of all fish, especially of the carp; and I have, besides experience, many testimonies of it. But Lebault allows water-frogs to be good meat, especially in some months, if they be fat: but you are to note that he is a Frenchman; and we English will hardly believe him, though we know frogs are usually eaten in his country: however, he advises to destroy them and kingfishers out of your ponds; and he advises not to suffer much shooting at wild fowl; for that (he says) affrightens, and harms, and destroys the fish.

Note, that carps and tench thrive and breed best when no other fish is put with them into the same pond; for all other fish devour their spawn, or at least the greatest part of it. And note, that clods of grass thrown into any pond, feed any carps in summer; and that garden-earth and parsley thrown into a pond recovers and refreshes the sick fish. And note, that when you store your pond, you are to put into it two or three melters for one spawner, if you put them into a breeding-pond; but if into a nurse-pond, or feeding pond, in which they will not breed, then no care is to be taken, whether there be most male or female carps.

It is observed that the best ponds to breed carps are those that be stony or sandy, and are warm and free from wind, and that are not deep, but have willow trees and grass on their sides, over which the water sometimes flows: and note, that carps do more usually breed in marle-pits, or pits that have clean clay-bottoms, or in new ponds, or ponds that lie dry a winter season, than in old ponds that be full of mud and weeds.

Well, scholar, I have told you the substance of all that either observation, or discourse, or a diligent survey of Dubravius and Lebault hath told me: not that they in their long discourses have not said more; but the most of the rest are so common observations, as if a man should tell a good arithmetician that twice two is four. I will therefore put an end to this discourse, and we will here sit down and rest us.

CHAPTER XXI

Directions for making a Line, and for the colouring of both Rod and Line

PISC. Well, scholar, I have held you too long about these cadis, and smaller fish, and rivers, and fishponds; and my spirits are almost spent, and so I doubt is your patience; but being, we are now almost at Tottenham, where I first met you, and where we are to part, I will lose no time, but give you a little direction how to make and order your lines, and to colour the hair of which you make your lines, for that is very needful to be known of an angler; and also how to paint your rod, especially your top; for a right grown top is a choice commodity, and should be preserved from the water soaking into it, which makes it in wet weather to be heavy, and fish ill-favouredly, and not true; and also it rots quickly for want of painting: and I think a good top is worth preserving, or I had not taken care to keep a top above twenty years. But first for your line.

First, note, that you are to take care that your hair be round and clear, and free from galls or scabs or frets; for a well-chosen, even, clear, round hair, of a kind of glass-colour, will prove as strong as three uneven scabby hairs, that are ill-chosen, and full of galls or unevenness. You shall seldom find a black hair but it is round, but many white are flat and uneven; therefore, if you get a lock of right, round, clear, glass-coloured hair, make much of it.

And for making your line, observe this rule: first let your hair be clean washed ere you go about to twist it; and then choose not only the clearest hair for it, but hairs that be of an equal bigness, for such do usually stretch altogether, and break altogether, which hairs of an unequal bigness never do, but break singly, and so deceive the angler that trusts to them.

When you have twisted your links, lay them in water for a quarter of an hour, at least, and then twist them over again before you tie them into a line: for those that do not so, shall usually find their line to have a hair or two shrink, and be shorter than the rest at the first fishing with it, which is so much of the strength of the line lost for want of first watering it, and then retwisting it; and this is most visible in a seven-hair line, one of those which hath always a black hair in the middle.

And for dyeing of your hairs, do it thus:

Take a pint of strong ale, half a pound of soot, and a little quantity of the juice of walnut tree leaves, and an equal quantity of alum; put these together into a pot, pan, or pipkin, and boil them half an hour; and having so done, let it cool; and being cold, put your hair into it, and there let it lie; it will turn your hair to be a kind of water or glass-colour, or greenish; and the longer you let it lie, the deeper it will be. You might be taught to make many other colours, but it is to little purpose; for doubtless the water-colour or glass-coloured hair is the most choice and the most useful for an angler, but let it not be too green.

But if you desire to colour hair greener, then do it thus: take a quart of small ale, half a pound of alum; then put these into a pan or pipkin, and your hair into it with them; then put it upon a fire, and let it boil softly for half an hour; and then take out your hair, and let it dry; and having so done, then take a pottle of water, and put into it two handfuls of marigolds, and cover it with a tile (or what you think fit), and set it again on the fire, where it is to boil again softly for half an hour, about which time the scum will turn yellow; then put into it half a pound of copperas, beaten small, and with it the hair that you intend to colour; then let the hair be boiled softly till half the liquor be wasted, and then let it cool three or four hours with your hair in it; and you are to observe that the more copperas you put into it, the greener it will be; but, doubtless, the pale green is best; but if you desire yellow hair (which is only good when the weeds rot), then put in the more marigolds, and abate most of the copperas, or leave it quite out, and take a little verdigrease instead of it.

This for colouring your hair. And as for painting your rod, which must be in oil, you must first make a size with glue and water, boiled together until the glue be dissolved, and the size of a lye-colour; then strike your size upon the wood with a bristle, or a brush, or pencil, whilst it is hot; that being quite dry, take white-lead, and a little red-lead, and a little coal-black, so much as altogether will make an ash-colour; grind these all together with linseed oil; let it be thick, and lay it thin upon the wood with a brush or pencil; this do for the ground of any colour to lie upon wood.

For a green.

Take pink and verdigrease, and grind them together in linseed oil, as thin as you can well grind it; then lay it smoothly on with your brush, and drive it thin; once doing for the most part will serve, if you lay it well; and if twice, be sure your first colour be thoroughly dry before you lay on a second.

Well, scholar, having now taught you to paint your rod, and we having still a mile to Tottenham High Cross, I will, as we walk towards it in the cool shade of this sweet honeysuckle hedge, mention to you some of the thoughts and joys that have possest my soul since we two met together. And these thoughts shall be told you, that you also may join with me in thankfulness to the Giver of every good and perfect gift, for our happiness. And that our present happiness may appear to be the greater, and we the more thankful for it, I will beg you to consider with me how many do, even at this very time, lie under the torment of the stone, the gout, and toothache; and this we are free from. And every misery that I miss is a new mercy, and therefore let us be thankful. There have been, since we met, others that have met disasters of broken limbs; some have been blasted, others thunder-strucken; and we have been freed from these, and all those many other miseries that threaten human nature; let us therefore rejoice, and be thankful. Nay, which is a far greater mercy, we are free from the unsupportable burden of an accusing tormenting conscience, a misery that none can bear; and therefore let us praise him for his preventing grace, and say, every misery that I miss is a new mercy: nay, let me tell you, there be many that have forty times our estates, that would give the greatest part of it to be healthful and cheerful like us; who, with the expense of a little money, have eat and drank, and laught, and angled, and sung, and slept securely; and rose next day, and cast away care, and sung and laught, and angled again; which are blessings rich men cannot purchase with all their money. Let me tell you, scholar, I have a rich neighbour that is always so busy that he has no leisure to laugh; the whole business of his life is to get money, and more money, that he may still get more and more money; he is still drudging on, and says that Solomon says, 'The diligent hand maketh rich:' and 'tis true indeed; but he considers not that 'tis not in the power of riches to make a man happy: for it was wisely said, by a man of great observation, 'That there be as many miseries beyond riches, as on this side them:' and yet God deliver us from pinching poverty; and grant that, having a competency, we may be content, and thankful. Let us not repine, or so much as think the gifts of God unequally dealt, if we see another abound with riches, when, as God knows, the cares that are the keys that keep those riches hang often so heavily at the rich man's girdle, that they clog him with weary days and restless nights, even when others sleep quietly. We see but the outside of the rich man's happiness: few consider him to be like the silk-worm, that, when she seems to play, is, at the very same time, spinning her own bowels, and consuming herself. And this many rich men do, loading themselves with corroding cares, to keep what they have (probably) unconscionably got. Let us, therefore, be thankful for

health and a competence; and, above all, for a quiet conscience.

Let me tell you, scholar, that Diogenes walked on a day, with his friend, to see a country fair; where he saw ribbons, and looking-glasses, and nut-crackers, and fiddles, and hobbyhorses, and many other gimcracks; and, having observed them and all the other finnimbruns that make a complete country fair, he said to his friend, 'Lord, how many things are there in this world of which Diogenes hath no need?' And truly, it is so, or might be so, with very many who vex and toil themselves to get what they have no need of. Can any man charge God that he hath not given him enough to make his life happy? No, doubtless; for nature is content with a little: and yet you shall hardly meet with a man that complains not of some want; though he, indeed, wants nothing but his will; it may be, nothing but his will of his poor neighbour, for not worshipping or not flattering him: and thus when we might be happy and quiet, we create trouble to ourselves. I have heard of a man that was angry with himself because he was no taller; and of a woman that broke her looking-glass because it would not show her face to be as young and handsome as her next neighbour's was. And I knew another to whom God had given health and plenty, but a wife that nature had made peevish, and her husband's riches had made purse-proud; and must, because she was rich (and for no other virtue) sit in the highest pew in the church; which being denied her, she engaged her husband into a contention for it; and at last into a lawsuit with a dogged neighbour who was as rich as he, and had a wife as peevish and purse-proud as the other: and this lawsuit begot higher oppositions, and actionable words, and more vexations and lawsuits; for you must remember that both were rich, and must therefore have their wills. Well, this wilful, purse-proud lawsuit lasted during the life of the first husband; after which his wife vext and chid, and chid and vext till she also chid and vext herself into her grave; and so the wealth of these poor rich people was curst into a punishment, because they wanted meek and thankful hearts; for those only can make us happy. I knew a man that had health and riches, and several houses, all beautiful, and ready furnished, and would often trouble himself and family to be removing from one house to another; and being asked by a friend, why he removed so often from one house to another, replied, 'It was to find content in some one of them.' But his friend, knowing his temper, told him, if he would find content in any of his houses he must leave himself behind him; for content will never dwell but in a meek and quiet soul. And this may appear, if we read and consider what our Saviour says in St Matthew's gospel; for he there says, 'Blessed be the merciful, for they shall obtain mercy. – Blessed be the pure in heart, for they shall see God. – Blessed be the poor in spirit, for theirs is

Baldock S⟂. Ware.

the kingdom of heaven.' And, 'Blessed be the meek, for they shall possess the earth.' Not that the meek shall not also obtain mercy, and see God, and be comforted, and at last come to the kingdom of heaven; but in the meantime he (and he only) possesses the earth, as he goes towards that kingdom of heaven, by being humble and cheerful, and content with what his good God has allotted him. He has no turbulent, repining, vexatious thoughts that he deserves better; nor is vext when he sees others possest of more honour or more riches than his wise God has allotted for his share; but he possesses what he has with a meek and contented quietness, such a quietness as makes his very dreams pleasing, both to God and himself.

My honest scholar, all this is told to incline you to thankfulness; and to incline you the more, let me tell you, that though the prophet David was guilty of murder and adultery, and many other of the most deadly sins; yet he was said to be a man after God's own heart, because he abounded more with thankfulness than any other that is mentioned in Holy Scripture, as may appear in his book of Psalms; where there is such a commixture of his confessing of his sins and unworthiness, and such thankfulness for God's pardon and mercies, as did make him to be accounted, even by God himself, to be a man after his own heart: and let us, in that, labour to be as like him as we can; let not the blessings we receive daily from God make us not to value, or not praise him because they be common; let us not forget to praise him for the innocent mirth and pleasure we have met with since we met together. What would a blind man give to see the pleasant rivers and meadows and flowers and fountains, that we have met with since we met together? I have been told that if a man that was born blind could obtain to have his sight for but only one hour during his whole life, and should, at the first opening of his eyes, fix his sight upon the sun when it was in its full glory, either at the rising or setting of it, he would be so transported and amazed, and so admire the glory of it, that he would not willingly turn his eyes from that first ravishing object, to behold all the other various beauties this world could present to him. And this, and many other like blessings, we enjoy daily. And for most of them, because they be so common, most men forget to pay their praises; but let not us, because it is a sacrifice so pleasing to Him that made that sun and us, and still protects us, and gives us flowers and showers, and stomachs and meat, and content and leisure to go a-fishing.

Well, scholar, I have almost tired myself, and, I fear, more than almost tired you; but I now see Tottenham High Cross, and our short walk thither shall put a period to my too long discourse, in which my meaning was and is, to plant that in your mind, with which I labour to possess my own soul: that is, a meek and thankful heart. And to that end, I have showed you that riches, without them, do not make any man happy. But let me tell you, that riches, with them, remove many fears and cares; and therefore my advice is, that you endeavour to be honestly rich, or contentedly poor: but be sure

The Cock Inn Ware.

that your riches be justly got, or you spoil all. For it is well said by Caussin, 'He that loses his conscience, has nothing left that is worth keeping.' Therefore be sure you look to that. And, in the next place, look to your health: and if you have it, praise God, and value it next to a good conscience; for health is the second blessing that we mortals are capable of; a blessing that money cannot buy, and therefore value it, and be thankful for it. As for money (which may be said to be the third blessing) neglect it not: but note, that there is no necessity of being rich; for I told you there be as many miseries beyond riches, as on this side them: and if you have a competence, enjoy it with a meek, cheerful, thankful heart. I will tell you, scholar, I have heard a grave divine say that God has two dwellings, one in heaven, and the other in a meek and thankful heart. Which Almighty God grant to me, and to my honest scholar; and so you are welcome to Tottenham High Cross.

VEN. Well, master, I thank you for all your good directions; but for none more than this last, of thankfulness, which I hope I shall never forget. And pray let's now rest ourselves in this sweet shady arbour, which nature herself has woven with her own fine finger; 'tis such a contexture of woodbines, sweet-briar, jasmine, and myrtle; and so interwoven, as will secure us both from the sun's violent heat, and from the approaching shower. And being sat down, I will requite a part of your courtesies with a bottle of sack, milk, oranges, and sugar; which, all put together, make a drink like nectar; indeed, too

good for anybody but us anglers. And so, master, here is a full glass
to you of that liquor; and when you have pledged me I will repeat
the verses which I promised you: it is a copy printed among some of
Sir Henry Wotton's, and doubtless made either by him or by a lover
of angling. Come, master, now drink a glass to me, and then I will
pledge you, and fall to my repetition; it is a description of such
country recreations as I have enjoyed since I had the happiness to
fall into your company.

> Quivering fears, heart-tearing cares,
> Anxious sighs, untimely tears,
> > Fly, fly to courts,
> > Fly to fond worldlings' sports,
> Where strain's Sardonic smiles are glosing still,
> And grief is forced to laugh against her will;
> > Where mirth's but mummery,
> > And sorrows only real be.
>
> Fly from our country's pastimes, fly,
> Sad troops of human misery.
> > Come, serene looks,
> > Clear as the crystal brooks,
> Or the pure azured heaven that smiles to see
> The rich attendance on our poverty;
> > Peace and a secure mind,
> > Which all men seek, we only find.
>
> Abused mortals, did you know
> Where joy, heart's ease, and comforts grow,
> > You'd scorn proud towers,
> > And seek them in these bowers;
> Where winds, sometimes, our woods perhaps may shake,
> But blustering care could never tempest make,
> > Nor murmur's e'er come nigh us,
> > Saving of fountains that glide by us.
>
> Here's no fantastic mask nor dance,
> But of our kids that frisk and prance;
> > Nor wars are seen,
> > Unless upon the green
> Two harmless lambs are butting one the other,
> Which done, both bleating run, each to his mother;

And wounds are never found,
Save what the ploughshare gives the ground.

Here are no entrapping baits,
To hasten to too hasty fates.
        Unless it be
        The fond credulity
Of silly fish, which (worldling like) still look
Upon the bait, but never on the hook;
        Nor envy, less among
        The birds, for prize of their sweet song.

Go, let the diving negro seek
For gems, hid in some forlorn creek:
        We all pearls scorn,
        Save what the dewy morn
Congeals upon each little spire of grass,
Which careless shepherds beat down as they pass:
        And gold ne'er here appears,
        Save what the yellow Ceres bears.

Bless'd silent groves, O may you be,
For ever, mirth's best nursery!
        May pure contents
        For ever pitch their tents
Upon these downs, these meads, these rocks,
        these mountains,
And peace still slumber by these purling fountains;
        Which we may every year
        Meet, when we come a-fishing here.

PISC. Trust me, scholar, I thank you heartily for these verses: they
be choicely good, and doubtless made by a lover of angling. Come,
now, drink a glass with me, and I will requite you with another very
good copy: it is a farewell to the vanities of the world, and some say
written by Sir Harry Wotton, who I told you was an excellent
angler. But let them be writ by whom they will, he that writ them
had a brave soul, and must needs be possest with happy thoughts at
the time of their composure.

Farewell, ye gilded follies, pleasing troubles;
Farewell, ye honour'd rags, ye glorious bubbles:
Fame's but a hollow echo, gold, pure clay;

Humour, the darling but of one short day;
Beauty (th' eye's idol) but a damask'd skin;
State, but a golden prison, to live in,
And torture free born minds; embroidered trains,
Merely but pageants for proud swelling veins:
And blood allied to greatness is alone
Inherited, not purchased, nor our own.
  Fame, honour, beauty, state, train, blood and birth,
  Are but the fading blossoms of the earth.

I would be great, but that the sun doth still
Level his rays against the rising hill:
I would be high, but see the proudest oak
Most subject to the rending thunder-stroke:
I would be rich, but see men (too unkind)
Dig in the bowels of the richest mind:
I would be wise, but that I often see
The fox suspected, whilst the ass goes free:
I would be fair, but see the fair and proud,
Like the bright sun, oft setting in a cloud:
I would be poor, but know the humble grass
Still trampled on by each unworthy ass:
Rich, hated: wise, suspected: scorn'd, if poor:
Great, fear'd: fair, tempted: high, still envied more:
  I have wish'd all; but now I wish for neither,
  Great, high, rich, wise, nor fair; poor I'll be rather.

Would the world now adopt me for her heir;
Would beauty's queen entitle me the fair;
Fame speak me fortune's minion; could I vie
Angels with India; with a speaking eye
Command bare heads, bow'd knees, strike justice dumb,
As well as blind and lame, or give a tongue
To stones by epitaphs; be call'd 'great master',
In the loose rhymes of every poetaster:
Could I be more than any man that lives,
Great, fair, rich, wise, all in superlatives:
Yet I more freely would these gifts resign,
Than ever Fortune would have made them mine;
  And hold one minute of this holy leisure

Beyond the riches of this empty pleasure.

Welcome, pure thoughts, welcome ye silent groves,
These guests, these courts, my soul most dearly loves;
Now the wing'd people of the sky shall sing
My cheerful anthems to the gladsome spring;
A prayer-book, now, shall be my looking glass,
In which I will adore sweet virtue's face,
Here dwell no hateful looks, no palace cares,
No broken vows well here, nor pale-faced fears;
Then here I'll sit, and sigh my hot love's folly,
And learn t'affect a holy melancholy;
    And if contentment be a stranger, then
    I'll ne'er look for it, but in heaven, again.

VEN. Well, master, these verses be worthy to keep a room in every man's memory. I thank you for them; and I thank you for your many instructions, which (Godwilling) I will not forget. And as St Austin, in his *Confessions* (book 4, chap. 5), commemorates the kindness of his friend Verecundus, for lending him and his companion a country house; because there they rested and enjoyed themselves, free from the troubles of the world: so, having had the like advantage, both by your conversation and the art you have taught me, I ought ever to do the like; for indeed, your company and discourse have been so useful and pleasant, that, I may truly say, I have only lived since I enjoyed them and turned angler, and not before. Nevertheless, here I must part with you, here in this now sad place where I was so happy as first to meet you: but I shall long for the ninth of May; for then I hope again to enjoy your beloved company at the appointed time and place. And now I wish for some somniferous potion, that might force me to sleep away the intermitted time, which will pass away with me as tediously, as it does with men in sorrow; nevertheless, I will make it as short as I can by my hopes and wishes. And, my good master, I will not forget the doctrine which you told me Socrates taught his scholars, that they should not think to be honoured so much for being philosophers, as to honour philosophy by their virtuous lives. You advised me to the like concerning angling, and I will endeavour to do so; and to live like those many worthy men of which you made mention in the former part of your discourse. This is my firm

At
Ware

resolution; and as a pious man advised his friend, that to beget mortification he should frequent churches, and view monuments, and charnel-houses, and then and there consider how many dead bones time had piled up at the gates of death: so when I would beget content, and increase confidence in the power, and wisdom, and providence of Almighty God, I will walk the meadows by some gliding stream, and there contemplate the lilies that take no care, and those very many other various little living creatures, that are not only created but fed (man knows not how) by the goodness of the God of nature, and therefore trust in him. This is my purpose; and so, let everything that hath breath praise the Lord: and let the blessing of St Peter's master be with mine.

PISC. And upon all that are lovers of virtue, and dare trust in his providence, and be quiet, and go a-angling.

'Study to be quiet.'

1 THESS. 4. 11

At
Ware

E·H·N·

A short Discourse by way of Postscript
Touching the Laws of Angling

My Good Friend – I cannot but tender my particular thanks to you for that you have been pleased by the editions of your *Compleat Angler*, freely to dispense your dear bought experiences to all the lovers of that art, and have thereby so excelling vindicated the legality thereof, as to devine approbation, that if I should go about to say more in that behalf, it indeed were to light a candle to the sun: but since all pleasures (though never so innocent in themselves) lose that stamp, when they are either pursued with inordinate affections, or to the prejudice of another; therefore as to the former, every man ought to endeavour, through a serious consideration of the vanity of worldly contentments, to moderate his affections thereunto, whereby they may be made of excellent use, as some poisons allayed are in physic: and as to the latter, we are to have recourse to the known laws, ignorance whereof excuseth no man, and therefore by their directions so to square our actions, that we hurt no man, but keep close to that golden rule, *To do to all men, as we would have ourselves be done unto*.

Now concerning the art of angling, we may conclude, Sir, that as you have proved it to be of great antiquity, so I find it favoured by the laws of this kingdom; for where provision is made by our statutes *primo Elizab. cap. 17*, against taking fish by the nets that be not of such and such a size there set down, yet, those lawnmakers had so much respect to anglers, as to except them; and leave them at liberty to catch as big as they could, and as little as they would catch. And yet though this apostolical recreation be simply in itself lawful, yet no man can go upon another man's ground to fish, without his licence to enter into a close or ground for such a space of time, there, though he practise angling all that time, he is not a trespasser, because his fishing is no abuse of his licence: but this is to be understood of running streams, and not of ponds or standing pools; for in case of a pond or standing pool, the owner thereof hath a property in the fish, and they are so far said to be his, that he may have trespass for the fish against anyone that shall take them without his licence, though it be upon a common, or adjoining to the king's highway, or adjoining to another man's ground, who gives licence: but in case of a river where one or more have *libera piscaria*, only it is otherwise, for there the fishes are said to be *ferae naturae*, and the taking of them with an angle is not trespass for that no man is said to have a property in them till he have caught them: and then it is a trespass for any to take them from him: but this is not to be understood of fishes confined to a man's own ground by gates or otherwise, so that they cannot pass away, but may be taken out or put in at pleasure, for in that way the party hath a property in them, as in the case of a standing pool, but where anyone hath *separalis piscaria*, as in Child and Greenhill's case in *Trin. 15, Car. 1*, in the King's Bench, there it seemeth that the fish may be said to be his, because no man else may take them whilst they are within his several fishing: therefore what is meant by a several fishing is necessary to be considered: and though the difference between a free-fishing, and a several fishing be often treated of in the ancient books of the law, and some opinions will have the difference to be great, and others small or nothing at all; yet the certainest definition of a several fishing is, where one hath the royalty, and owneth the ground on each side of the water, which agreeth with Sir William Calthrop's case, *Mich. 17, E. 4, 6, & Pasc. 18, E. 44*, where an action was brought by him against another for fishing in his several fishing, &c., to which the defendant pleaded, that the place wherein the trespass was supposed to be done, contained ten perches of land in length, and twenty perches in breadth, which was his own freehold at the time when the trespass was supposed to be done, and that he fished there as was lawful for him to do, and this was adjudged a good plea by the whole court, and upon argument in that very case it was agreed, that no one could have a several fishing except in his own soil, and that free fishing may be in the soil of another man, which was all agreed unto by Littleton, our famous English lawyer. So that from all this may be drawn this short conclusion, that if the angler take care that if he offend not with his feet, there is no great danger of his hands.

But there are some covetous, rigid persons, whose souls hold no sympathy with those of the innocent anglers, having either got to be lords of royalties, or owners of land adjoining to rivers, and these do, by some apted clownish nature and education for the purpose, insult and domineer over the innocent angler, beating him, breaking his rod, or at least taking it from him, and sometimes imprisoning his person as if he were a felon. Whereas a true-bred gentleman scorns those spider-like attempts, and will rather refresh a civil stranger at his table, than warn him from coming on his ground upon so innocent an occasion. It would therefore be considered how far such furious drivers are warranted by the law and what the angler may (in case of such violence) do in defence of himself. If I come upon another man's ground without his licence, or the licence of the law, I am a trespasser, for which the owner may have an action of trespass against me, and if I continue there after warning to depart by the owner, or his servant thereunto author-ised, the owner, or his servant by his command, may put me off by force, but not beat me, for then I (by resisting) make the assault; but if he beat me, I not resisting, in that case, he makes the assault, and I may beat him in defence of myself, and to free myself from his violence: and in case I shall leave my rod behind in his ground, he may take it *damage feasant*, but he can neither take it from my person by force, nor break it, but he is a trespasser to me: which seems clear by the case of Reynell and Champernoon, *Mich*. 7, *Car*. *1*, where Reynell brought an action of trespass against Champernoon for taking and cutting his nets, the defendant justified for that he was seized in fee of a several fishing, and that the plaintive with others endeavoured to row upon his waters, and with the nets to catch his fish, and that for the safeguard of his fishing he took and cut the nets and oars: to which plea the plaintive demurred; and there was adjudged by the whole court, that he could not by such colour cut the nets and oars; and judgement was therefore given for the plaintive.

Doubtless our forefathers well considered, that man to man was a wolf, and therefore made good laws to keep us from devouring one another, and amongst the rest a very good statute was made in the three and fortieth year of Queen Elizabeth, whereby it is provided, that in personal actions in the courts at Westminster (being not for land or battery), when it shall appear to the judge (and be so by them signified), that the debt or damages to be recovered amount not to the sum of forty shillings or above, the said judges shall award the plaintive no more costs than damages, but less at their discretion.

And now with my acknowledgement of the advantage I have had both by your friendship and your book: I wish nothing may ever be that looks like an alteration in the first; nor anything in the last, unless, by reason of the useful pleasure of it, you had called it *The Arcadia of Angling*; for it deserves that title, and I would deserve the continuance of your friendship.

Meadow
Sweet

Part Two

Being Directions how to
Angle for Trout or Grayling
in a Clear stream

Qui mihi non credit, faciat licet ipse periclum;
Et fuerit scriptis aequior ille meis.

Beresford
Hall
E·H·N

Cotton of Beresford

TO
MY MOST WORTHY
FATHER AND FRIEND,
MR IZAAK WALTON, THE ELDER

Sir – Being you were pleased, some years past, to grant me your free leave to do what I have here attempted; and observing you never retract any promise when made in favour of your meanest friends; I accordingly expect to see these following articular directions for the taking of a trout, to wait upon your better and more general rules for all sorts of angling. And though mine be neither so perfect, so well digested, nor indeed so handsomely couch'd as they might have been, in so long a time as since your leave was granted; yet I dare affirm them to be generally true: and they had appeared too in something a neater dress, but that I was surprised with the sudden news of a sudden new edition of your *Compleat Angler*; so that, having little more than ten days' time to turn me in, and rub up my memory (for, in truth, I have not, in all this long time, though I have often thought on't, and almost as often resolved to go presently about it), I was forced, upon the instant, to scribble what I here present you: which I have also endeavoured to accommodate to your own method. And, if mine be clear enough for the honest brothers of the angle readily to understand (which is the only thing I aim at) then I have my end, and shall need to make no further apology; a writing of this kind not requiring (if I were master of any such thing) any eloquence to set it off, or recommend it; so that if you, in your better judgement, or kindness rather, can allow it passable for a thing of this nature, you will then do me the honour if the cypher fixed and carved in the front of my little fishing-house, may be here explained: and to permit me to attend you in public, who, in private have ever been, am, and ever resolve to be,

Sir,

Your most affectionate son and servant,

CHARLES COTTON
Beresford, 10th of March, 1675–76

Arrow Heads

Beresford Hall

TO MY MOST HONOURED FRIEND,
CHARLES COTTON, ESQ.

Sir – You now see I have returned you your very pleasant, and useful discourse of *The Art of Fly-fishing*, printed just as it was sent me; for I have been so obedient to your desires, as to endure all the praises you have ventured to fix upon me in it. And when I have thanked you for them, as the effects of an undissembled love, then, let me tell you, sir, that I will readily endeavour to live up to the character you have given of me, if there were no other reason, yet for this alone, that you, that love me so well, and always think what you speak, may not, for my sake, suffer by a mistake in your judgement.

And, sir, I have ventured to fill a part of your margin, by way of paraphrase, for the reader's clearer understanding the situation both of your fishing-house, and the pleasantness of that you dwell in. And I have ventured also to give him a 'Copy of Verses' that you were pleased to send me, now some years past, in which he may see a good picture of both; and so much of your own mind too, as will make any reader, that is blessed with a generous soul, to love you the better. I confess, that for doing this you may justly judge me too bold: if you do, I will say so too; and so far commute for my offence, that, though I be more than a hundred miles from you, and in the eighty-third year of my age, yet I will forget both, and the next month begin a pilgrimage to beg your pardon; for I would die in your favour, and till then will live,

Sir,

Your most affectionate father and friend,

IZAAK WALTON
London, April 29th, 1676

Beresford Arms

CHAPTER I

Conference betwixt a country Gentleman proficient in the Art of Fly-fishing and a Traveller who becomes his Pupil

PISCATOR JUNIOR AND VIATOR

PISC. You are happily overtaken, sir; may a man be so bold as to enquire how far you travel this way?

VIAT. Yes sure, sir, very freely, though it be a question I cannot very well resolve you, as not knowing myself how far it is to Ashborn, where I intend tonight to take up my inn.

PISC. Why then, sir, seeing I perceive you to be a stranger in these parts, I shall take upon me to inform you, that from the town you last came through, called Brailsford, it is five miles; and you are not yet above half a mile on this side.

VIAT. So much? I was told it was but ten miles from Derby; and, methinks, I have rode almost so far already.

PISC. O sir, find no fault with large measure of good land, which Derbyshire abounds in, as much as most counties of England.

VIAT. It may be so; and good land, I confess, affords a pleasant prospect: but, by your good leave, sir, large measure of foul way is not altogether so acceptable.

Pisc. True, sir; but the foul way serves to justify the fertility of the soil, according to the proverb, 'There is good land where there is foul way;' and is of good use to inform you of the riches of the country you are come into, and of its continual travel and traffic to the country town you came from; which is also very observable by the fullness of its road, and the laden horses you meet everywhere upon the way.

Viat. Well, sir, I will be content to think as well of your country as you would desire; and I shall have a great deal of reason both to think, and to speak very well of you, if I may obtain the happiness of your company to the forementioned place, provided your affairs lead you that way, and that they will permit you to slack your pace, out of complacency to a traveller utterly a stranger in these parts, and who am still to wander further out of my own knowledge.

Pisc. Sir, you invite me to my own advantage, and I am ready to attend you, my way lying through that town; but my business, that is, my home, some miles beyond it: however, I shall have time enough to lodge you in your quarters, and afterward to perform my own journey. In the meantime, may I be so bold as to enquire the end of your journey?

Viat. 'Tis into Lancashire, sir; and about some business of concern to a near relation of mine; for I assure you I do not use to take such long journeys as from Essex upon the single account of pleasure.

Pisc. From thence, sir! I do not then wonder you should appear dissatisfied with the length of the miles, and the foulness of the way: though I am sorry you should begin to quarrel with them so soon; for, believe me, sir, you will find the miles much longer, and the way much worse, before you come to your journey's end.

Viat. Why! truly, sir! for that I am prepared to expect the worst; but methinks the way is mended since I had the good fortune to fall into your good company.

Pisc. You are not obliged to my company for that, but because you are already past the worst, and the greatest part of your way to your lodging.

Viat. I am very glad to hear it, both for the ease of myself and my horse; but especially, because I may then expect a freer enjoyment of your conversation; though the shortness of the way will, I fear, make me lose it the sooner.

Pisc. That, sir, is not worth your care; and I am sure you deserve much better for being content with so ill company. But we have

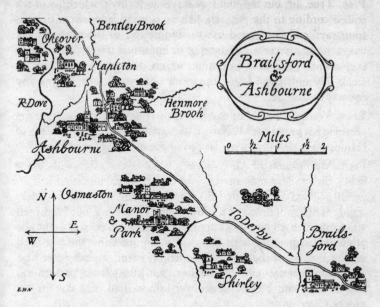

already talked away two miles of your journey; for, from the brook before us, that runs at the foot of this sandy hill, you have but three miles to Ashborn.

VIAT. I meet, everywhere in this country, with these little brooks; and they look as if they were full of fish: have they not trouts in them?

PISC. That is a question which is to be excused in a stranger, as you are: otherwise, give me leave to tell you, it would seem a kind of affront to our country, to make a doubt of what we pretend to be famous for, next, if not before, our malt, wool, lead, and coal; for you are to understand, that we think we have as many fine rivers, rivulets, and brooks, as any country whatever; and they are all full of trouts, and some of them the best (it is said), by many degrees, in England.

VIAT. I was first, sir, in love with you; and now shall be so enamoured of your country by this account you give me of it, as to wish myself a Derbyshire man, or at least that I might live in it: for you must know I am a pretender to the angle, and, doubtless, a trout affords the most pleasure to the angler of any sort of fish whatever; and the best trouts must needs make the best sport; but this brook, and some others I have met with upon this way, are too full of wood for that recreation.

PISC. This, sir! why this, and several others like it, which you have passed, and some that you are like to pass, have scarce any name amongst us; but we can show you as fine rivers, and as clear from wood, or any other encumbrance to hinder an angler, as any you ever saw; and for clear, beautiful streams, Hampshire itself, by Mr Izaak Walton's good leave, can show none such; nor I think any country in Europe.

VIAT. You go far, sir, in the praise of your country rivers, and I perceive have read Mr Walton's *Compleat Angler*, by your naming of Hampshire; and I pray what is your opinion of that book?

PISC. My opinion of Mr Walton's book is the same with every man's that understands anything of the art of angling, that it is an excellent good one, and that the fore-mentioned gentleman understands as much of fish, and fishing, as any man living: but I must tell you further, that I have the happiness to know his person, and to be intimately acquainted with him, and in him to know the worthiest man, and to enjoy the best, and the truest friend any man ever had; nay, I shall yet acquaint you further, that he gives me leave to call him Father, and I hope is not yet ashamed to own me for his adopted Son.

VIAT. In earnest, sir, I am ravished to meet with a friend of Mr Izaak Walton's, and one that does him so much right in so good and true a character; for I must boast to you, that I have the good fortune to know him too, and came acquainted with him much after the same manner I do with you; that he was my Master, who first taught me to love angling, and then to become an angler; and to be plain with you, I am the very man deciphered in his book under the name of Venator; for I was wholly addicted to the chace, till he taught me as good, a more quiet, innocent, and less dangerous diversion.

PISC. Sir, I think myself happy in your acquaintance, and before we part shall entreat leave to embrace you; you have said enough to recommend you to my best opinion; for my father Walton will be seen twice in no man's company he does not like, and likes none but such as he believes to be very honest men; which is one of the best arguments, or at least of the best testimonies I have, that I either am, or that he thinks me, one of those, seeing I have not yet found him weary of me.

VIAT. You speak like a true friend, and in doing so render yourself worthy of his friendship. May I be so bold as to ask your name?

ASH-
BOVRNE   CHVRCH

E·H·N·

Pisc. Yes surely, sir, and if you please a much nicer question; my
name —, and I intend to stay long enough in your company, if I find
you do not dislike mine, to ask yours too. In the meantime, because
we are now almost at Ashborn, I shall freely and bluntly tell you,
that I am a brother of the angle too, and, peradventure, can give you
some instructions how to angle for a trout in a clear river, that my
father Walton himself will not disapprove, though he did either
purposely omit, or did not remember them, when you and he sat

Ashbourne

discoursing under the sycamore tree. And, being you have already told me whither your journey is intended, and that I am better acquainted with the country than you are; I will heartily and earnestly entreat you will not think of staying at this town, but go on with me six miles farther to my house, where you shall be extremely welcome; it is directly in your way, we have day enough to perform our journey, and, as you like your entertainment, you may there repose yourself a day or two, or as many more as your occasions will permit, to recompense the trouble of so much a longer journey.

VIAT. Sir, you surprise me with so friendly an invitation upon so short acquaintance; but how advantageous soever it would be to me, and that my haste, perhaps, is not so great but it might dispense with such a divertisement as I promise myself in your company, yet I cannot, in modesty, accept your offer, and must therefore beg your pardon: I could otherwise, I confess, be glad to wait upon you, if upon no other account but to talk of Mr I. Walton, and to receive those instructions you say you are able to give me for the deceiving a trout; in which art I will not deny but that I have an ambition to be one of the greatest deceivers; though I cannot forbear freely to tell you, that I think it hard to say much more than has been read to me upon that subject.

Brailsford

Pisc. Well, sir, I grant that too; but you must know that the variety of rivers require different ways of angling: however, you shall have the best rules I am able to give, and I will tell you nothing I have not made myself as certain of as any man can be in a thirty years' experience (for so long I have been a dabbler in that art); and that, if you please to stay a few days, you shall, in a very great measure, see made good to you. But of that hereafter; and now, sir, if I am not mistaken, I have half overcome you; and that I may wholly conquer that modesty of yours, I will take upon me to be so familiar as to say, you must accept my invitation, which, that you may the more easily be persuaded to do, I will tell you that my house stands upon the margin of one of the finest rivers for trouts and grayling in England; that I have lately built a little fishing-house upon it, dedicated to anglers, over the door of which you will see the two first letters of my father Walton's name and mine twisted in cipher; that you shall lie in the same bed he has sometimes been contented with, and have such country entertainment as my friends sometimes accept, and be as welcome, too, as the best friend of them all.

Viat. No doubt, sir, but my master Walton found good reason to be satisfied with his entertainment in your house; for you who are so friendly to a mere stranger, who deserves so little, must needs be exceeding kind and free to him who deserves so much.

Brailsford Brook

PISC. Believe me, no: and such as are intimately acquainted with that gentleman know him to be a man who will not endure to be treated like a stranger. So that his acceptation of my poor entertainment has ever been a pure effect of his own humility, and good-nature, and nothing else. But, sir, we are now going down the Spittle Hill, into the town; and therefore let me importune you suddenly to resolve, and most earnestly not to deny me.

VIAT. In truth, sir, I am so overcome by your bounty, that I find I cannot, but must render myself wholly to be disposed of by you.

PISC. Why, that's heartily and kindly spoken, and I as heartily thank you; and, being you have abandoned yourself to my conduct, we will only call and drink a glass on horseback at the Talbot, and away.

VIAT. I attend you. But what pretty river is this, that runs under this stone bridge? Has it a name?

PISC. Yes, 'tis called Henmore, and has in it both trout and grayling; but you will meet with one or two better anon. And so soon as we are past through the town, I will endeavour, by such discourse as best likes you, to pass away the time till you come to your ill quarters.

VIAT. We can talk of nothing with which I shall be more delighted than of rivers and angling.

PISC. Let those be the subjects, then; but we are now come to the Talbot. What will you drink, sir, ale or wine?

VIAT. Nay, I am for the country liquor, Derbyshire ale, if you please; for a man should not, methinks, come from London to drink wine in the Peak.

PISC. You are in the right; and yet, let me tell you, you may drink worse French wine in many taverns in London, than they have sometimes at this house. What ho! bring us a flagon of your best ale; and now, sir, my service to you, a good health to the honest gentleman you know of, and you are welcome into the Peak.

VIAT. I thank you, sir, and present you my service again, and to all the honest brothers of the angle.

PISC. I'll pledge you, sir: so, there's for your ale, and farewell. Come, sir, let us be going, for the sun grows low, and I would have you look about you as you ride; for you will see an odd country, and sights that will seem strange to you.

Bentley Brook

Spittle Hill
from the Bridge

E·H·N·

CHAPTER II

Observations of the principal Rivers in Derbyshire;
Viator lodges at Piscator Junior's House

Pisc. So, sir, now we have got to the top of the hill out of town, look about you, and tell me how you like the country.

Viat. Bless me, what mountains are here! Are we not in Wales?

Pisc. No, but in almost as mountainous a country; and yet these hills, though high, bleak, and craggy, breed and feed good beef and mutton, above ground, and afford good store of lead within.

Viat. They had need of all those commodities to make amends for the ill landskip: but I hope our way does not lie over any of these, for I dread a precipice.

Pisc. Believe me, but it does, and down one, especially, that will appear a little terrible to a stranger: though the way is passable enough, and so passable, that we who are natives of these mountains and acquainted with them, disdain to alight.

VIAT. I hope, though, that a foreigner is privileged to use his own discretion, and that I may have the liberty to entrust my neck to the fidelity of my own feet, rather than to those of my horse, for I have no more at home.

PISC. 'Twere hard else. But in the meantime, I think 'twere best, while this way is pretty even, to mend our pace, that we may be past that hill I speak of; to the end your apprehension may not be doubled for want of light to discern the easiness of the descent.

VIAT. I am willing to put forward as fast as my beast will give me leave, though I fear nothing in your company. But what pretty river is this we are going into?

PISC. Why this, sir, is called Bently-brook, and is full of very good trout and grayling; but so encumbered with wood in many places, as is troublesome to an angler.

VIAT. Here are the prettiest rivers, and the most of them in this country that ever I saw; do you know how many you have in the country?

PISC. I know them all, and they were not hard to reckon, were it worth the trouble; but the most considerable of them I will presently name you. And to begin where we now are (for you must know we are now upon the very skirts of Derbyshire) we have first the river Dove, that we shall come to by and by, which divides the two counties of Derby and Stafford for many miles together; and is so called from the swiftness of its current, and that swiftness occasioned by the declivity of its course, and by being so straitened in that course betwixt the rocks; by which, and those very high ones, it is, hereabout, for four or five miles, confined into a very narrow stream; a river that from a contemptible fountain (which I can cover with my hat) by the confluence of other rivers, rivulets, brooks, and rills, is swelled before it falls into Trent, a little below Eggington, where it loses the name, to such a breadth and depth as to be in most places navigable, were not the passage frequently interrupted with fords and weirs; and has as fertile banks as any river in England, none excepted. And this river, from its head for a mile or two, is a black water (as all the rest of the Derbyshire rivers of note originally are, for they all spring from the mosses); but is in a few miles' travel so clarified by the addition of several clear and very great springs (bigger than itself) which gush out of the limestone rocks, that before it comes to my house, which is but six or seven miles from its source, you will find it one of the purest crystalline streams you have seen.

VIAT. Does Trent spring in these parts?

PISC. Yes, in these parts; not in this country, but somewhere towards the upper end of Staffordshire, I think not far from a place called Trentham; and thence runs down, not far from Stafford, to Wolsly Bridge, and, washing the skirts and purlieus of the forest of Needwood, runs down to Burton, in the same county; thence it comes into this, where we now are, and running by Swarkston and Dunnington, receives Derwent at Wildon; and, so, to Nottingham; thence, to Newark; and, by Gainsborough, to Kingston-upon-Hull, where it takes the name of Humber, and thence falls into the sea; but that the map will best inform you.

VIAT. Know you whence this river Trent derives its name?

PISC. No, indeed; and yet I have heard it often discoursed upon, when some have given its denomination from the forenamed Trentham, though that seems rather a derivative from it; others have said 'tis so called from thirty rivers that fall into it, and there lose their names, which cannot be neither, because it carries that name from its very fountain, before any other rivers fall into it; others derive it from thirty several sorts of fish that breed there; and that is the most likely derivation: but be it how it will, it is doubtless one of the finest rivers in the world, and the most abounding with excellent salmon, and all sorts of delicate fish.

VIAT. Pardon me, sir, for tempting you into this digression; and then proceed to your other rivers, for I am mightily delighted with this discourse.

PISC. It was no interruption, but a very seasonable question; for Trent is not only one of our Derbyshire rivers, but the chief of them, and into which all the rest pay the tribute of their names, which I had, perhaps, forgot to insist upon, being got to the other end of the county, had you not awoke my memory. But I will now proceed. And the next river of note (for I will take them as they lie eastward from us) is the river Wye; I say of note, for we have two lesser betwixt us and it, namely, Lathkin and Bradford; of which Lathkin is, by many degrees, the purest and most transparent stream that I ever yet saw, either at home or abroad, and breeds 'tis said, the reddest and the best trouts in England; but neither of these are to be reputed rivers, being no better than great springs. The river Wye, then, has its source near unto Buxton, a town some ten miles hence, famous for a warm bath, and which you are to ride through in your way to Manchester; a black water, too, at the

fountain; but, by the same reason with Dove, becomes very soon a most delicate, clear river, and breeds admirable trout and grayling, reputed by those who, by living upon its banks, are partial to it, the best of any; and this, running down by Ashford, Bakewell, and Hadden, at a town a little lower, called Rowsly, falls into Derwent, and there loses its name. The next in order is Derwent, a black water, too, and that not only from its fountain, but quite through its progress, not having these crystal springs to wash and cleanse it which the two fore-mentioned have; but abounds with trout and grayling (such as they are) towards its source, and with salmon below; and this river, from the upper and utmost part of the county, where it springs, taking its course by Chatsworth, Darley, Matlock, Derby, Burrow-Ash, and Awberson, falls into Trent at a place called Wildon, and there loses its name. The east side of this county of Derby, is bounded by little inconsiderable rivers, as Awber, Eroways, and the like, scarce worth naming, but trouty, too; and further we are not to enquire. But, sir, I have carried you, as a man may say, by water, till we are now come to the descent of the formidable hill I told you of, at the foot of which runs the river Dove, which I cannot

but love above all the rest; and therefore prepare yourself to be a little frighted.

VIAT. Sir, I see you would fortify me, that I should not shame myself: but I dare follow where you please to lead me; and I see no danger yet; for the descent, methinks, is thus far green, even, and easy.

PISC. You will like it worse presently, when you come to the brow of the hill; and now we are there, what think you?

VIAT. What do I think? Why I think it is the strangest place that ever, sure, men and horses went down; and that (if there be any safety at all) the safest way is to alight.

PISC. I think so too, for you, who are mounted upon a beast not acquainted with these slippery stones; and though I frequently ride down, I will alight, too, to bear you company, and to lead you the way; and, if you please, my man shall lead your horse.

VIAT. Marry, sir, and thank you too, for I am afraid I shall have enough to do to look to myself; and, with my horse in my hand should be in a double fear, both of breaking my neck, and my horse's falling on me; for it is as steep as a penthouse.

Ashbourne from the S.E.

Pisc. To look down from hence it appears so, I confess; but the path winds and turns, and will not be found so troublesome.

Viat. Would I were well down though! Hoist thee! there's one fair 'scape! these stones are so slippery I cannot stand! yet again! I think I were best lay my heels in my neck, and tumble down.

Pisc. If you think your heels will defend your neck, that is the way to be soon at the bottom; but give me your hand at this broad stone, and then the worst is past.

Viat. I thank you, sir, I am now past it, I can go myself. What's here the sign of a bridge? Do you use to travel with wheelbarrows in this country?

Pisc. Not that I ever saw, sir. Why do you ask that question?

Viat. Because this bridge certainly was made for nothing else; why, a mouse can hardly go over it: 'tis not two fingers broad.

Pisc. You are pleasant, and I am glad to see you so: but I have rid over the bridge many a dark night.

Viat. Why, according to the French proverb, and 'tis a good one among a great many of worse sense and sound that language abounds in, *Ce que Dieu garde, est bien gardé*. 'They whom God takes care of are in safe protection:' but, let me tell you, I would not ride over it for a thousand pounds, nor fall off it for two; and yet I think I dare venture on foot, though if you were not by to laugh at me, I should do it on all fours.

PISC. Well, sir, your mirth becomes you, and I am glad to see you safe over; and now you are welcome into Staffordshire.

VIAT. How, Staffordshire! What do I there, trow? there is not a word of Staffordshire in all my direction.

PISC. You see you are betrayed into it; but it shall be in order to something that will make amends; and 'tis but an ill mile or two out of your way.

VIAT. I believe all things, sir, and doubt nothing. Is this your beloved river, Dove? 'Tis clear and swift, indeed, but a very little one.

PISC. You see it here at the worst; we shall come to it anon again, after two miles riding, and so near as to lie upon the very banks.

VIAT. Would we were there once; but I hope we have no more of these Alps to pass over.

PISC. No, no, sir; only this ascent before you, which you see is not very uneasy, and then you will no more quarrel with your way.

VIAT. Well, if ever I come to London (of which many a man there, if he were in my place, would make a question) I will sit down and write my travels; and, like Tom Coriate, print them at my own charge. Pray, what do you call this hill we came down?

PISC. We call it Hanson Toot.

VIAT. Why, farewell, Hanson Toot! I'll no more on thee; I'll go twenty miles about first: Puh! I sweat that my shirt sticks to my back.

PISC. Come, sir, now we are up the hill; and now how do you?

VIAT. Why, very well, I humbly thank you, sir; and warm enough, I assure you. What have we here, a church? As I'm an honest man, a very pretty church? Have you churches in this country, sir?

PISC. You see we have: but had you seen none, why should you make that doubt, sir?

VIAT. Why, if you will not be angry, I'll tell you: I thought myself a stage or two beyond Christendom.

PISC. Come, come, we'll reconcile you to our country before we part with you; if showing you good sport with angling will do it.

VIAT. My respect to you, and that together, may do much, sir; otherwise, to be plain with you, I do not find myself much inclined that way.

PISC. Well, sir, your raillery upon our mountains has brought us almost home; and look you where the same river of Dove has again met us to bid you welcome, and to invite you to a dish of trouts tomorrow.

VIAT. Is this the same we saw at the foot of Penmen-Maure? It is a much finer river here.

PISC. It will appear yet much finer tomorrow. But look you, sir, here appears the house, that is now like to be your inn, for want of a better.

VIAT. It appears on a sudden, but not before 'twas looked for; it stands prettily, and here's wood about it too, but so young, as appears to be of your own planting.

PISC. It is so; will it please you to alight, sir? And now permit me, after all your pains and dangers, to take you in my arms, and to assure you, that you are infinitely welcome.

VIAT. I thank you, sir, and am glad with all my heart I am here; for, in downright truth, I am exceeding weary.

PISC. You will sleep so much the better; you shall presently have a light supper, and to bed. Come, sirs, lay the cloth, and bring what you have presently, and let the gentleman's bed be made ready in the meantime, in my father Walton's chamber; and now, sir, here is my service to you, and once more welcome.

Smith's yard

VIAT. Ay marry, sir, this glass of good sack has refreshed me, and I'll make as bold with your meat, for the trot has got me a good stomach.

PISC. Come, sir, fall to, then, you see my little supper is always ready when I come home; and I'll make no stranger of you.

VIAT. That your meal is so soon ready is a sign your servants know your certain hours, sir; I confess I did not expect it so soon; but now 'tis here, you shall see I will make myself no stranger.

PISC. Much good do your heart, and I thank you for that friendly word: and now, sir, my service to you in a cup of More-Lands ale: for you are now in the More-Lands, but within a spit and a stride of the Peak; fill my friend his glass.

VIAT. Believe me, you have good ale in the More-Lands, far better than that at Ashborn.

PISC. That it may soon be: for Ashborn has (which is a kind of riddle) always in it the best malt, and the worst ale in England. Come, take away, and bring us some pipes, and a bottle of ale, and go to your own suppers. Are you for this diet, sir?

VIAT. Yes, sir, I am for one pipe of tobacco; and I perceive yours is very good by the smell.

PISC. The best I can get in London, I assure you. But, sir, now you have thus far complied with my designs, as to take a troublesome journey into an ill country, only to satisfy me; how long may I hope to enjoy you?

VIAT. Why truly, sir, as long as I conveniently can; and longer, I think, you would not have me.

PISC. Not to your inconvenience by any means, sir: but I see you are weary, and therefore I will presently wait on you to your chamber, where, take counsel of your pillow, and tomorrow resolve me. Here, take the lights; and pray follow them, sir; here you are like to lie; and now I have showed you your lodging, I beseech you, command anything you want, and so I wish you good rest.

VIAT. Good-night, sir.

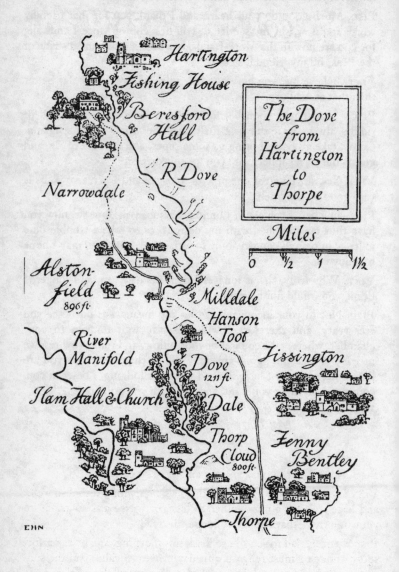

The Dove
from
Hartington
to
Thorpe

Miles

0 ½ 1 1½

Hartington
Fishing House
Beresford Hall
R Dove
Narrowdale
Alstonfield
896 ft.
Milldale
Hanson Toot
River Manifold
Fissington
Ilam Hall & Church
Dove 1211 ft.
Dale
Thorp Cloud 800 ft.
Fenny Bentley
Thorpe

EHN

SECOND DAY

The Fishing House.

CHAPTER III

Conference containing an account of Mr Cotton's Fishing-house

PISC. Good-morrow, sir, what up and drest so early?

VIAT. Yes, sir, I have been drest this half-hour; for I rested so well, and have so great a mind either to take, or to see a trout taken in your fine river, that I could no longer lie abed.

PISC. I am so glad to see you so brisk this morning, and so eager for sport; though I must tell you, this day proves so calm, and the sun rises so bright, as promises no great success to the angler; but, however, we'll try, and, one way or other, we shall sure do something. What will you have to your breakfast, or what will you drink this morning?

VIAT. For breakfast, I never eat any, and for drink am very indifferent; but if you please to call for a glass of ale, I'm for you; and let it be quickly, if you please, for I long to see the little fishing-house you spoke of, and to be at my lesson.

PISC. Well, sir, you see the ale is come without calling; for though I do not know yours, my people know my diet, which is always one glass so soon as I am drest, and no more till dinner: and so my servants have served you.

VIAT. My thanks! And now, if you please, let us look out this fine morning.

PISC. With all my heart. Boy, take the key of my fishing-house, and carry down those two angle-rods in the hall window, thither, with my fish-pannier, pouch, and landing-net; and stay you there till we come. Come, sir, we'll walk after, where, by the way, I expect you should raise all the exceptions against our country you can.

VIAT. Nay, sir, do not think me so ill-natured, nor so uncivil; I only made a little bold with it last night to divert you, and was only in jest.

PISC. You were then in as good earnest as I am now with you: but had you been really angry at it, I could not blame you: for, to say the truth, it is not very taking at first sight. But look you, sir, now you are abroad, does not the sun shine as bright here as in Essex, Middlesex, or Kent, or any of your southern counties?

VIAT. 'Tis a delicate morning, indeed; and I now think this a marvellous pretty place.

PISC. Whether you think so or no, you cannot oblige me more than to say so; and those of my friends who know my humour, and are so kind as to comply with it, usually flatter me that way. But look you, sir, now you are at the brink of the hill, how do you like my river, the vale it winds through like a snake, and the situation of my little fishing-house?

VIAT. Trust me, 'tis all very fine, and the house seems at this distance a neat building.

PISC. Good enough for that purpose; and here is a bowling green too, close by it; so, though I am myself no very good bowler, I am not totally devoted to my own pleasure; but that I have also some regard to other men's. And now, sir, you are come to the door, pray walk in, and there we will sit and talk as long as you please.

VIAT. Stay, what's here over the door? PISCATORIBUS SACRUM.

Thorpe Cloud

Why then, I perceive I have some title here; for I am one of them, though one of the worst; and here below it is the cypher too you speak of, and 'tis prettily contrived. Has my master Walton ever been here to see it, for it seems new built?

PISC. Yes, he saw it cut in the stone before it was set up; but never in the posture it now stands; for the house was but building when he was last here, and not raised so high as the arch of the door. And I am afraid he will not see it yet; for he has lately writ me word, he doubts his coming down this summer; which, I do assure you, was the worst news he could possibly have sent me.

VIAT. Men must sometimes mind their affairs to make more room for their pleasures; and 'tis odds he is as much displeased with the business that keeps him from you, as you are that he comes not. But I am most pleased with this little house of anything I ever saw: it stands in a kind of peninsula too, with a delicate clear river about it. I dare hardly go in, lest I should not like it so well within as without; but, by your leave, I'll try. Why, this is better and better, fine lights, fine wainscoted, and all exceeding neat, with a marble table and all in the middle!

PISC. Enough, sir, enough; I have laid open to you the part where I can worst defend myself, and now you attack me there. Come boy, set two chairs; and whilst I am taking a pipe of tobacco, which is always my breakfast, we will, if you please, talk of some other subject.

VIAT. None fitter, then, sir, for the time and place, than those instructions you promised.

PISC. I begin to doubt, by something I discover in you, whether I am able to instruct you, or no; though, if you are really a stranger to our clear

The Channel
Ashbourne

northern rivers, I still think I can; and therefore, since it is yet too early in the morning at this time of the year, today being but the seventh of March, to cast a fly upon the water, if you will direct me what kind of fishing for a trout I shall read you a lecture on, I am willing and ready to obey you.

VIAT. Why, sir, if you will so far oblige me, and that it may not be too troublesome to you, I would entreat you would run through the whole body of it; and I will not conceal from you that I am so far in love with you, your courtesy, and pretty More-Land seat, as to resolve to stay with you long enough by intervals (for I will not oppress you) to hear all you can say upon that subject.

PISC. You cannot oblige me more than by such a promise; and therefore, without more ceremony, I will begin to tell you, that my father Walton having read to you before, it would look like a presumption in me and, peradventure, would do so in any other man, to pretend to give lessons for angling after him, who, I do really believe, understands as much of it at least as any man in England, did I not preacquaint you, that I am not tempted to it by any vain opinion of myself, that I am able to give you better directions; but having, from my childhood, pursued the recreation of angling in very clear rivers, truly I think by much (some of them at least) the clearest in this kingdom, and the manner of angling here with us, by reason of that exceeding clearness, being something different from the method commonly used in others, which by being not near so bright, admit of stronger tackle, and allow a nearer approach to the stream; I may peradventure give you some instructions that may be of use, even in your own rivers, and shall bring you acquainted with more flies, and show you how to make them, and with what dubbing too, than he has taken notice of in his *Compleat Angler*.

VIAT. I beseech you, sir, do; and if you will lend me your steel, I will light a pipe the while; for that is commonly my breakfast in a morning too.

Okeover Hall & Church

At Thorpe

CHAPTER IV

Of Angling for Trout or Grayling at the 'Top', at the 'Middle' and the 'Bottom'

PISC. Why then, sir, to begin methodically, as a master in any art should do (and I will not deny but that I think myself a master in this) I shall divide angling for trout or grayling into these three ways: *at the top, at the bottom, in the middle.* Which three ways, though they are all of them (as I shall hereafter endeavour to make it appear) in some sort common to both those kinds of fish; yet are they not so generally and absolutely so, but that they will necessarily require a distinction, which, in due place, I will also give you.

That which we call angling at the top is with a fly; at the bottom, with a ground-bait; in the middle, with a minnow or ground-bait.

Angling at the top is of two sorts; *with a quick fly,* or *with an artificial fly.*

That we call angling at the bottom is also of two sorts; *by hand,* or *with a cork or float.*

That we call angling in the middle is also of two sorts; *with a minnow for a trout, or with a ground-bait for a grayling.*

Of all which several sorts of angling, I will, if you can have the patience to hear me, give you the best account I can.

Viat. The trouble will be yours, and mine the pleasure and the obligation: I beseech you therefore to proceed.

Pisc. Why then, first of fly-fishing.

Dovedale from Thorpe Cloud

Ashbourne

CHAPTER V

Of Fly-fishing and Fly-making

Pisc. Fly-fishing, or fishing at the top, is, as I said before, of two sorts; *with a natural and living fly, or with an artificial and made fly.*

First, then, of the natural fly; of which we generally use but two sorts; and those but in the two months of May and June only: namely, the green drake and the stone-fly; though I have made use of a third that way, called the camlet-fly, with very good success, for grayling, but never saw it angled with by any other after this manner, my master only excepted, who died many years ago, and was one of the best anglers that ever I knew.

These are to be angled with, with a short line, not much more than half the length of your rod, if the air be still; or with a longer very near, or all out, as long as your rod, if you have any wind to carry it from you. And this way of fishing we call daping, dabbing, or dibbing; wherein you are always to have your line flying before you up or down the river, as the wind serves, and to angle as near as you can to the bank of the same side whereon you stand, though where you see a fish rise near you, you may guide your quick fly over him, whether in the middle, or on the contrary side; and if you are pretty well out of sight, either by kneeling or the interposition of a bank, or bush, you may almost be sure to raise, and take him too, if it be presently done; the fish will, otherwise, peradventure be removed to some other place, if it be in the still deeps, where he is always in motion, and roving up and down to look for prey, though, in a stream, you may always almost, especially if there be a good stone near, find him in the same place. Your line ought in this case to be three good hairs next the hook, both by reason you are in this kind of angling to expect the biggest fish, and also that wanting length to give him line after he is struck, you must be forced to tug for it; to which I will also add, that not an inch of your line being to be suffered to touch the water in dibbing, it may be allowed to be the stronger. I should now give you a description of those flies, their shape and colour, and then give you an account of their breeding, and withal show you how to keep and use them; but shall defer them to their proper place and season.

VIAT. In earnest, sir, you discourse very rationally of this affair, and I am glad to find myself mistaken in you; for in truth I did not expect so much from you.

PISC. Nay, sir, I can tell you a great deal more than this, and will conceal nothing from you. But I must now come to the second way of angling at the top, which is with an artificial fly, which also I will show you how to make before I have done, but first shall acquaint you, that with this you are to angle with a line longer by a yard and a half, or sometimes two yards, than your rod; and with both this and the other, in a still day in the streams, in a breeze that curls the water in the still deeps, where (excepting in May and June, that the best trouts will lie in shallow streams to watch for prey, and even then too) you are like to hit the best fish.

For the length of your rod, you are always to be governed by the breadth of the river you shall choose to angle at; and for a trout-river one of five or six yards long is commonly enough; and longer (though never so neatly and artificially made) it ought not to be, if you intend to fish at ease; and if otherwise, where lies the sport?

Of these, the best that ever I saw are made in Yorkshire, which are all of one piece; that is to say, of several, six, eight, ten or twelve pieces, so neatly pieced and tied together with fine thread below, and silk above, as to make it taper like a switch, and to ply with a true bent to your hand; and these are too light, being made of fir-wood for two or three lengths nearest to the hand, and of other wood nearer to the top, that a man might very easily manage the longest of them that ever I saw with one hand; and these, when you have given over angling for a season, being taken to pieces, and laid up in some dry place, may afterwards be set together again in their former postures, and will be as straight, sound, and good as the first hour they were made; and being laid in oil and colour, according to your master Walton's direction, will last many years.

The length of your line, to a man that knows how to handle his rod, and to cast it, is no manner of encumbrance, excepting in woody places, and in landing of a fish, which everyone that can afford to angle for pleasure, has somebody to do for him; and the length of line is a mighty advantage to the fishing at distance; and to fish fine, and far off, is the first and principal rule for trout-angling.

Your line in this case should never be less, nor ever exceed two hairs next to the hook; for one (though some, I know, will pretend to more art than their fellows) is indeed too few, the least accident, with the finest hand, being sufficient to break it: but he that cannot kill a trout of twenty inches long with two, in a river clear of wood and weeds, as this and some others of ours are, deserves not the name of an angler.

Now to have your whole line as it ought to be, two of the first lengths nearest the hook should be of two hairs a-piece; the next three lengths above them of three; the next three above them of four; and so of five, and six, and seven, to the very top: by which means your rod and tackle will, in a manner, be taper from your very hand to your hook; your line will fall much better and straighter, and cast your fly to any certain place, to which the hand and eye shall direct it, with less weight and violence, than would otherwise circle the water, and fright away the fish.

In casting your line, do it always before you, and so that your fly may first fall upon the water, and as little of your line with it as is possible; though if the wind be stiff, you will then of necessity be compelled to drown a good part of your line to keep your fly in the water: and in casting your fly, you must aim at the further or nearer bank as the wind serves your turn, which also will be with and against you, on the same side, several times in an hour, as the river winds in its course, and you will be forced to angle up and down by turns accordingly; but are to endeavour, as much as you can, to have the wind, evermore, on your back. And always be sure to stand as far off the bank as your length will give you leave when you throw to the contrary side; though when the wind will not permit you so to

Tissington

E·H·N·

do, and that you are constrained to angle on the same side whereon you stand, you must then stand on the very brink of the river, and cast your fly to the utmost length of your rod and line, up or down the river, as the gale serves.

It only remains, touching your line, to enquire whether your two hairs next to the hook are better twisted or open; and for that I should declare that I think the open way the better, because it makes less show in the water, but that I have found an inconvenience, or two, or three, that have made me almost weary of that way; of which, one is, that, without dispute, they are not so strong open as twisted; another, that they are not easily to be fastened of so exact an equal length in the arming that the one will not cause the other to bag, by which means a man has but one hair upon the matter to trust to; and the last is that these loose flying hairs are not only more apt to catch upon every twig or bent they meet with; but, moreover, the hook, in falling upon the water, will, very often, rebound and fly back betwixt the hairs, and there stick (which, in a rough water especially, is not presently to be discerned by the angler), so as the point of the hook shall stand reversed; by which means your fly swims backward, makes a much greater circle in the water, and till taken home to you, and set right, will never raise any fish, or, if it should, I am sure, but by a very extraordinary chance, can hit none.

Having done with both these ways of fishing at the top, the length of your rod, and line and all, I am next to teach you how to make a fly; and afterwards of what dubbing you are to make the several flies I shall hereafter name to you.

In making a fly then (which is not a hackle or palmer-fly, for of those, and their several kinds, we shall have occasion to speak every month in the year), you are first to hold your hook fast betwixt the forefinger and thumb of your left hand, with the back of the shank upwards, and the point towards your finger's end; then take a strong small silk, of the colour of the fly you intend to make, wax it well with wax of the same colour too (to which end you are always, by the way, to have wax of all colours about you), and draw it betwixt your finger and thumb, to the head of the shank, and then whip it twice or thrice about the bare hook, which you must know is done, both to prevent slipping, and also that the shank of the hook may not cut the hairs of your towght, which sometimes it will otherwise do; which being done, take your line, and draw it likewise betwixt your finger and thumb, holding the hook so fast as only to suffer it to pass by, until you have the knot of your towght almost to the middle of the shank of your hook, on the inside of it; then whip your silk twice or thrice about both hook and line, as hard as the strength of the silk will permit; which being done, strip the feather for the wings proportionable to the bigness of your fly, placing that side downwards which grew uppermost before, upon the back of the hook, leaving so much only as to serve for the length of the wing of the point of the plume, lying reversed from the end of the shank upwards; then whip your silk twice or thrice about the root-end of

Below Thorpe Cloud

the feather, hook, and towght; which being done, clip off the root-end of the feather close by the arming, and then whip the silk fast and firm about the hook and towght, until you come to the bend of the hook, but not further (as you do at London, and so make a very unhandsome, and, in plain English, a very unnatural and shapeless fly); which being done, cut away the end of your towght, and fasten it, and then take your dubbing, which is to make the body of your fly, as much as you think convenient, and holding it lightly with your hook betwixt the finger and thumb of your left hand, take your silk with the right, and twisting it betwixt the finger and thumb of that hand, the dubbing will spin itself about the silk, which when it has done, whip it about the armed hook backward, till you come to the setting on of the wings, and then take the feather for the wings, and divide it equally into two parts, and turn them back towards the bend of the hook, the one on the one side and the other on the other of the shank, holding them fast in that posture betwixt the forefinger and thumb of your left hand; which done, warp them so down as to stand and slope towards the bend of the hook; and having warped up to the end of the shank, hold the fly fast betwixt the finger and thumb of your left hand, and then take the silk betwixt the finger and thumb of your right hand, and where the warping ends, pinch or nip it with your thumb-nail against your finger, and strip away the remainder of your dubbing from the silk, and then with the bare silk whip it once or twice about, make the wings to stand in due order, fasten, and cut it off; after which, with the point of a needle, raise up the dubbing gently from the warp, twitch off the superfluous hairs of your dubbing; leave the wings of an equal length (your fly will never else swim true), and the work is done. And this way of making a fly (which is certainly the best of all other) was taught me by a kinsman of mine, one Captain Henry Jackson, a near neighbour, an admirable fly-angler, by many degrees the best fly-maker that ever I yet met with. And now that I have told you how a fly is to be made, you shall presently see me make one, with which you may peradventure take a trout this morning, notwithstanding the unlikeliness of the day; for it is now nine of the clock, and fish will begin to rise, if they will rise today: I will walk along by you, and look on, and after dinner I will proceed in my lecture of fly-fishing.

VIAT. I confess I long to be at the river, and yet I could sit here all day to hear you: but some of the one, and some of the other, will do well; and I have a mighty ambition to take a trout in your river Dove.

PISC. I warrant you shall: I would not for more than I will speak of but you should, seeing I have so extolled my river to you: nay, I will keep you here a month, but you shall have one good day of sport before you go.

VIAT. You will find me, I doubt, too tractable that way; for in good earnest, if business would give me leave, and that it were fit, I could find in my heart to stay with you for ever.

PISC. I thank you, sir, for that kind expression; and now let me look out my things to make this fly.

CHAPTER VI

A Practical Lesson in Fly-fishing for Trout and Grayling

PISC. Boy, come, give me my dubbing bag here presently; and now, sir, since I find you so honest a man, I will make no scruple to lay open my treasure before you.

VIAT. Did ever anyone see the like! What a heap of trumpery is here! Certainly never an angler in Europe has his shop half so well furnished as you have.

PISC. You, perhaps, may think now, that I rake together this trumpery, as you call it, for show only, to the end that such as see it (which are not many I assure you) may think me a great master in the art of angling: but, let me tell you, here are some colours (as contemptible as they seem here) that are very hard to be got; and scarce any one of them which, if it should be lost, I should not miss, and be concerned about the loss of it too, once in the year. But look you, sir, amongst all these I will choose out these two colours only, of which this is bear's hair, this darker, no great matter what; but I am sure I have killed a great deal of fish with it; and with one or both of these you shall take trout or grayling this very day, notwithstanding all disadvantages, or my art shall fail me.

VIAT. You promise comfortably, and I have a great deal of reason to believe everything you say; but I wish the fly were made that we were at it.

PISC. That will not be long in doing: and pray observe then. You see first how I hold my hook, and thus I begin. Look you, here are my first two or three whips about the bare hook; thus I join hook and line; thus I put on my wings; thus I twirl and lap on my dubbing; thus I work it up towards the head; thus I part my wings; thus I nip my superfluous dubbing from my silk; thus fasten; thus trim and adjust my fly; and there's a fly made; and now how do you like it?

VIAT. In earnest, admirably well, and it resembles a fly: but we about London make the bodies of our flies both much bigger and longer, so long as even almost to the very beard of the hook.

PISC. I know it very well, and had one of those flies given me by an honest gentleman, who came with my father Walton to give me a visit; which (to tell you the truth) I hung in my parlour window to laugh at: but, sir, you know the proverb, 'Those who go to Rome must do as they at Rome do;' and believe me, you must here make your flies after this fashion, or you will take no fish. Come, I will look you out a line, and you shall put it on, and try it. There, sir, I think you are fitted; and now beyond the further end of the walk you shall begin: I see, at that bend of the water above, the air crisps the water a little: knit your line first here, and then go up thither, and see what you can do.

VIAT. Did you see that, sir?

PISC. Yes, I saw the fish: and he saw you too, which made him turn short. You must fish further off, if you intend to have any sport here; this is no New River, let me tell you. That was a good trout, believe me: did you touch him?

VIAT. No, I would I had, we would not have parted so. Look you, there was another; this is an excellent fly.

PISC. That fly I am sure would kill fish, if the day were right; but they only chew at it, I see, and will not take it. Come, sir, let us return back to the fishing-house; this still water, I see, will not do our business today: you shall now, if you please, make a fly yourself, and

Milldale

try what you can do in the streams with that; and I know a trout taken with a fly of your own making will please you better than twenty with one of mine. Give me that bag again, sirrah; look you, sir, there is a hook, towght, silk, and a feather for the wings; be doing with those, and I will look you out a dubbing that I think will do.

VIAT. That is a very little hook.

PISC. That may serve to inform you that it is for a very little fly, and you must make your wings accordingly; for as the case stands, it must be a little fly, and a very little one too, that must do your business. Well said! believe me, you shift your fingers very handsomely; I doubt I have taken upon me to teach my master. So here's your dubbing now.

VIAT. This dubbing is very black.

PISC. It appears so in hand; but step to the door and hold it up betwixt your eye and the sun, and it will appear a shining red; let me tell you, never a man in England can discern the true colour of a dubbing any way but that, and therefore choose always to make your flies on such a bright sunshine day as this, which also you may the better do, because it is worth nothing to fish in: here, put it on, and be sure to make the body of your fly as slender as you can. Very good! upon my word you have made a marvellous handsome fly.

VIAT. I am very glad to hear it; 'tis the first that ever I made of this kind in my life.

PISC. Away, away! you are a doctor at it; but I will not commend you too much, lest I make you proud. Come, put it on, and you shall now go downward to some streams betwixt the rocks below the little footbridge you see there, and try your fortune. Take heed of slipping into the water as you follow me under this rock: so, now you are over, and now throw in.

VIAT. This is a fine stream indeed: there's one! I have him.

PISC. And a precious catch you have of him; pull him out! I see you have a tender hand: this is a diminutive gentleman, e'en throw him in again, and let him grow till he be more worthy your anger.

VIAT. Pardon me, sir, all's fish that comes to the hook with me now. Another.

PISC. And of the same standing.

VIAT. I see I shall have good sport now: another! and a grayling. Why, you have fish here at will.

PISC. Come, come, cross the bridge, and go down the other side lower, where you will find finer streams and better sport, I hope, than this. Look you, sir, here is a fine stream now, you have length enough, stand a little further off, let me entreat you, and do but fish this stream like an artist, and peradventure a good fish may fall to your share. How now! what! is all gone?

VIAT. No, but I touched him; but that was a fish worth taking.

PISC. Why now, let me tell you you lost that fish by your own fault, and through your own eagerness and haste; for you are never to offer to strike a good fish, if he do not strike himself, till you first see him turn his head after he has taken your fly, and then you can

In Dovedale

never strain your tackle in the striking, if you strike with any manner of moderation. Come, throw in once again, and fish me this stream by inches; for I assure you here are very good fish; both trout and grayling lie here; and at that great stone on the other side, 'tis ten to one a good trout gives you the meeting.

VIAT. I have him now, but he is gone down towards the bottom: I cannot see what he is, yet he should be a good fish by his weight; but he makes no great stir.

PISC. Why then, by what you say, I dare venture to assure you 'tis a grayling, who is one of the deadest-hearted fishes in the world, and the bigger he is, the more easily taken. Look you, now you see him plain; I told you what he was: bring hither that landing-net, boy: and now, sir, he is your own; and believe me a good one, sixteen inches long, I warrant him: I have taken none such this year.

VIAT. I never saw a grayling before look so black.

PISC. Did you not? Why then, let me tell you, that you never saw one before in right season; for then a grayling is very black about his head, gills, and down his back, and has his belly of a dark grey, dappled with black spots, as you see this is; and I am apt to conclude that from thence he derives his name of umber. Though I must tell you this fish is past his prime, and begins to decline, and was in better season at Christmas than he is now. But move on: for it grows towards dinner-time; and there is a very great and fine stream below, under that rock, that fills the deepest pool in all the river, where you are almost sure of a good fish.

VIAT. Let him come, I'll try a fall with him. But I had thought that the grayling had been always in season with the trout, and had come in and gone out with him.

PISC. Oh, no! assure yourself a grayling is a winter fish; but such a one as would deceive any but such as know him very well indeed; for his flesh, even in his worst season, is so firm, and will so easily calver, that in plain truth he is very good meat at all times; but in his perfect season (which, by the way, none but an overgrown grayling will ever be), I think him so good a fish, as to be little inferior to the best trout that ever I tasted in my life.

VIAT. Here's another skipjack; and I have raised five or six more at least while you were speaking. Well, go thy way, little Dove! thou art the finest river that ever I saw, and the fullest of fish. Indeed, sir, I like it so well that I am afraid you will be troubled with me once a year, so long as we two live.

PISC. I am afraid I shall not, sir; but were you once here a May or a June, if good sport would tempt you, I should then expect you would sometimes see me; for you would then say it were a fine river indeed, if you had once seen the sport at the height.

VIAT. Which I will do, if I live, and that you please to give me leave. There was one, and there another.

PISC. And all this in a strange river, and with a fly of his own making! why, what a dangerous man are you!

VIAT. I, sir: but who taught me? and as Damaetas says by his man Dorus, so you may say by me,

> If any man such praises have,
> What then have I, that taught the knave!

But what have we got here? a rock springing up in the middle of the river! this is one of the oddest sights that ever I saw.

PISC. Why, sir, from that pike that you see standing up there distant from the rock, this is called Pike Pool: and young Mr Izaak Walton was so pleased with it, as to draw it in landscape, in black and white, in a blank book I have at home, as he has done several prospects of my house also, which I keep for a memorial of his favour, and will show you when we come up to dinner.

VIAT. Has young master Izaak Walton been here, too?

PISC. Yes, marry has he, sir, and that again and again, too, and in France since, and at Rome, and at Venice, and I can't tell where: but I intend to ask him a great many hard questions so soon as I can see him, which will be, God willing, next month. In the meantime, sir, to come to this fine stream at the head of this great pool, you must venture over these slippery, cobbling stones; believe me, sir, there you were nimble, or else you had been down; but now you are got over, look to yourself; for, on my word, if a fish rise here, he is like to be such a one as will endanger your tackle: how now!

VIAT. I think you have such command here over the fishes, that you can raise them by your word, as they say conjurers can do spirits, and afterward make them do what you bid them; for here's a trout has taken my fly, I had rather have lost a crown. What luck's this! he was a lovely fish, and turned up a side like a salmon.

PISC. O, sir, this is a war where you sometimes win, and must sometimes expect to lose. Never concern yourself for the loss of your fly, for ten to one I teach you to make a better. Who's that calls?

SERV. Sir, will it please you to come to dinner?

PISC. We come. You hear, sir, we are called, and now take your choice, whether you will climb this steep hill before you, from the top of which you will go directly into the house, or back again over these stepping-stones, and about by the bridge.

VIAT. Nay, sure, the nearest way is best; at least my stomach tells me so; and I am now so well acquainted with your rocks, that I fear them not.

PISC. Come, then, follow me; and so soon as we have dined, we will down again to the little house, where I will begin at the place I left off about fly-fishing, and read you another lecture; for I have a great deal more to say upon that subject.

VIAT. The more the better; I could never have met with a more obliging master, my first excepted; nor such sport can all the rivers about London ever afford, as is to be found in this pretty river.

PISC. You deserve to have better, both because I see you are willing to take pains, and for liking this little so well; and better I hope to show you before we part.

Hanson Grange

CHAPTER VII

On Artificial Flies for the Months of January, February, March, April and May; showing also how to dib or dape with the Green-drake or May-fly and how to make that famous Fly artificially

VIAT. Come, sir, having now well dined, and being again set in your little house, I will now challenge your promise, and entreat you to proceed in your instruction for fly-fishing; which that you may be the better encouraged to do, I will assure you that I have not lost, I think, one syllable of what you have told me; but very well retain all your directions, both for the rod, line, and making a fly; and now desire an account of the flies themselves.

PISC. Why, sir, I am ready to give it you, and shall have the whole afternoon to do it in, if nobody come in to interrupt us; for you must know (besides the unfitness of the day) that the afternoons, so early in March, signify very little for angling with a fly, though with a minnow, or a worm, something might (I confess) be done.

To begin, then, where I left off, my father Walton tells us but of twelve artificial flies only, to angle with at the top, and gives their names; of which some are common with us here; and I think I guess at most of them by his description, and I believe they all breed and are taken in our rivers, though we do not make them either of the same dubbing or fashion. And it may be in the rivers about London, which I presume he has most frequented, and where 'tis likely he has done most execution, there is not much notice taken of many more: but we are acquainted with several others here, though perhaps I may reckon some of his by other names too; but if I do, I shall make you amends by an addition to his catalogue. And although the forenamed great master in the art of angling (for so in truth he is) tells you that no man should, in honesty, catch a trout in the middle of March, yet I hope he will give a man leave sooner to take a grayling, which, as I told you, is in the dead months in his best season; and do assure you (which I remember by a very remarkable token), I did once take, upon the sixth day of December, one, and only one, of the biggest graylings, and the best in season, that ever I yet saw or tasted; and do usually take trouts too, and with a fly, not only before the middle of this month, but almost every year in February, unless it be a very ill spring indeed; and have sometimes in January, so early as New-year's tide, and in frost and snow, taken grayling in a warm sunshine day for an hour or two about noon; and to fish for him with a grub, it is then the best time of all.

I shall therefore begin my fly-fishing with that month (though I must confess very few begin so soon, and that such as are so fond of the sport as to embrace all opportunities, can rarely in that month find a day fit for their purpose); and tell you, that upon my knowledge these flies in a warm sun, for an hour or two in the day, are certainly taken.

JANUARY

1. A red brown, with wings of the male of a mallard almost white: the dubbing of the tail of a black long-coated cur, such as they commonly make muffs of; for the hair on the tail of such a dog dies and turns to a red-brown, but the hair of a smooth-coated dog of the same colour will not do, because it will not die, but retains its natural colour, and this fly is taken in a warm sun, this whole month through.

Alstonfield Manor House

2. There is also a very little bright dun gnat, as little as can possibly be made, so little as never to be fished with, with above one hair next the hook; and this is to be made of a mixed dubbing of marten's fur, and the white of a hare's scut; with a very white and small wing; and 'tis no great matter how fine you fish, for nothing will rise in this month, but a grayling; and of them I never, at this season, saw any taken with a fly, of above a foot long in my life; but of little ones about the bigness of a smelt, in a warm day, and a glowing sun, you may take enough with these two flies, and they are both taken the whole month through.

FEBRUARY

1. Where the red-brown of the last month ends, another almost of the same colour begins, with this saving, that the dubbing of this must be of something a blacker colour, and both of them wrapped on with red silk. The dubbing that should make this fly, and that is the truest colour, is to be got off the black spot off a hog's ear: not that a black spot in any part of the hog will not afford the same

colour, but that the hair in that place is, by many degrees, softer, and more fit for the purpose. His wing must be as the other; and this kills all this month, and is called the lesser red-brown.

2. This month, also, a plain hackle, or palmer-fly, made with a rough black body, either of black spaniel's fur, or the whirl of an ostrich feather, and the red hackle of a capon over all, will kill, and, if the weather be right, make very good sport.

3. Also, a lesser hackle, with a black body, also silver twist over that, and a red feather over all, will fill your pannier, if the month be open, and not bound up in ice and snow, with very good fish; but, in case of a frost and snow, you are to angle only with the smallest gnats, browns, and duns you can make; and with those are only to expect graylings no bigger than sprats.

4. In this month, upon a whirling round water, we have a great hackle, the body black, and wrapped with a red feather of a capon untrimmed; that is, the whole length of the hackle staring out (for we sometimes barb the hackle-feather short all over; sometimes barb it only a little, and sometimes barb it close underneath), leaving the whole length of the feather on the top or back of the fly, which makes it swim better, and, as occasion serves, kills very great fish.

5. We make use, also, in this month, of another great hackle, the body black, and ribbed over with gold twist, and a red feather over all; which also does great execution.

6. Also a great dun, made with dun bear's hair, and the wings of the grey feather of a mallard near unto his tail; which is absolutely the best fly can be thrown upon a river this month, and with which an angler shall have admirable sport.

7. We have also this month the great blue dun, the dubbing of the bottom of bear's hair next to the roots, mixed with a little blue camlet, the wings of a dark grey feather of a mallard.

8. We have also this month a dark-brown, the dubbing of the brown hair off the flank of a brended cow, and the wings of the grey drake's feather.

And note, that these several hackles, or palmer-flies, are some for one water and one sky, and some for another; and, according to the change of those, we alter their size and colour; and note also, that both in this, and all other months of the year, when you do not certainly know what fly is taken, or cannot see any fish to rise, you are then to put on a small hackle, if the water be clear, or a bigger if

Alstonfield ch:

something dark, until you have taken one; and then thrusting your finger through his gills, to pull out his gorge, which being opened with your knife, you will then discover what fly is taken, and may fit yourself accordingly.

For the making of a hackle, or palmer-fly, my father Walton has already given you sufficient direction.

MARCH

For this month you are to use all the same hackles and flies with the other; but you are to make them less.

1. We have, besides, for this month, a little dun, called a whirling dun (though it is not the whirling dun, indeed, which is one of the best flies we have); and for this the dubbing must be of the bottom fur of a squirrel's tail; and the wing of the grey feather of a drake.

2. Also a bright brown; the dubbing either of the brown of a spaniel, or that of a red cow's flank, with a grey wing.

3. Also a whitish dun; made of the roots of camel's hair; and the wings, of the grey feather of a mallard.

4. There is also for this month a fly called the thorn tree fly: the dubbing an absolute black, mixed with eight or ten hairs of Isabella-coloured mohair; the body as little as can be made; and the wings of a bright mallard's feather. An admirable fly, and in great repute amongst us for a killer.

5. There is, besides this, another blue dun, the dubbing of which it is made being thus to be got. Take a small-tooth comb, and with it comb the neck of a black greyhound, and the down that sticks in the teeth will be the finest blue that ever you saw. The wings of this fly can hardly be too white, and he is taken about the tenth of this month, and lasteth till the four-and-twentieth.

6. From the tenth of this month also, till towards the end, is taken a little black gnat; the dubbing either of the fur of a black water-dog, or the down of a young black water-coot, the wing of the male of a mallard as white as may be, the body as little as you possibly can make it, and the wings as short as his body.

7. From the sixteenth of this month also to the end of it we use a bright brown; the dubbing for which is to be had out of a skinner's lime-pits, and of the hair of an abortive calf, which the lime will turn to be so bright as to shine like gold; for the wings of this fly, the feather of a brown hen is best: which fly is also taken till the tenth of April.

APRIL

All the same hackles and flies that were taken in March will be taken in this month also, with this distinction only concerning the flies, that all the browns be lapped with red silk, and the duns with yellow.

1. To these a small bright brown, made of spaniel's fur, with a light grey wing; in a bright day, and a clear water, is very well taken.

2. We have too a little dark brown, the dubbing of that colour, and some violet camlet mixed, and the wing, of the grey feather of a mallard.

3. From the sixth of this month to the tenth, we have also a fly called the violet fly, made of a dark violet stuff, with the wings of the grey feather of a mallard.

4. About the twelfth of this month comes in the fly called the whirling dun, which is taken every day, about the midtime of day, all this month through, and, by fits, from thence to the end of June, and is commonly made of the down of the fox-cub, which is of an ash colour at the roots next the skin, and ribbed about with yellow silk; the wings, of the pale grey feather of a mallard.

5. There is also a yellow dun, the dubbing of camel's hair, and yellow camlet or wool, mixed, and a white-grey wing.

6. There is also this month

Hanson Toot

another little brown, besides that mentioned before, made with a very slender body, the dubbing of dark brown and violet camlet, mixed, and a grey wing, which, though the direction for the making be near the other, is yet another fly, and will take when the other will not, especially in a bright day and a clear water.

7. About the twentieth of this month comes in a fly called the horse-flesh fly, the dubbing of which is a blue mohair, with pink coloured and red tammy mixed, a light coloured wing, and a dark brown head. This fly is taken best in an evening, and kills from two hours before sunset till twilight, and is taken the month through.

MAY

And now, sir, that we are entering into the month of May, I think it requisite to beg not only your attention, but also your best patience; for I must now be a little tedious with you, and dwell upon this month longer than ordinary; which, that you may the better endure, I must tell you, this month deserves, and requires to be insisted on; forasmuch as it alone, and the next following, afford more pleasure to the fly-angler than all the rest; and here it is, that you are to expect an account of the green-drake, and stone-fly, promised you so long ago, and some others that are peculiar to this month, and part of the month following; and that (though not so great either in bulk, or name) do yet stand in competition with the two before-named; and so, that it is yet undecided amongst the anglers, to which of the pretenders to the title of the May-fly it does properly and duly belong; neither dare I (where so many of the learned in this art of angling are got in dispute about the controversy) take upon me to determine; but I think I ought to have a vote amongst them, and according to that privilege, shall give you my free opinion; and peradventure when I have told you all, you may incline to think me in the right.

VIAT. I have so great a deference to your judgement in these matters, that I must always be of your opinion; and the more you speak, the faster I grow to my attention, for I can never be weary of hearing you upon this subject.

PISC. Why, that's encouragement enough; and now prepare yourself for a tedious lecture; but I will first begin with the flies of less esteem (though almost anything will take a trout in May), that I may afterwards insist the longer upon those of greater note and reputation; know therefore, that the first fly we take notice of in this month, is called the turkey-fly;

1. The dubbing ravelled out of some blue stuff, and lapt about with yellow silk; the wings of a grey mallard's feather.

2. Next, a great hackle or palmer fly, with a yellow body ribbed with gold twist, and large wings, of a mallard's feather dyed yellow, with a red capon's hackle over all.

The Pike Pool

3. Then a black fly, the dubbing of a black spaniel's fur; and the wings, of a grey mallard's feather.

4. After that, a light brown, with a slender body, the dubbing twirled upon small red silk, and raised with the point of a needle, that the ribs or rows of silk may appear through; the wings, of the grey feather of the mallard.

5. Next, a little dun, the dubbing of a bear's dun whirled upon yellow silk; the wings, of the grey feather of a mallard.

6. Then a white gnat, with a pale wing, and a black head.

7. There is also in this month, a fly called the peacock fly; the body made of a whirl of a peacock's feather, with a red head; and wings of a mallard's feather.

8. We have then another very killing fly, known by the name of the dun-cut; the dubbing of which is a bear's dun, with a little blue and yellow mixed with it; a large dun wing, and two horns at the head, made of the hairs of a squirrel's tail.

9. The next, is a cow-lady, a little fly; the body of a peacock's feather; the wing, of a red feather, or strips of the red hackle of a cock.

10. We have then, the cow-turd-fly: the dubbing, light brown and yellow mixed; the wing, the dark grey feather of a mallard. And note, that besides these above-mentioned, all the same hackles and flies, the hackles only brighter, and the flies smaller, that are taken in April, will also be taken this month, as also all browns and duns: and now I come to my stone-fly and green-drake, which are the matadores for trout and grayling, and in their season kill more fish in our Derbyshire rivers than all the rest, past and to come, in the whole year besides.

But first I am to tell you, that we have four several flies which contend for the title of the May-fly; namely,

Beresford Hall

E·H·N

The Green-drake,
The Stone-fly,
The Black-fly, and
The little yellow May-fly.

And all these have their champions and advocates to dispute and plead their priority; though I do not understand why the two last named should; the first two having so manifestly the advantage, both in their beauty, and the wonderful execution they do in their season.

11. Of these the green-drake comes in about the twentieth of this month, or betwixt that and the latter end (for they are sometimes sooner, and sometimes later, according to the quality of the year); but never well taken till towards the end of this month, and the beginning of June. The stone-fly comes much sooner, so early as the middle of April; but is never well taken till towards the middle of May, and continues to kill much longer than the green-drake stays with us, so long as to the end almost of June; and indeed, so long as there are any of them to be seen upon the water; and sometimes in an artificial fly, and late at night, or before sunrise in the morning, longer.

Now both these flies (and I believe many others, though I think not all) are certainly, and demonstratively bred in the very rivers where they are taken: our cadis or cod-bait which lie under stones in the bottom of the water, most of them turning into those two flies, and being gathered in the husk, or crust, near the time of their maturity, are very easily known and distinguished, and are, of all other, the most remarkable, both for their size, as being of all other the biggest (the shortest of them being a full inch long or more), and for the execution they do, the trout and grayling being much more greedy of them than of any others; and indeed the trout never feeds fat, nor comes into his perfect season, till these flies come in.

Of these the green-drake never discloses from his husk, till he be first there grown to full maturity, body, wings, and all; and then he creeps out of his cell, but with his wings so crimpt and ruffled, by being prest together in that narrow room, that they are, for some hours, totally useless to him; by which means he is compelled either to creep upon the flags, sedges, and blades of grass (if his first rising from the bottom of the water be near the banks of the river) till the air and sun stiffen and smooth them; or, if his first appearance above water happened to be in the middle, he then lies upon the surface of the water like a ship at hull (for his feet are totally useless to him there, and he cannot creep upon the water as the stone-fly can) until his wings have got stiffness to fly with, if by some trout or grayling he be not taken in the interim (which ten to one he is), and then his wings stand high, and closed exact upon his back, like the butterfly, and his motion in flying is the same. His body is, in some, of a paler, in others, of a darker yellow (for they are not all exactly of a colour), ribbed with rows of green, long, slender, and growing sharp towards the tail, at the end of which he has three long small whisks of a very dark colour, almost black, and his tail turns up towards his back like a mallard; from whence, questionless he has his name of the green-drake. These (as I think I told you before) we commonly dape, or dibble with, and having gathered great store of them into a long draw-box, with holes in the cover to give them air (where also they will continue fresh and vigorous a night or more), we take them out thence by the wings, and bait them thus upon the hook. We first take one (for we commonly fish with two of them at a time), and putting the point of the hook into the thickest part of his body, under one of his wings, run it directly through, and out at the other side, leaving him spitted cross upon the hook; and then taking the other, put him on after the same manner, but with his head the contrary way; in which posture they will live upon the hook, and play with their wings, for a quarter of an hour, or more: but you must have a care to keep their wings dry, both from the water, and also that your fingers be not wet when you take them out to bait them, for then your bait is spoiled.

Having now told you how to angle with this fly alive, I am now to tell you next how to make an artificial fly, that will so perfectly resemble him, as to be taken in a rough windy day, when no flies can lie upon the water, nor are to be found about the banks and sides of the river, to a wonder; and with which you shall certainly kill the best trout and grayling in the river.

The artificial green-drake, then, is made upon a large hook, the dubbing, camel's hair, bright bear's hair, the soft down that is combed from a hog's bristles, and yellow camlet, well mixed together; the body long, and ribbed about with green silk, or rather yellow, waxed with green wax; the whisks of the tail, of the long hairs of sables, or fitchet; and the wings, of a white-grey feather of a mallard, dyed yellow, which is also to be dyed thus:

Take the root of a barbary tree, and shave it, and put to it woody viss, with as much alum as a walnut, and boil your feathers in it with rain water; and they will be of a very fine yellow.

I have now done with the green-drake, excepting to tell you, that he is taken at all hours during his season, whilst there is any day

The Fishing House

E·H·N·

upon the sky; and with a made-fly I once took, ten days after he was absolutely gone, in a cloudy day, after a shower, and in a whistling wind, five-and-thirty very great trouts and graylings, betwixt five and eight of the clock in the evening, and had no less than five or six flies, with three good hairs a-piece, taken from me in despite of my heart, besides.

12. I should now come next to the stone-fly, but there is another gentleman in my way, that must of necessity come in between, and that is the grey-drake, which in all shapes and dimensions is perfectly the same with the other, but quite almost of another colour, being of a paler and more livid yellow and green, and ribbed with black quite down his body, with black shining wings, and so diaphanous and tender, cob-web like, that they are of no manner of use for daping; but come in, and are taken after the green-drake, and in an artificial fly kill very well; which fly is thus made, the dubbing of the down of a hog's bristles, and black spaniel's fur, mixed, and ribbed down the body with black silk, the whisks of the hairs of the beard of a black cat, and the wings of the black-grey feather of a mallard.

And now I come to the stone-fly; but I am afraid I have already wearied your patience, which if I have, I beseech you freely tell me so, and I will defer the remaining instructions for fly angling till some other time.

VIAT. No, truly, sir, I can never be weary of hearing you: but if you think fit, because I am afraid I am too troublesome, to refresh yourself with a glass, and a pipe, you may afterwards proceed, and I shall be exceedingly pleased to hear you.

ruins of
Beresford Hall

The Pike Pool

PISC. I thank you, sir, for that motion; for, believe me, I am dry with talking: here, boy, give us here a bottle and a glass; and, sir, my service to you, and to all our friends in the south.

VIAT. Your servant, sir, and I'll pledge you as heartily; for the good powdered beef I eat at dinner, or something else, has made me thirsty.

Hartington Hall

E·H·N·

CHAPTER VIII

Of the Stone-fly; also a list of Flies for
June, July, August, September, October,
November and December; with some
remarks on the Green-drake and
Stone-fly and on Poaching

VIAT. So, sir, I am now ready for another lesson, so soon as you please to give it me.

PISC. And I, sir, as ready to give you the best I can. Having told you the time of the stone-fly's coming in, and that he is bred of a cadis in the very river where he is taken, I am next to tell you that,

13. This same stone-fly has not the patience to continue in his crust, or husk, till his wings be full grown; but so soon as ever they begin to put out, that he feels himself strong (at which time we call him a jack), squeezes himself out of prison, and crawls to the top of some stone, where, if he can find a chink that will receive him, or can creep betwixt two stones, the one lying hollow upon the other

(which, by the way, we also lay so purposely to find them), he there lurks till his wings be full grown, and there is your only place to find him (and from thence doubtless he derives his name), though, for want of such convenience, he will make shift with the hollow of a bank, or any other place where the wind cannot come to fetch him off. His body is long, and pretty thick, and as broad at the tail almost as in the middle; his colour a very fine brown, ribbed with yellow, and much yellower on the belly than the back; he has two or three whisks also at the tag of his tail, and two little horns upon his head; his wings, when full grown, are double, and flat down his back, of the same colour, but rather darker than his body, and longer than it, though he makes but little use of them; for you shall rarely see him flying, though often swimming, and paddling with several feet he has under his belly, upon the water, without stirring a wing: but the drake will mount steeple-high into the air, though he is to be found upon flags and grass, too, and indeed everywhere, high and low, near the river; there being so many of them in their season, as, were they not a very inoffensive insect, would look like a plague; and these drakes (since I forgot to tell you before, I will tell you here) are taken by the fish to that incredible degree, that, upon a calm day, you shall see the still deeps continually all over circles by the fishes rising, who will gorge themselves with those flies, till they purge again out of their gills; and the trouts are at that time so lusty and strong, that one of eight or ten inches long, will then more struggle, and tug, and more endanger your tackle, than one twice as big in winter; but pardon this digression.

This stone-fly then, we dape or dibble with, as with the drake, but with this difference, that whereas the green-drake is common both to stream and still, and to all hours of the day, we seldom dape with this but in the streams (for in a whistling wind a made-fly in the deep is better), and rarely, but early and late, it not being so proper for the midtime of the day; though a great grayling will then take it very well in a sharp stream, and here and there, a trout too; but much better towards eight, nine, ten, or eleven of the clock at night, at which time also the best fish rise, and the later the better, provided you can see your fly; and when you cannot, a made-fly will murder, which is to be made thus: the dubbing of bear's dun, with a little brown and yellow camlet very well mixed, but so placed that your fly may be more yellow on the belly and towards the tail, underneath, than in any other part; and you are to place two or three hairs of a black cat's beard on the top of the hook, in your arming, so as to be turned up when you warp on your dubbing, and to stand almost upright, and staring one from another; and note, that your fly is to be ribbed with yellow silk; and the wings long and very large, of the dark grey feather of a mallard.

14. The next May-fly is the black-fly; made with a black body, of the whirl of all ostrich-feather, ribbed with silver-twist, and the black hackle of a cock over all; and is a killing fly, but not to be named with either of the other.

15. The last May-fly (that is, of the four pretenders) is the little yellow May-fly; in shape exactly the same with the green-drake, but a very little one, and of as bright a yellow as can be seen; which is made of a bright yellow camlet, and the wings of a white-grey feather dyed yellow.

16. The last fly for this month (and which continues all June, though it comes in the middle of May) is the fly called the camlet-fly, in shape like a moth, with fine diapered or water wings, and with which (as I told you before) I sometimes used to dibble; and grayling will rise mightily at it. But the artificial fly (which is only in use amongst our anglers) is made of a dark brown shining camlet, ribbed over with a very small light green silk, the wings of the double grey feather of a mallard; and it is a killing fly for small fish; and so much for May.

JUNE

From the first to the four-and-twentieth, the green-drake and stone-fly are taken (as I told you before).

1. From the twelfth to the four-and-twentieth, late at night, is taken a fly, called the owl-fly; the dubbing of a white weasel's tail, and a white grey wing.

2. We have then another dun, called the barm-fly, from its yeasty colour; the dubbing of the fur of a yellow-dun cat, and a grey wing of a mallard's feather.

3. We have also a hackle with a purple body, whipt about with a red capon's feather.

4. As also a gold-twist hackle with a purple body, whipt about with a red capon's feather.

5. To these we have this month a flesh-fly; the dubbing of a black spaniel's fur, and blue wool mixed, and a grey wing.

6. Also another little flesh-fly; the body made of the whirl of a peacock's feather, and the wings of the grey feather of a drake.

CHARLES COTTON'S
PEW IN ALSTON-
FIELD CHVRCH·

7. We have then the peacock-fly; the body and wing both made of the feather of that bird.

8. There is also the flying-ant or ant-fly; the dubbing of brown and red camlet mixed, with a light grey wing.

9. We have likewise a brown-gnat, with a very slender body of brown and violet camlet well mixed, and a light grey Wing.

10. And another little black-gnat; the dubbing of black mohair, and a white grey wing.

11. As also a green grasshopper; the dubbing of green and yellow wool mixed, ribbed over with green silk, and a red capon's feather over all.

12. And, lastly, a little dun grasshopper; the body slender, made of a dun camlet, and a dun hackle at the top.

JULY

First, all the small flies that were taken in June are also taken in this month.

1. We have then the orange-fly; the dubbing of orange wool, and the wing of a black feather.

2. Also a little white-dun; the body made of white mohair, and the wings blue, of a heron's feather.

3. We have likewise this month a wasp-fly; made either of a dark brown dubbing, or else the fur of a black cat's tail, ribbed about with yellow silk; and the wing, of the grey feather of a mallard.

4. Another fly taken this month is a black hackle; the body made of the whirl of a peacock's feather, and a black hackle-feather on the top.

5. We have also another, made of a peacock's whirl without wings.

6. Another fly also is taken this month, called the shell-fly; the dubbing of yellow-green Jersey wool, and a little white hog's-hair mixed, which I call the palm-fly, and do believe it is taken for a palm, that drops off the willows into the water; for this fly I have seen trouts take little pieces of moss, as they have swam down the river; by which I conclude that the best way to hit the right colour is to compare your dubbing with the moss, and mix the colours as near as you can.

7. There is also taken, this month, a black-blue dun; the dubbing of the fur of a black rabbit mixed with a little yellow; the wings, of the feather of a blue pigeon's wing.

AUGUST

The same flies with July.

1. Then another ant-fly; the dubbing of the black brown hair of a cow, some red wrapt in for the tug of his tail, and a dark wing; a killing fly.

2. Next a fly called the fern-fly; the dubbing of the fur of a hare's neck, that is, of the colour of fern, or bracken, with a darkish grey wing of a mallard's feather; a killer, too.

3. Besides these we have a white hackle; the body of white mohair and wrapped about with a white hackle-feather, and this is assuredly taken for thistle-down.

4. We have also this month a Harry-long-legs; the body made of bear's dun, and blue wool mixed, and a brown hackle-feather over all.

Lastly. In this month all the same browns and duns are taken that were taken in May.

SEPTEMBER

This month the same flies are taken that are taken in April.

1. To which I shall only add a camel-brown-fly; the dubbing pulled out of the lime of a wall, whipped about with red silk, and a darkish grey mallard's feather for the wing.

2. And one other for which we have no name; but it is made of the black hair of a badger's skin, mixed with the yellow softest down of a sanded hog.

OCTOBER

The same flies are taken this month as were taken in March.

NOVEMBER

The same flies that were taken in February are taken this month also.

DECEMBER

Few men angle with the fly this month, no more than they do in January; but yet, if the weather be warm (as I have known it sometimes in my life to be, even in this cold country, where it is least expected), then a brown, that looks red in the hand, and yellowish betwixt your eye and the sun, will both raise and kill in a clear water and free from snow-broth; but, at the best, it is hardly worth a man's labour.

And now, sir, I have done with fly-fishing, or angling at the top, excepting once more, to tell you, that of all these (and I have named you a great many very killing flies) none are fit to be compared with the drake and stone-fly, both for many and for very great fish; and yet there are some days that are by no means proper for the sport. And in a calm you shall not have near so much sport, even with daping, as in a whistling gale of wind, for two reasons, both because you are not then so easily discovered by the fish, and also because there are then but few flies that can lie upon the water; for where they have so much choice, you may easily imagine they will not be so eager and forward to rise at a bait, that both the shadow of your body, and that of your rod, nay of your very line, in a hot calm day, will, in spite of your best caution, render suspected to them; but even then, in swift streams, or by sitting down patiently behind a willow bush, you shall do more execution than at almost any other time of the year with any other fly; though one may sometimes hit of a day, when he shall come home very well satisfied with sport with several other flies: but with these two, the green-drake and the stone-fly, I do verily believe I could, some days in my life, had I not been weary of slaughter, have laden a lusty boy; and have sometimes, I do honestly assure you, given over upon the mere account of satiety of sport; which will be no hard matter to believe, when I likewise assure you, that with this very fly, I have in this very river that runs by us, in three or four hours taken thirty, five-and-thirty, and forty of the best trouts in the river. What shame and pity it is, then, that such a river should be destroyed by the basest sort of people, by those unlawful ways of fire and netting in the night, and of damming, groping, spearing, hanging, and hooking by day, which are now grown so common, that, though we have very good laws to punish such offenders, every rascal does it, for aught I see, *impunè*.

To conclude, I cannot now in honesty but frankly tell you, that many of these flies I have named, at least so made as we make them here, will peradventure do you no great service in your southern rivers; and will not conceal from you, but that I have sent flies to several friends in London, that for aught I could ever hear, never did any great feats with them; and therefore if you intend to profit by my instructions, you must come to angle with me here in the Peak: and so, if you please, let us walk up to supper, and tomorrow, if the day be windy, as our days here commonly are, 'tis ten to one but we shall take a good dish of fish for dinner.

Walton's Chamber Beresford Hall

Third Day

CHAPTER IX

A Short Dialogue; Viator fishes by himself

PISC. A good-day to you, sir; I see you will always be stirring before me.

VIAT. Why, to tell you the truth, I am so allured with the sport I had yesterday, that I long to be at the river again; and when I heard the wind sing in my chamber window, could forbear no longer, but leapt out of bed, and had just made an end of dressing myself as you came in.

PISC. Well, I am both glad you are so ready for the day, and that the day is so fit for you; and look you, I have made you three or four flies this morning; this silver-twist hackle, this bear's dun, this light brown, and this dark brown, any of which I dare say will do; but you may try them all, and see which does best; only I must ask your pardon that I cannot wait upon you this morning, a little business being fallen out, that for two or three hours will deprive me of your company: but I'll come and call you home to dinner, and my man shall attend you.

VIAT. Oh, sir, mind your affairs by all means. Do but lend me a little of your skill to these fine flies, and, unless it have forsaken me since yesterday, I shall find luck of my own, I hope, to do something.

PISC. The best instructions I can give you is, that seeing the wind curls the water, and blows the right way, you would now angle up the still deep today; for betwixt the rocks where the streams are, you will find it now too brisk; and besides, I would have you take fish in both waters.

VIAT. I'll obey your direction, and so good-morning to you. Come, young man, let you and I walk together. But hark you, sir, I have not done with you yet; I expect another lesson for angling at the bottom, in the afternoon.

PISC. Well, sir, I'll be ready for you.

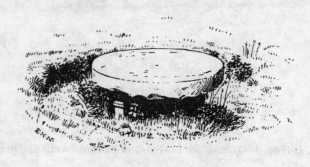

At Beresford Hall

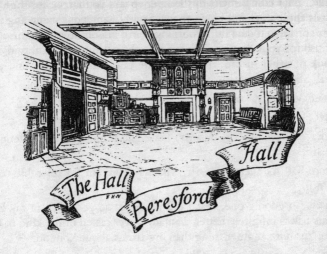

The Hall Beresford Hall

CHAPTER X

Directions how to Dress a Trout or Grayling

Pisc. Oh, sir, are you returned? you have but just prevented me. I was coming to call you.

Viat. I am glad then I have saved you the labour.

Pisc. And how have you sped?

Viat. You shall see that, sir, presently; look you, sir, here are three brace of trouts, one of them the biggest but one that ever I killed with a fly in my life; and yet I lost a bigger than that, with my fly to boot; and here are three graylings, and one of them longer by some inches than that I took yesterday, and yet I thought that a good one, too.

Pisc. Why you have made a pretty good morning's work on't; and now, sir, what think you of our river Dove?

Viat. I think it to be the best trout river in England; and am so far in love with it, that if it were mine, and that I could keep it to myself, I would not exchange that water for all the land it runs over, to be totally debarred from it.

Pisc. That compliment to the river speaks you a true lover of the art of angling; and now, sir, to make part of amends for sending you so uncivilly out alone this morning, I will myself dress you this dish of fish for your dinner; walk but into the parlour, you will find one book or other in the window to entertain you the while, and you shall have it presently.

Viat. Well, sir, I obey you.

Pisc. Look you, sir, have I not made haste?

Viat. Believe me, sir, that you have; and it looks so well, I long to be at it.

Pisc. Fall to, then; now, sir, what say you, am I a tolerable cook or no?

Viat. So good a one, that I did never eat so good fish in my life. This fish is infinitely better than any I ever tasted of the kind in my life; 'tis quite another thing than our trouts about London.

Pisc. You would say so, if that trout you eat of were in right season: but pray eat of the grayling, which upon my word, at this season is by much the better fish.

Viat. In earnest and so it is: and I have one request to make to you, which is, that as you have taught me to catch trout and grayling, you will now teach me how to dress them as these are dressed, which questionless is of all other the best way.

Pisc. That I will, sir, with all my heart, and am glad you like them so well as to make that request, and they are dressed thus:

Take your trout, wash, and dry him with a clean napkin; then open him, and having taken out his guts, and all the blood, wipe him very clean within, but wash him not, and give him three scotches with a knife to the bone, on one side only. After which take a clean kettle, and put in as much hard stale beer (but it must not be dead), vinegar, and a little white wine and water as will cover the fish you intend to boil; then throw into the liquor a good quantity of salt, the rind of a lemon, a handful of sliced horseradish root, with a handsome little faggot of rosemary, thyme, and winter savory. Then set your kettle upon a quick fire of wood; and let your liquor boil up to the height before you put in your fish; and then, if there be many, put them in one by one, that they may not so cool the liquor as to make it fall: and whilst your fish is boiling, beat up the butter for your sauce with a ladleful or two of the liquor it is boiling in; and being boiled enough, immediately pour the liquor from the fish; and being laid in a dish, pour your butter upon it; and strewing it plentifully over with shaved horseradish, and a little pounded ginger, garnish the sides of your dish, and the fish itself, with a sliced lemon or two, and serve it up.

A grayling is also to be dressed exactly after the same manner, saving that he is to be scaled, which a trout never is: and that must be done either with one's nails, or very lightly and carefully with a knife, for fear of bruising the fish. And note, that these kinds of fish, a trout especially, if he is not eaten within four or five hours after he be taken, is worth nothing.

But come, sir, I see you have dined; and therefore, if you please, we will walk down again to the little house, and there I will read you a lecture of angling at the bottom.

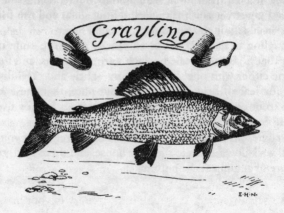

CHAPTER XI

Of Angling at the Bottom for Trout or Grayling

VIAT. So, sir, now we are here, and set, let me have my instructions for angling for trout and grayling at the bottom; which though not so easy, so cleanly, nor (as 'tis said) so genteel a way of fishing as with a fly, is yet (if I mistake not) a good holding way, and takes fish when nothing else will.

PISC. You are in the right, it does so: and a worm is so sure a bait at all times, that, excepting in a flood, I would I had laid a thousand pounds that I killed fish, more or less, with it, winter or summer, every day throughout the year; those days always excepted, that upon a more serious account always ought so to be. But not longer to delay you, I will begin, and tell you, that angling at the bottom is also commonly of two sorts (and yet there is a third way of angling with a ground-bait, and to very great effect too, as shall be said hereafter), namely, *by hand; or with a cork, or float.*

That we call angling by hand is of three sorts.

The first, with a line about half the length of the rod, a good weighty plumb, and three hairs next the hook, which we call a running-line, and with one large brandling, or a dew-worm of a moderate size, or two small ones of the first, or any other sort, proper for a trout, of which my father Walton has already given you the names, and saved me labour; or, indeed, almost any worm whatever; for if a trout be in the humour to bite, it must be such a worm as I never yet saw, that he will refuse; and if you fish with two, you are then to bait your hook thus. You are first to run the point of your hook in at the very head of your first worm, and so down through his body, till he be past the knot, and then let it out, and strip the worm above the arming (that you may not bruise it with your fingers) till you have put on the other, by running the point of the hook in below the knot, upwards through his body towards his head, till it be just covered with the head; which being done, you are then to slip the first worm down over the arming again, till the knots of both worms meet together.

The second way of angling by hand, and with a running line, is with a line something longer than the former, and with tackle made after this same manner. At the utmost extremity of your line, where the hook is always placed in all other ways of angling, you are to have a large pistol or carabine bullet, into which the end of your line is to be fastened with a peg, or pin, even and close with the bullet; and, about half a foot above that, a branch of line, of two or three handfuls long, or more for a swift stream, with a hook at the end thereof, baited with some of the fore-named worms, and half a foot above that, another armed and baited after the same manner, but with another sort of worm, without any lead at all above: by which means you will always certainly find the true bottom in all depths; which with the plumbs upon your line above you can never do, but that your bait must always drag whilst you are sounding (which in this way of angling must be continually), by which means you are like to have more trouble, and peradventure worse success. And both these ways of angling at the bottom are most proper for a dark and muddy water, by reason, that in such a condition of the stream, a man may stand as near as he will, and neither his own shadow, nor the roundness of his tackle will hinder his sport.

The third way of angling by hand with a ground-bait, and by much the best of all other, is, with a line full as long, or a yard and a half longer, than your rod; with no more than one hair next the hook, and for two or three lengths above it; and no more than one small pellet or shot for your plumb; your hook, little; your worms of the smaller brandlings, very well secured, and only one upon your hook at a time; which is thus to be baited. The point of your hook is to be put in at the very tag of his tail, and run up his body quite over all the arming, and still stripped on an inch at least upon the hair, the head and remaining part hanging downward; and with this line and hook thus baited you are evermore to angle in the streams, always in a clear rather than a troubled water, and always up the river, still casting out your worm before you with a light one-handed rod, like an artificial fly; where it will be taken sometimes at the top, or within a very little of the superficies of the water, and almost always before that light plumb can sink it to the bottom, both by reason of the stream, and also, that you must always keep your worm in motion by drawing still back towards you, as if you were angling with a fly; and believe me, whoever will try it, shall find this the best way of all other to angle with a worm, in a bright water especially; but then his rod must be very light and pliant, and very true and finely made, which, with a skilful hand, will do wonders, and in a clear stream is undoubtedly the best way of angling for a trout, or grayling with a worm, by many degrees, that any man can make choice of, and of most ease and delight to the angler. To which, let me add, that if the angler be of a constitution that will suffer him to wade, and will slip into the tail of a shallow stream, to the calf of the leg, or the knee, and so keep off the bank, he shall almost take what fish he pleases.

The second way of angling at the bottom is with a cork or float; and that is also of two sorts; with a worm; or with a grub or cadis.

With a worm, you are to have your line within a foot, or a foot and a half as long as your rod; in a dark water, with two, or if you will with three, but in a clear water never with above one hair next the hook, and two or three for four or five lengths above it, and a worm of what size you please, your plumbs fitted to your cork, your cork to the condition of the river (that is, to the swiftness or slowness of it), and both when the water is very clear, as fine as you can, and then you are never to bait with above one of the lesser sort of brandlings; or, if they are very little ones indeed, you may then bait with two, after the manner before directed.

When you angle for a trout, you are to do it as deep, that is, as near the bottom as you can, provided your bait do not drag, or if it do, a trout will sometimes take it in at that posture: if for a grayling, you are then to fish further from the bottom, he being a fish that usually swims nearer the middle of the water, and lies always loose; or however, is more apt to rise than a trout, and more inclined to rise than to descend even to a ground-bait.

With a grub or cadis, you are to angle with the same length of line, or if it be all out as long as your rod 'tis not the worse, with never above one hair, for two or three lengths next the hook, and with the smallest cork, or float, and the least weight of plumb you can that will but sink, and that the swiftness of your stream will allow; which also you may help, and avoid the violence of the current, by angling in the returns of a stream, or the eddies betwixt two streams, which also are the most likely places wherein to kill a fish in a stream, either at the top or bottom.

Of grubs for a grayling, the ash-grub, which is plump, milk-white, bent round from head to tail, and exceeding tender, with a red head, or, the dock-worm, or grub of a pale yellow, longer, lanker, and tougher than the other, with rows of feet all down his belly, and a red head also, are the best; I say, for a grayling, because, although a trout will take both these (the ash-grub especially), yet he does not do it so freely as the other, and I have usually taken ten graylings for one trout with that bait; though if a trout come, I have observed that he is commonly a very good one.

These baits we usually keep in bran, in which an ash-grub commonly grows tougher, and will better endure baiting; though he is yet so tender, that it will be necessary to warp in a piece of a stiff hair with your arming, leaving it standing out about a straw-breadth at the head of your hook, so as to keep the grub either from slipping totally off when baited, or at least down to the point of the hook; by which means your arming will be left wholly naked and bare, which is neither so sightly, nor so likely to be taken; though to help that (which will however very oft fall out), I always arm the hook I design for this bait with the whitest horse-hair I can choose, which itself will resemble, and shine like that bait, and consequently will do more good, or less harm, than an arming of any other colour. These grubs are to be baited thus: the hook is to be put under the head or chaps of the bait, and guided down the middle of the belly (without suffering it to peep out by the way, for then the ash-grub especially will issue out water and milk, till nothing but the skin shall remain, and the bend of the hook will appear black, through it) till the point of your hook come so low that the head of your bait may rest, and stick upon the hair that stands out to hold it; by which means it can neither slip of itself, neither will the force of the stream, nor quick pulling out, upon any mistake, strip it off.

Now the cadis, or cod-bait (which is a sure killing bait, and, for the most part, by much surer than either of the other) may be put upon the hook, two or three together, and is sometimes (to very great effect) joined to a worm, and sometimes to an artificial fly, to cover the joint of your hook; but is always to be angled with at the bottom (when by itself especially) with the finest tackle; and is, for all times of the year, the most holding bait of all other whatever, both for trout and grayling.

There are several other baits besides these few I have named you, which also do very great execution at the bottom, and some that are peculiar to certain countries and rivers, of which every angler may in his own place make his own observation; and some others that I do not think fit to put you in mind of, because I would not corrupt you, and would have you, as in all things else I observe you to be a very honest gentleman, a fair angler. And so much for the second sort of angling for a trout at the bottom.

VIAT. But, sir, I beseech you give me leave to ask you one question: is there no art to be used to worms, to make them allure the fish, and in a manner compel them to bite at the bait?

PISC. Not that I know of; or did I know any such secret, I would not use it myself, and therefore would not teach it you. Though I will not deny to you, that in my younger days, I have made trial of oil of osprey, oil of ivy, camphire, asafoetida, juice of nettles, and several other devices that I was taught by several anglers I met with; but could never find any advantage by them; and can scarce believe there is anything to be done that way; though I must tell you, I have seen some men who I thought went to work no more artificially than I, and have yet, with the same kind of worms I had, in my own sight taken five, and sometimes ten to one. But we'll let that business alone, if you please; and because we have time enough, and that I would deliver you from the trouble of any more lectures, I will, if you please, proceed to the last way of angling for a trout or grayling, which is in the middle; after which I shall have no more to trouble you with.

VIAT. 'Tis no trouble, sir, but the greatest satisfaction that can be: and I attend you.

ruins of
Beresford
Hall

CHAPTER XII

Of Angling in the Middle for Trout or Grayling; Farewell of Viator with Piscator Junior

PISC. Angling in the middle, then, for a trout or grayling, is of two sorts: with a penk or minnow for a trout; or with a worm, grub, or cadis, for a grayling.

For the first. It is with a minnow, half a foot or a foot within the superficies of the water. And as to the rest that concerns this sort of angling, I shall wholly refer you to Mr Walton's directions, who is undoubtedly the best angler with a minnow in England; only, in plain truth, I do not approve of those baits he keeps in salt, unless where the living ones are not possibly to be had (though I know he frequently kills with them, and peradventure, more than with any other; nay, I have seen him refuse a living one for one of them); and much less of his artificial one; for though we do it with a counterfeit fly, me thinks it should hardly be expected that a man should deceive a fish with a counterfeit fish. Which having said, I shall only add, and that out of my own experience, that I do believe a bull-head, with his gill-fins cut off (at some times of the year especially), to be a much better bait for a trout than a minnow, and a loach much better than that; to prove which I shall only tell you, that I have much oftener taken trouts with a bull-head or a loach in their throats (for there a trout has questionless his first digestion) than a minnow; and that one day especially, having angled a good part of the day with a minnow, and that in as hopeful a day, and as fit a water, as could be wished for that purpose, without raising any one fish; I at last fell to with the worm, and with that took fourteen in a very short space; amongst all which there was not, to my remembrance, so much as one that had not a loach or two, and some of them three, four, five, and six loaches, in his throat and stomach; from whence I concluded, that had I angled with that bait, I had made a notable day's work of it.

But after all, there is a better way of angling with a minnow, than perhaps is fit either to teach or to practise; to which I shall only add, that a grayling will certainly rise at, and sometimes take a minnow, though it will be hard to be believed by anyone, who shall consider the littleness of that fish's mouth, very unfit to take so great a bait: but it is affirmed by many, that he will sometimes do it; and I myself know it to be true, for though I never took a grayling so, yet a man of mine once did, and within so few paces of me, that I am as certain of it, as I can be of anything I did not see, and (which made it appear the more strange) the grayling was not above eleven inches long.

I must here also beg leave of your master, and mine, not to controvert, but to tell him, that I cannot consent to his way of throwing in his rod to an over-grown trout, and afterwards recovering his fish with his tackle. For though I am satisfied he has sometimes done it, because he says so, yet I have found it quite otherwise; and though I have taken with the angle, I may safely say, some thousands of trout in my life, my top never snapt (though my line still continued fast to the remaining part of my rod by some lengths of my line curled round about my top, and there fastened, with waxed silk, against such an accident), nor my hand never slacked, or slipped by any other chance, but I almost always infallibly lost my fish, whether great or little, though my hook came home again. And I have often wondered how a trout should so suddenly disengage himself from so great a hook, as that we bait with a minnow, and so deep bearded as those hooks commonly are, when I have seen by the forenamed accidents, or the slipping of a knot in the upper part of the line, by sudden and hard striking, that though the line has immediately been recovered, almost before it

could be all drawn into the water, the fish cleared and gone in a moment. And yet, to justify what he says, I have sometimes known a trout, having carried away a whole line, found dead three or four days after with the hook fast sticking in him; but then it is to be supposed he had gorged it, which a trout will do, if you be not too quick with him when he comes at a minnow, as sure and much sooner than a pike: and I myself have also, once or twice in my life, taken the same fish, with my own fly sticking in his chaps, that he had taken from me the day before, by the slipping of a hook in the arming: but I am very confident a trout will not be troubled two hours with any hook that has so much as one handful of line left behind with it, or that is not struck through a bone, if it be in any part of his mouth only; nay, I do certainly know that a trout, so soon as ever he feels himself pricked, if he carries away the hook, goes immediately to the bottom, and will there root, like a hog upon the gravel, till he either rub out or break the hook in the middle. And so much for this sort of angling in the middle for a trout.

The second way of angling in the middle is with a worm, grub, cadis, or any other ground-bait for a grayling; and that is with a cork, and a foot from the bottom, a grayling taking it much better there, than at the bottom, as has been said before; and this always in a clear water, and with the finest tackle.

To which we may also, and with very good reason, add the third way of angling by hand with a ground-bait, as a third way of fishing in the middle, which is common to both trout and grayling, and (as I said before) the best way of angling with a worm, of all other I ever tried whatever.

And now, sir, I have said all I can at present think of concerning angling for a trout and grayling, and I doubt not have tired you sufficiently; but I will give you no more trouble of this kind, whilst you stay, which I hope will be a good while longer.

Viat. That will not be above a day longer; but if I live till May come twelvemonth, you are sure of me again, either with my master Walton, or without him; and in the meantime shall acquaint him how much you have made of me for his sake, and I hope he loves me well enough to thank you for it.

Pisc. I shall be glad, sir, of your good company at the time you speak of, and shall be loath to part with you now; but when you tell me you must go, I will then wait upon you more miles on your way than I have tempted you out of it, and heartily wish you a good journey.

WORDSWORTH CLASSICS

The Mill on the Floss
Middlemarch
Silas Marner

HENRY FIELDING
Tom Jones

RONALD FIRBANK
*Valmouth & other
stories*

TRANSLATED BY
EDWARD FITZGERALD
*The Rubaiyat of Omar
Khayyam*

F. SCOTT FITZGERALD
*The Diamond as Big as
the Ritz & other stories*
The Great Gatsby
Tender is the Night

GUSTAVE FLAUBERT
Madame Bovary

JOHN GALSWORTHY
In Chancery
The Man of Property
To Let

ELIZABETH GASKELL
Cranford
North and South

GEORGE GISSING
New Grub Street

KENNETH GRAHAME
*The Wind in the
Willows*

**GEORGE & WEEDON
GROSSMITH**
Diary of a Nobody

RIDER HAGGARD
She

THOMAS HARDY
*Far from the
Madding Crowd*
Jude the Obscure
*The Mayor of
Casterbridge*

A Pair of Blue Eyes
*The Return of the
Native*
Selected Short Stories
Tess of the D'Urbervilles
The Trumpet Major
*Under the Greenwood
Tree*
Wessex Tales
The Woodlanders

**NATHANIEL
HAWTHORNE**
The Scarlet Letter

O. HENRY
Selected Stories

JAMES HOGG
*The Private Memoirs
and Confessions of a
Justified Sinner*

HOMER
The Iliad
The Odyssey

E. W. HORNUNG
*Raffles: The Amateur
Cracksman*

VICTOR HUGO
*The Hunchback of
Notre Dame*
Les Misérables
IN TWO VOLUMES

HENRY JAMES
The Ambassadors
*Daisy Miller & other
stories*
The Europeans
The Golden Bowl
The Portrait of a Lady
*The Turn of the Screw
& The Aspern Papers*

M. R. JAMES
Ghost Stories

JEROME K. JEROME
Three Men in a Boat

JAMES JOYCE
Dubliners
*A Portrait of the Artist
as a Young Man*

RUDYARD KIPLING
The Best Short Stories
Captains Courageous
Kim
*The Man Who Would
Be King & other stories*
*Plain Tales from the
Hills*

D. H. LAWRENCE
Lady Chatterley's Lover
The Plumed Serpent
The Rainbow
Sons and Lovers
*The Virgin and the
Gypsy & selected stories*
Women in Love

SHERIDAN LE FANU
(EDITED BY M. R. JAMES)
*Madam Crowl's Ghost
& other stories*
In a Glass Darkly

GASTON LEROUX
*The Phantom of the
Opera*

JACK LONDON
*Call of the Wild &
White Fang*

**GUY DE
MAUPASSANT**
The Best Short Stories

HERMAN MELVILLE
Moby Dick
Typee

GEORGE MEREDITH
The Egoist

H. H. MUNRO
*The Complete Stories of
Saki*

WORDSWORTH CLASSICS

**THOMAS LOVE
PEACOCK**
*Headlong Hall &
Nightmare Abbey*

EDGAR ALLAN POE
*Tales of Mystery and
Imagination*

FREDERICK ROLFE
Hadrian the Seventh

SIR WALTER SCOTT
*Ivanhoe
Rob Roy*

**WILLIAM
SHAKESPEARE**
*All's Well that Ends Well
Antony and Cleopatra
As You Like It
The Comedy of Errors
Coriolanus
Hamlet
Henry IV Part 1
Henry IV Part 2
Henry V
Julius Caesar
King John
King Lear
Love's Labours Lost
Macbeth
Measure for Measure
The Merchant of Venice
The Merry Wives of
Windsor
A Midsummer Night's
Dream
Much Ado About Nothing
Othello
Pericles
Richard II
Richard III
Romeo and Juliet
The Taming of the Shrew
The Tempest
Titus Andronicus
Troilus and Cressida*

*Twelfth Night
Two Gentlemen of
Verona
A Winter's Tale*

MARY SHELLEY
Frankenstein

TOBIAS SMOLLETT
Humphry Clinker

LAURENCE STERNE
*A Sentimental Journey
Tristram Shandy*

**ROBERT LOUIS
STEVENSON**
*Dr Jekyll and Mr Hyde
The Master of Ballantrae
& Weir of Hermiston*

BRAM STOKER
Dracula

R. S. SURTEES
*Mr Sponge's
Sporting Tour*

JONATHAN SWIFT
Gulliver's Travels

W. M. THACKERAY
Vanity Fair

TOLSTOY
*Anna Karenina
War and Peace*

ANTHONY TROLLOPE
*Barchester Towers
Can You Forgive Her?
Dr Thorne
The Eustace Diamonds
Framley Parsonage
The Last Chronicle
of Barset
Phineas Finn
Phineas Redux
The Small House at
Allington
The Way We Live Now
The Warden*

**IVAN SERGEYEVICH
TURGENEV**
Fathers and Sons

MARK TWAIN
*Tom Sawyer &
Huckleberry Finn*

JULES VERNE
*Around the World in
Eighty Days & Five
Weeks in a Balloon
Journey to the Centre
of the Earth
Twenty Thousand
Leagues Under the Sea*

VIRGIL
The Aeneid

VOLTAIRE
Candide

LEW WALLACE
Ben Hur

ISAAC WALTON
The Compleat Angler

EDITH WHARTON
The Age of Innocence

GILBERT WHITE
*The Natural History
of Selborne*

OSCAR WILDE
*Lord Arthur Savile's
Crime & other stories
The Picture of
Dorian Gray
The Plays*
IN TWO VOLUMES

VIRGINIA WOOLF
*Mrs Dalloway
Orlando
To the Lighthouse*

P. C. WREN
Beau Geste

Bhagavad Gita

DISTRIBUTION

AUSTRALIA & PAPUA NEW GUINEA
Peribo Pty Ltd
58 Beaumont Road, Mount Kuring-Gai
NSW 2080, Australia
Tel: (02) 457 0011 Fax: (02) 457 0022

CZECH REPUBLIC
Bohemian Ventures s r. o.,
Delnicka 13, 170 00 Prague 7
Tel: 042 2 877837 Fax: 042 2 801498

FRANCE
Copernicus Diffusion
23 Rue Saint Dominique, Paris 75007
Tel: 1 44 11 33 20 Fax: 1 44 11 33 21

GERMANY & AUSTRIA
**GLBmbH (Bargain, Promotional
& Remainder Shops)**
Zollstockgürtel 5, 50969 Köln
Tel: 0221 34 20 92 Fax: 0221 38 40 40

**Tradis Verlag und Vertrieb GmbH
(Bookshops)**
Postfach 90 03 69, D-51113 Köln
Tel: 022 03 31059 Fax: 022 03 3 93 40

GREAT BRITAIN & IRELAND
Wordsworth Editions Ltd
Cumberland House, Crib Street
Ware, Hertfordshire SG12 9ET

INDIA
OM Book Service
1690 First Floor, Nai Sarak, Delhi – 110006
Tel: 3279823-3265303 Fax: 3278091

ISRAEL
Timmy Marketing Limited
Israel Ben Zeev 12, Ramont Gimmel, Jerusalem
Tel: 02-865266 Fax: 02-880035

ITALY
Magis Books s.p.a.
Via Raffaello 31/C, Zona Ind Mancasale
42100 Reggio Emilia
Tel: 0522 920999 Fax: 0522 920666

NEW ZEALAND & FIJI
Allphy Book Distributors Ltd
4-6 Charles Street, Eden Terrace, Auckland,
Tel: (09) 3773096 Fax: (09) 3022770

MALAYSIA & BRUNEI
Vintrade SDN BHD
5 & 7 Lorong Datuk Sulaiman 7
Taman Tun Dr Ismail
60000 Kuala Lumpur, Malaysia
Tel: (603) 717 3333 Fax: (603) 719 2942

MALTA & GOZO
Agius & Agius Ltd
42A South Street, Valletta VLT 11
Tel: 234038 - 220347 Fax: 241175

NORTH AMERICA
Universal Sales & Marketing
230 Fifth Avenue, Suite 1212
New York, NY 10001, USA
Tel: 212 481 3500 Fax: 212 481 3534

PHILIPPINES
I J Sagun Enterprises
P O Box 4322 CPO Manila
2 Topaz Road, Greenheights Village,
Taytay, Rizal
Tel: 631 80 61 TO 66

PORTUGAL
International Publishing Services Ltd
Rua da Cruz da Carreira, 4B, 1100 Lisbon
Tel: 01 570051 Fax: 01 3522066

SOUTHERN & CENTRAL AFRICA
Southern Book Publishers (Pty) Ltd
P.O.Box 3103
Halfway House 1685, South Africa
Tel: (011) 315-3633/4/5/6
Fax: (011) 315-3810

EAST AFRICA & KENYA
P.M.C. International Importers & Exporters CC
Unit 6, Ben-Sarah Place, 52-56 Columbine Place,
Glen Anil, Kwa-Zulu Natal 4051,
P.O.Box 201520,
Durban North, Kwa-Zulu Natal 4016
Tel: (031) 844441 Fax: (031) 844466

SINGAPORE
Paul & Elizabeth Book Services Pte Ltd
163 Tanglin Road No 03-15/16
Tanglin Mall, Singapore 1024
Tel: (65) 735 7308 Fax: (65) 735 9747

SLOVAK REPUBLIC
Slovak Ventures s r. o.,
Stefanikova 128, 949 01 Nitra
Tel/Fax: 042 87 525105/6/7

SPAIN
Ribera Libros, S.L.
Poligono Martiartu, Calle 1 - no 6
48480 Arrigorriaga, Vizcaya
Tel: 34 4 6713607 (Almacen)
　　　34 4 4418787 (Libreria)
Fax: 34 4 6713608 (Almacen)
　　　34 4 4418029 (Libreria)

UNITED ARAB EMIRATES
Nadoo Trading LLC
P.O.Box 3186
Dubai
United Arab Emirates
Tel: 04-359793 Fax: 04-487157

DIRECT MAIL Bibliophile Books
5 Thomas Road, London E14 7BN,
Tel: 0171-515 9222 Fax: 0171-538 4115
Order hotline 24 hours Tel: 0171-515 9555
Cash with order + £2.00 p&p (UK)